Belief and Religion in Barbarian Europe c. 350–700

Belief and Religion in Barbarian Europe c. 350–700

Marilyn Dunn

BLOOMSBURY

LONDON • NEW DELHI • NEW YORK • SYDNEY

Bloomsbury Academic
An imprint of Bloomsbury Publishing Plc

50 Bedford Square
London
WC1B 3DP
UK

1385 Broadway
New York
NY 10018
USA

www.bloomsbury.com

Bloomsbury is a registered trade mark of Bloomsbury Publishing Plc

First published 2013

© Marilyn Dunn, 2013

British Library Cataloguing-in-Publication Data
A catalogue record for this book is available from the British Library.

ISBN: HB: 978-1-4411-3160-7
PB: 978-1-4411-6532-9
ePDF: 978-1-4411-0023-8
ePub: 978-1-4411-2382-4

Library of Congress Cataloging-in-Publication Data
Dunn, Marilyn.
Belief and Religion in Barbarian Europe c. 350 – 700 /
Marilyn Dunn.
pages cm.
Includes bibliographical references and index.
ISBN 978-1-4411-3160-7(hardcover) – ISBN 978-1-4411-6532-9(paperback) –
ISBN 978-1-4411-0023-8(ebook(pdf)) ISBN 978-1-4411-2382-4(ebook(epub))
1. Christianity and other religions – Germanic. 2. Germanic Peoples – Religion.
3. Conversion – Christianity – History. 4. Europe – Church history. 5. Europe –
Church history– 600-1500. 6. Paganism – Europe – History. I Title.
BR128.G4D86 2014
274'.02--dc23
2013031536

Typeset by Fakenham Prepress Solutions, Fakenham, Norfolk NR21 8NN

Contents

Abbreviations

AASS	*Acta Sanctorum*
AHR	*American Historical Review*
Annales ESC	*Annales, Économies, Sociétés, Civilisations*
GC	Gregory of Tours, *Glory of the Confessors*
GM	Gregory of Tours, *Glory of the Martyrs*
DLH	Gregory of Tours, *Decem Libri Historiarum* ('*History of the Franks*')
HL	Paul the Deacon, *History of the Lombards*
MGH	*Monumenta Germaniae Historica*
VP	Gregory of Tours, *Life of the Fathers*
ZKG	*Zeitschrift für Kirchengeschichte*

Acknowledgements

First of all, I would like to thank Ben Hayes, formerly of Continuum Publishing, who provided unfailing support when I was writing my previous book, *The Christianization of the Anglo-Saxons* and who commissioned this volume. I am also grateful to Claire Lipscomb and Michael Greenwood for their help in its early stages and to Ian Buck, Charlotte Loveridge and Dhara Patel for seeing it through to production.

I want to take this occasion to express my warmest thanks to Tony Goodman and Brenda Bolton for their encouragement and support throughout. I am also deeply grateful to Judith George, who read the whole manuscript and made sage suggestions for its improvement.

The work for this volume took place in the national libraries of France, Italy, Spain and Portugal and in regional libraries and museums in all these countries. Further research and writing was mainly carried out in two great libraries: Glasgow University Library and the National Library of Scotland. I am greatly indebted to the staff of both. In particular, I want to thank the DDS department of the former, whose labours extend the vast range of materials available in GUL even further; and most of all the Reading Room staff of the latter who have looked after me so very well over the years. Thanks too to Rachel Douglas and Nikki Macdonald for their supportive intellectual companionship at Table B of the NLS Reading Room.

I dedicate this book to Michael Baron, without whom it would not have been completed.

MD

1

Introduction

From the late fourth century onwards, Germanic peoples entered the Roman Empire in large numbers. The first to do so were groups of Tervingi and Greuthungi, who were permitted to cross the Danube in 376, followed by further groups of Greuthungi in 386 and 405/6. All were fleeing Hunnic attack and hoped to find greater security inside the imperial frontiers.[1] In December 405, a 'huge body' of peoples from the interior of Germania crossed the Rhine: Sueves, Vandals and Alans.[2] The Sueves moved south, settling ultimately in north-western Iberia, while the Alans and Vandals who reached Iberia about the same time would cross over into Africa in the 420s. Beyond the Rhine, the Burgundes were also subject to Hunnic pressure: victorious against a Hunnic army in 429, they were then defeated by the Roman general Aëtius and his Hunnic allies in the 430s and were resettled within imperial frontiers.[3] Salian Franks, who unsuccessfully helped defend the Empire against some of these incursions would themselves move within its frontiers where a Frankish state would begin to emerge in north-eastern Gaul later in the fifth century.[4] In the 450s, Gothic groups escaping Hunnic hegemony entered imperial territories: first the Balkans and then Italy. And in the late 560s, not long after the Gothic state created in Italy in the 490s had been destroyed by the armies of the East Roman Empire, the Lombards began to move into Italy.

This book is concerned with belief and religion among the 'barbarians' who settled and created states in Western Europe: Tervingi and Greuthungi, who eventually became the Visigoths of southern Gaul and Spain; Sueves, Burgundians and Franks; the Balkan groups who became Italian Ostrogoths; and the Lombards. Who the 'barbarians' were, where they originally came from and the manner in which they settled in Western Europe has been much discussed.[5] Historians have increasingly focused in recent years on questions of ethnicity. This is no longer regarded as a simple matter of belonging to a particular descent group.[6] We are now told – rather as we are told of gender – that ethnicity is multi-layered, performative, situational and dynamic.[7] The process by which Visigoths and Ostrogoths emerged in the fifth century is complex, controversial and still unclear: Peter Heather writes of the emergence of these Gothic 'supergroups' as a result of military activity; 'proper' migration; the adhesion at different times of minorities of Huns, Alans and Taifali (recruits were not refused); social status, both claimed and recognized; and 'the overriding press of circumstance'.[8] Such observations are confirmed by the discovery of individuals in Germanic cemeteries with dental traits characteristic of Hunnic populations: in one Burgundian cemetery excavated in the 1970s, one-third of the skeletons exhibited such enamel formations. This seems to indicate a mixture of Hunnic and Burgundian populations before the Burgundes were settled in the Empire.[9] If this is the case, it seems that the written sources afford only very limited indications of the way major population groups were formed (or dissolved) in this period.

In these debates over the issues of ethnogenesis, ethnicity, identity and state formation in 'barbarian' Europe we can find some discussion of aspects of religious history of the 'barbarians' and their conversion to Christianity; and religion is examined in a number of recent volumes devoted to the study of individual peoples.[10] Scholars have also produced a few brief studies of conversion; and we are still indebted to older classic works such as that of E. A. Thompson on the Goths in the time of Ulfila, which examines both the pre-Christian religion and the conversion of this people.[11] The conversion of the Germanic peoples has also featured in several major books in English covering the religious history of Late Antiquity and the Early Middle Ages. Richard Fletcher and Peter Brown have treated it as part of their broader canvases – the conversion of Europe up to the fourteenth century and the 'triumph and diversity' of the 'rise of western Christendom'.[12] Non-Christian Germanic religion is also examined in Ken Dowden's study of European paganism and 'the realities of cult', a survey ranging from the early Greeks to fifteenth-century Lithuania. Carole Cusack has provided a major region-by-region treatment of European conversion in the period 300–1000 CE.[13] But since the 1990s, there has been no attempt to propose any broad interpretative framework that might help us achieve a greater understanding of the way in which Germanic pagan peoples on the continent gradually became Catholic Christians in Late Antiquity and Early Middle Ages. The two major works in the 1990s which attempted a fundamental examination of religious change have both proved controversial. The first was Valerie Flint's study of the 'rise of magic', a concept defined very broadly, in the Early Middle Ages. In setting out the scope of her study, Flint acknowledged the risks of her approach, which involved claiming that non-Christian 'magic' – *auguria* and *auspicia* (soothsaying), *incantatio* (incantation) and *astrologia* (astrology) – would be rehabilitated in Christian terminology as miracles (*miracula*), wonders (*mirabilia*), mystery (*mysterium*) and even grace (*gratia*). Predictably this attracted much criticism, though recently it appears to have found some followers.[14] James C. Russell's 'socio-historical approach', suggesting the 'inculturation' or 'Germanization' of Christianity by 'barbarians' was also contested: his ideas of 'Christianity' and 'Germanization' were attacked as static and his use of medieval sources, as opposed to modern theory, thin.[15]

This book offers something new. It focuses on the beliefs of continental Germanic peoples – Goths, Sueves, Burgundes, Franks and Lombards – in the period between c. 350 and c. 700, in which they settled in the territories – or former territories – of the Western Roman Empire and gradually accepted Catholic Christianity. It presents a study of belief based on the cognitive turn in the study of religion of recent years, expanding and developing the approaches pioneered in *The Christianization of the Anglo-Saxons c. 597–c. 700*.[16] It offers fresh insights into familiar texts; ways out of apparent conceptual impasses; and new understandings of the beliefs and religions of these groups.[17]

The starting point for this study, in Chapter 2, 'Intuitions of Divinity', is the pagan beliefs of the Germanic peoples. This is an area which poses considerable problems for the historian as these were religions with no written doctrines and what evidence we have for them is not only very limited, but was produced by a variety of outsiders. The restricted and problematic nature of evidence relating to rituals, sacred places and deities has made this a no-go area for some historians, though philologists continue diligently to sift the evidence of language and literature in an attempt to identify gods.[18] However, a cognitive approach offers viable alternatives. As long ago as 1994, one of the leading exponents of the cognitive science of religion, Pascal Boyer, suggested that there are some universal characteristics of human cognition and that these account for the recurrence throughout history of certain religious features transcending ideas of 'culture' or 'cultures'.[19] Rather than thinking in terms of 'cultures', the cognitive study of religion looks for the 'underlying templates that underwrite our variable concepts'.[20] This enables a supra-cultural approach allowing us to compare, contextualize and extrapolate from limited information.

Another useful conceptual tool provided by the cognitive study of religion is the idea of 'abductive' reasoning. Boyer coined this expression in the 1990s to explain the way in which people 'make surprising data unsurprising'. It is a variety of *post hoc, propter hoc* reasoning used to 'explain' the healing powers of natural features or the intervention of supernatural beings.[21] As Chapter 2 shows, 'abductive' reasoning underlies the idea of sacrifices and offerings to supernatural beings or to natural features believed to have special powers. It is a particularly useful template that helps us understand not only sacrifices and offerings in Germanic paganism (see pp. 23–9 below) but also *ex-voto* offerings amongst Christians (Chapter 5). Elsewhere, Boyer has provided another useful template for the study of the rituals of the pagan Germanic peoples. He suggests that, contrary to what we might expect, gods and other supernatural beings are 'add-ons', in the sense that the ritual is intended to do something else in the first place, thus shedding some light on the meagre descriptions that have come down to us of pagan rites.[22]

The cognitive study of religion also highlights the importance of intuitions of supernatural beings. This arises from what theorists regard as the human propensity to detect agency: that is, for individuals to seek reasons or forces behind events that affect them. Our mental architecture is 'geared up' for the detection of agency in general.[23] Justin Barrett has even coined the term 'hypersensitive agency detection device' to describe this predisposition,[24] which means, in terms of religion, that people intuit the presence or actions of gods, spirits and ancestors. In belief-systems with no written doctrine, intuitions of divinity are paramount and central. A common intuition is that of a supremely powerful god who has created the world – but has no regular cult or worship. This may seem surprising or paradoxical to those familiar only with religion as doctrine: but it is likely that people form the intuition that he is simply too important to concern himself with human concerns and frailties: these are the business of a range of lesser gods and spirits. Using this template,

Chapter 2 offers new ways of interpreting the diverse and scanty evidence for the supernatural beings venerated by the Germanic peoples.

Chapter 3 takes a fresh look at 'Arianism'. There is general consensus that Goths, Sueves, Burgundes, Franks and Lombards as they all arrived and settled in western Europe followed a trajectory from paganism, through 'Arianism' to Catholicism – though the Franks missed out the 'Arian' stage. Scholarship in English seems gradually to be coming to terms with the fact that 'Arianism' should really be described as Homoian Christianity, as it was only indirectly related to the theology of Arius, the Alexandrian presbyter whose views on the Trinity threw the fourth-century Church into theological turmoil.[25] Whether it is called 'Arianism' or Homoianism, it is still viewed as an aberrant theology adopted by the Goths only because it happened to be the creed of the reigning emperor when they began to enter the Empire in large numbers – a view of the Goths which portrays them as mere passive recipients of Christian doctrine. But a close look at the development of Homoian doctrine, combined with an understanding of the Germanic intuition of supernatural beings suggests something quite different: that Homoianism was a version of Christianity constructed by ecclesiastics on the Danube frontier to appeal to Gothic intuitions of divinity, thus creating an 'entry-level' Christianity. The evidence suggests that it was originally conceived of as dynamic and that Ulfila, the famous 'apostle of the Goths', intended to move his people beyond an understanding of the Christian God founded on intuition to doctrinal orthodoxy.[26] Chapter 3 also looks at the way in which the abandonment of the Homoian creed by the Empire in 381 effectively condemned Gothic Christianity to the margins and stifled its doctrinal development. Although it would prove a viable means of introducing other Germanic groups, such as the Sueves and Burgundians to Christianity, Homoianism would gradually become static and conservative, remaining an 'entry-level Christianity' when 'barbarian' rulers wanted to become full members of the Catholic club.

Chapter 4 turns the spotlight on the interaction between religion and politics as the Germanic peoples one by one accepted Catholicism. It draws on an interpretative framework first suggested by the Africanist Robin Horton in the 1970s. Examining religious change in West Africa, Horton characterized rulers as occupying a pivotal position between the microcosm of their native beliefs and polities on one hand and the world religions of Islam and Christianity, with the fresh political and economic opportunities they offered, on the other.[27] Building on this insight, this chapter offers a fresh view of the relationship between religion and politics as rulers opted, or attempted to opt, for Catholicism. It adds an extra dimension to current understandings of the tensions between kings and their warriors, suggesting that 'Arianism'/ Homoianism was favoured by the sections of the latter who felt threatened by the potential for a ruler to expand his power and prestige and fundamentally change his relationship with them if he succeeded in entering the Catholic macrocosm. It also suggests why Clovis, the ruler of the Franks, was able to make a direct transition from paganism to Catholicism. And a combination of the perspectives offered by Horton and by the cognitive study of religion sheds new light on the phenomenon of Lombard 'Arianism', as well as on Lombard rulers' acceptance of Catholicism in the seventh century.

Chapter 5, 'Bringing God to Mind', looks at the ways in which the Church sought to achieve a Christianity that was more than superficial. It offers a way out of one of the most notable impasses in the study of early medieval religion: the question of whether we should accept or dismiss testimonies about the continuation of practices disapproved of by the Church long after Christianization. The question of their reliability has divided scholars, with some rejecting them altogether, others accepting them cautiously: acceptance or rejection has up to now been very much a matter of personal opinion. However, the cognitive study of religion indicates that rituals have common features across vastly different cultures, thus providing support for the idea that the apparent similarities between practices condemned over wide geographical areas and long periods are not simply a result of lazy ecclesiastics copying earlier writings.

A cognitive approach also enables us to move away from the misleading idea of 'pagan survivals' amongst the Catholic Franks and Sueves. A survey of legislation indicates that after the Franks officially accepted Catholicism, practices involving major non-Christian deities seem to have died out relatively quickly (except perhaps on the north-eastern borders). The practices condemned by the Church are based on the continued intuition of certain natural features as being special. They involve what Justin Barrett has called 'nonreflective' belief, belief that is not necessarily conscious or explicit, is produced automatically and rapidly, is expressed mainly by behaviour and is typified by strong in-group uniformity.[28] The practice of making vows at springs, trees, groves and shrines is typical of such 'nonreflective' belief: it is not one based on reflection or doctrine – as is Christian theology – but on the 'abductive' reasoning which attributes healing or other supernatural powers to them. However, as Barrett also underlines, 'nonreflective' belief works to make 'reflective' belief – such as Christian doctrine and theology – more plausible.[29] This opens up new ways of looking at behaviours which the Church sought to discourage or encourage. The sermons of Cæsarius of Arles, works such as Martin of Braga's *On the Castigation of Rustics* and Gregory of Tours' treatises *Glory of the Martyrs* and *Glory of the Confessors* appear in this light as part of the Church's attempts to divert people from non-Christian 'nonreflective' belief and replace it with attractive Christian alternatives, in the hope of strengthening their attachment to Christianity.

Chapter 5 also suggests that we should consider the cognitive aspect of the penitentials, handbooks of penance which enabled the clergy to administer penances tailored to a range of offences and which enjoyed a widespread circulation on the continent from the early seventh century onwards. The first work of this type was produced in sixth-century Ireland, where conversion to Christianity was not yet fully accomplished: part of its aim appears to have been to convince people that the Christian God had access to what is termed 'strategic information' – that He could see into their innermost thoughts. An equally important development, which would survive as the concept of the penitential was transmitted to the continent, was to make penance repeatable, thus playing an important role in reinforcing the key 'nonreflective' level of belief.

The final chapter, 'Rest In Peace' examines the very important area of beliefs about death and the afterlife. According to Pascal Boyer, the souls of the dead, or their 'shadows' or 'presences', are the most commonly intuited of all supernatural agents.[30] He points to the common feeling that something has to be done with a corpse and also to anthropological observations of the way in which the dead body is regarded as polluting: in cognitive terms people, however vague their notions about the dead in general might be, have much more detailed feelings and intuitions about the recently dead – and what they can do to the living.[31] This chapter highlights the differing pagan and Christian views of the relationship between body and soul and afterlife and the very different types of funerary ritual which this produced. It surveys a wide range of archaeological evidence suggesting that Christian funerary rites were perceived as inadequate by the Germanic peoples in terms of ensuring that the dead would remain safely in their graves and would not return to harm the living. It offers a fresh understanding of the way in which the Church, by around 700 CE, was gradually beginning to develop ways of reassuring people that their souls would safely pass into a Christian afterlife where they would be united with their long-dead ancestors.

Intuitions of Divinity

Searching for gods

Templates provided by the cognitive study of religion are particularly useful
in enabling us to understand the deities and rituals of the Germanic peoples.
Over recent decades, we have seen the emergence of sharply differing
opinions as to how much we can know about their beliefs – and how we can
know it. There have been numerous earlier attempts at interpretation of the
evidence by scholars as diverse as Georges Dumézil, Claude Lévi-Strauss and
Mircea Eliade, some of which have stood the test of time better than others.[1]
One major book on the conversion of Europe announces our 'ignorance' of
Germanic paganism and of the way in which its traces were 'diligently oblit-
erated' by its Christian supplanter. This, it adds, has not deterred modern
scholars from writing many weighty books about the topic.[2] Others have
taken a more positive view and have attempted to chart the evolution of the
Germanic and Scandinavian pantheon of major deities across the centuries.[3]
A cognitive approach allows us to interpret such findings further and also to
extend our understanding of the shape and characteristics of the religions of
the Germanic peoples.

Traditionally, discussion of the continental Germanic peoples' pre-Christian
beliefs centres round what might be called 'the search for gods'.[4] For our scant
evidence of the major supernatural beings worshipped by the Germanic
peoples, we are chiefly dependent on a handful of written sources: principally
the *Germania* of the pagan Roman author Tacitus, written at the end of the
first century CE, which gives some glimpses into the religious world of the
Germanic peoples three hundred years or so before they settled in the Empire;
the *Getica* of the Christian Jordanes (mid-sixth century); and the anonymous
text from the seventh century known as the *Origo Gentis Langobardorum*.

These are all what cultural anthropologists would term 'etic' accounts, written from the point of view of the outsider. All their information is at the very least, second-hand. The sources' purposes are diverse: Tacitus is writing in the tradition of classical ethnography and he also creates idealized descriptions of 'noble savages', presented as 'endowed with desirable qualities of simplicity and uprightness that the Romans had lost'.[5] Jordanes, a Catholic of Gothic descent writing in Latin c. 550 CE, claimed access to Gothic oral traditions as well as to a now lost and presumably propagandistic *Gothic History* composed for Theoderic the Great by Cassiodorus; and also to the work of an otherwise unknown Gothic writer, Ablabius.[6] The anonymous *Origo Gentis Langobardorum* (*Origin of the People of the Lombards*) is, as its title suggests, a legendary account of the beginnings of the Lombards, set down in Latin in the second half of the seventh century. Despite this late date, its most recent editor describes it as originating in a 'pagan or paganizing' milieu, suggesting that the Lombards' non-Christian past was still a reasonably vivid memory when it was committed to writing.[7] We are also able to also glean some fragmentary information about the Franks from the writings of Gregory, Bishop of Tours, who died in the 590s (see below) and a very little from sixth-century ecclesiastical legislation.

The *locus classicus* for the religion of Germanic tribes in earlier Roman times, long before groups moved into the Empire en masse, is the work of Tacitus – principally the *Germania*, composed at the end of the first century CE. Where major deities are concerned, he states that the Reudingi, Aviones, Anglii, Varini, Eudoses, Suarines and Huitones, tribes 'protected by rivers and forests' and neighbours of the Langobards, and living north of the Elbe in Schleswig-Holstein, Jutland and perhaps Mecklenburg, all worship a fertility goddess, Nerthus.[8] He names the deities of the Naharvali, identified by some modern scholars as the Siling Vandals, from the regions of the Czech Republic and Silesia, as 'the Alci', whom he says are 'worshipped as brothers and young men'.[9] For the other major deities of the Germanic people, the *Germania* offers no native names and does not associate them with any particular group. Tacitus makes Mercury the chief deity to whom the first-century German tribes offered cult: on certain days, he claimed, they even sacrificed humans to him. As well as Mercury, they venerated Mars and Hercules. Some of the Sueves, he adds, had imported the cult of the eastern goddess, Isis.[10]

The deities named by Tacitus as Mercury, Mars and Hercules have been identified as Woden, Tiw and Thunor. Mercury's day – *dies Mercurii* in Latin, Mercredi in French – is Wednesday, Woden's day in English, originally Wodenstag in German (now the neutral Mittwoch). *Dies Martii* is the English Tuesday, the day of the god Tiw. As for Hercules, it seems he is to be identified with the god Thunor, who is more usually equated with Jove, as in Thursday – Jeudi in French and Giovedì in Italian.[11]

Our main authority for the major gods of the Lombards is the text known as the *Origo Gentis Langobardorum* composed in the seventh century. It contains the oldest written version of the traditional tale of how the Lombards got their name, a story encompassing a number of valuable references to Lombard deities. The *Origo* relates how, in the era before they entered Italy, the people known as the Winniles found themselves in conflict with the Vandals in a crucial struggle over the payment of tribute. The Vandals petitioned the god Godan – that is, Woden – to help them and Godan answered that he would award victory to whomever he first saw at sunrise. Meanwhile the leaders of the Winniles, the legendary Ibor and Agio, together with their mother Gambara, resorted to the goddess Frea for help. Frea advised that the women of the Winniles should first let their hair down, arrange it to imitate a beard and line up beside their husbands. She then turned her husband's bed around while he was asleep so that when he awoke, he was facing eastwards and saw the Winniles. He asked Frea who these 'long-beards' were – and she answered that as he had given them the name, he should award them the victory – which he duly did.[12] And so the Lombards – *Langobardi* or 'long-beards' – got their name.

There is no comparable source for the deities venerated by the pagan Franks; but there is a little information to be gleaned from the *Ten Books of Histories* – better known as the *History of the Franks* – of Gregory, Bishop of Tours, writing in the late sixth century. Gregory narrates the conversion to Catholic Christianity of the Frankish leader Clovis. As a source of information on this event, Gregory has considerable limitations. His account is highly circumstantial, but he is not always reliable. His narrative makes Clovis' Burgundian Catholic wife Clothild reprove her husband for his paganism, casting aspersions on the moral character of his gods.[13] Disappointingly for the historian, the gods she names are the Roman deities and her speech is clearly made up by Gregory as it repeats the highly unflattering characterization of the Roman pantheon given by Christian authors such as Bishops Cæsarius of Arles and Martin of Braga (see Chapter 5 below). But Gregory does let slip one vital detail: Clovis and Clothild's firstborn was a son called Ingomer. The 'Ing' element is important. Later in his work Gregory also mentions the consort of Charibert, a slightly later Merovinigian ruler, whose name is Ingoberg; as well as Ingund, daughter of King Sigibert and Brunichildis and another Ingund who was the second wife of Chlothar I; and Ingitrude, a relation of King Charibert.[14] All this suggests that amongst the gods known to and worshipped by the Franks was Ingui, otherwise known as Ing or Inguec. The Ripuarian Franks along with the 'Ingvaeones' and the Anglii venerated Ing/Ingui as a fertility deity: it is possible that for the Franks, as for the Angles in seventh-century Northumbria, he was associated with the sea, sky and earth.[15] Some scholars believe that that he was a male personification of the female fertility deity mentioned by Tacitus, Nerthus.[16]

Apart from these major written sources there are other fragmentary clues to the identity of the deities of the Germanic peoples. There are indications that Goths and perhaps also the Sueves worshipped Thunor, the god of thunder. Some Latin authors equated him, as we will see, with Jove or Jupiter, another thunder deity and it is noticeable that sixth-century Christian sources from the Suevic and Gothic areas of Gallaecia and Septimania (Visigothic Southern France) inveigh against the custom of taking the 'day of Jove' as a holiday.[17]

Tacitus and the 'interpretatio romana'

Tacitus' account suggests a Germanic pantheon consisting of a fertility goddess, twin male gods, a god of war, a god of strength and a god of invention and communication. However, there are many difficulties in accepting it at face value. In the first part of the *Germania*, his description of Mercury as the chief deity of the Germans is clearly dependent on Cæsar (who himself was indebted to Herodotus) on the Gauls. Cæsar describes the Mercury of the Gauls as

> the discoverer of all arts, the ruler of roads and journeys and they believe that he has the greatest power in getting wealth and for merchants.[18]

Not only does Tacitus use Cæsar on the Gauls, he also follows the practice of what he himself designates the *interpretatio romana*: the identification of Germanic or other non-Roman deities by the names of Roman divinities. This technique of association should not be taken as a straightforward indication of equivalence. It is, rather, a discourse of power, an assimilation of foreign divinities to those of Rome, based on whichever of their aspects and abilities approximated most closely to those of a Roman god.[19] Thus it is possible for Tacitus to substitute Hercules for Thunor – presumably on account of the strength that they have in common and the resemblance between weapons associated with them (club and 'hammer') – while the more familiar association between Jove and Thunor is based on the circumstance that both were gods of thunder. Neither 'interpretation' represents an absolute fit. The fact that Jove was regarded as the chief of the Roman gods, while no such status has been claimed for Thunor, creates an additional complication and a barrier to accepting Tacitus' information as it stands. However, the use of a cognitive approach helps us achieve a more complete understanding both of what Tacitus has to say and also of the early Germanic gods in general.

Intuiting gods: a cognitive approach

The cognitive study of religion teaches us that the powers and accessibility of supernatural beings may vary a great deal. A common intuition is that of a supremely powerful god who has created the world and everything in it. A crucial part of this intuition is that he is too important to concern himself with everyday goings-on and the affairs of humans. This leads to the important consequence that he has no regular worship or cult. The classic example of such gods known to ethnographers and anthropologists is the African deity Nzame.[20] The Germanic peoples also appear to have regarded one god as superior to the others: in the eighth century, the Anglo-Saxon Bishop Daniel of Winchester, giving advice to his compatriot St Boniface in Germany, noted that pagans were careful not to offend the one god whom they thought more powerful than the rest.[21] This god is originally likely to have been an Indo-European deity, *Tiwaz: his name means both 'god' and 'heaven'; he was a sky god, creator of light and of the world, day-father (*dies-pater* in Latin).

His name is cognate with the Greek Zeus and the Latin Jove, both regarded as fathers of the gods in their respective pantheons. He was known both to continental Germans and to the Anglo-Saxons as Tiw.

Given that Tiw and Jove are essentially the same deity, why did Tacitus and others equate Tiw with Mars? In his *Annals*, Tacitus provides us with a valuable clue when he specifically associates two tribes, the Chatti and the Hermunduri (Thuringians?) with the cults of both Mars (*Tiwaz/Tiw) and Mercury (*Wodanaz/Woden):

> The same summer [58 CE] the Hermunduri and Chatti fought a great battle. Each wanted to seize the rich salt-producing river which flowed between them. Besides their passion for settling everything by force, they held a religious conviction that this region was close to heaven so that men's prayers received ready access [*agendi religione insita eos maxime locos propinquare caelo precesque mortalium a deis nusquam propius audiri*]. And by divine favour, they believed, salt in this river and these woods was produced, not as in other countries by the evaporation of water left by the sea, but by pouring it on heaps of burning wood and thus uniting the two opposed elements, fire and water. In the battle, the Chatti were defeated – with catastrophic effects. For both sides, in the event of victory, had vowed their enemies to Mars and Mercury. This vow implied the sacrifice of the entire beaten side with their horses and all their possessions.[22]

Both Mercury and *Wodanaz/Woden were regarded as psychopomps, conductors of souls to the otherworld and this link with death probably explains the development of Woden's association with war. We cannot be absolutely sure of the extent to which this connection had developed in Tacitus' era. Even so, the passage shows that the struggle was felt by both groups to require the invocation of two gods, one associated with movement between the worlds of the living and the dead and the other who was the supreme deity. While the most powerful gods are intuited as generally disinterested in human affairs, sacrifices to them may be attempted in extreme life-or-death situations.[23] Tacitus' account makes clear the extraordinary nature of the contest over a region that was both economically important and sacred.

Tacitus exhibits no awareness of Tiw's position as sky god and would have been influenced in his 'interpretation' of Tiw as Mars because of the way he had been invoked in a famous conflict situation. He may also have been aware of a militarization of Tiw in the form of dedicatory inscriptions to 'Mars' raised by Germans who had risen through the ranks of the imperial armies. As they integrated into imperial forces, these officers picked up the 'epigraphic habit': in inscriptions of this nature, Germanic gods were 'increasingly worshipped in the form of Roman counterparts'.[24] (The same phenomenon has been observed of the Celtic gods in Roman Britain, where 'native deities are likely to have been squeezed, with varying degrees of discomfort, into imported conceptual moulds'.[25]) Upwardly mobile soldiers or other officials of Germanic origin were ready to 'squeeze' Tiw into Mars. In doing so they Romanized and altered his significance, highlighting his ability to intervene in war or his protective dimension, making him active rather than remote.[26] We can only speculate to what extent this gradual transformation was produced by the victory of the Chatti over the Hermunduri, or the assimilation of Roman values and intuitions of divinity – or by a combination of the two. But we find an expression of the older understanding of Tiw – 'Mars' – as supreme deity by Germans in the armies of the Roman Empire in the second century CE in two Latin inscriptions from the Roman fort at Housesteads on Hadrian's Wall:

> To the god Mars Thincsus and the two Alaisiagae Beda and Fimmilena, and to the *numen* (godhood) of Augustus Germanicus, the citizens of Tuihantus have paid their vow freely and deservedly.

> To the god Mars and the two Alaisiagae and the godhood of Augustus Germanicus, the citizens of Tuihantus, of the troop of the Frisians of Ver(covicium) of Severus Alexander's paid their vow deservedly.[27]

According to Ken Dowden, these dedications date from the reign of Alexander Severus (222–35 CE) and were made by troops from the region of Twente in the Netherlands. Mars is not represented here just as a war-god. Instead he appears at the head of a hierarchy of divinities, superior to the Alaisiagae (for whom see below) and also to the deified Roman Emperor Augustus Germanicus. Crucially, in the first inscription, he is also designated *Thincsus*, god of the Thing. This was the assembly of free male German warriors and the inscription can be read as reflecting an understanding of him as a paramount deity 'uniting a variety of people who claim to belong to the same stock'.[28]

The mutations in Tiw's identity represented in both Tacitus and the dedications reflect different types of assimilations to Rome – one top-down, the other bottom-up, both the product of contacts between the western Germanic peoples and Rome. The second part of *Germania*, where Tacitus warns against the threat posed by Germans and enumerates the German tribes, is closer in many respects to classical ethnographic traditions than the first. Tacitus sketches some of the rituals of the tribes who worshipped Nerthus as well as those of the Semnones, who formed part of the Suebes (see below). Thus as he moves into areas were there were fewer direct contacts between Germans and Romans, he appears at first to provide marginally less stereotyped information. Nevertheless, it is still very thin and continues to present problems, not least as we do not know how it was originally obtained. When discussing the Alci, Tacitus concentrates on the aspects in which they most resemble the Dioscuri, while his account of Nerthus, a female fertility goddess, raises many questions, not least about her gender. Richard North has argued that Nerthus was a masculine fertility god and that Tacitus misunderstood the information given him by his (unknown) source, mistakenly imposing an *interpretatio romana* making him female. He also sees in Nerthus the origin of the fertility deity Ing, who was worshipped by the Franks and Angles.[29] However, Tacitus' description of the religion of the Semnones also refers to a supreme god. He claims that the Semnones believed this divinity was connected to the grove where the tribe had been created and where a grisly ritual symbolically re-enacting that creation took place at irregular intervals. Tacitus offers no name for, or *interpretatio* of, this 'god who reigns over all', but the evidence suggests that we are looking at *Tiwaz/Tiw.[30]

Philologists have confirmed the Goths' worship of Tiw from the ninth-century manuscript giving the rune *Tyz*.[31] The sixth-century author of the *Getica*, Jordanes, not only identifies their major deity as 'Mars', but also states that the Goths used to sacrifice captured enemies to him and to hang spoils of war on trees in his honour.[32] Is he simply following the Tacitean *interpretatio*? Jordanes has never been regarded as the most reliable source: as Peter Heather has pointed out, not one of the central theses of his *Getica* has won simple acceptance from historians and archaeologists;[33] while E. A. Thompson went so far as to write of his 'genius for misunderstanding'.[34] Historians still debate the extent to which he is dependent not only on the lost Gothic history of Cassiodorus, but also on Gothic traditions.[35] His work certainly shows awareness of some of Tacitus' writings, in particular the *Agricola*.[36] However, he makes the association between the Goths and Mars in a section of the *Getica* which describes a period in which the Goths resided in Thrace. Thrace is particularly associated in Virgil's *Æneid* with Mars;[37] and Jordanes appears to have picked up the association of Thrace with Mars after following the earlier Spanish historian Orosius in assimilating the ethnonym of the ancient Thracian people, the Getae, to the Goths.[38]

Jordanes makes no mention of 'Mercury'; and the idea that Goths worshipped *Wodanaz/Woden is controversial for a number of reasons. An inscription on a gold torque found in the Gothic Pietroasa hoard, possibly buried in the confusion of a Hunnic attack in 376, may read *gutaniowi hailag*. This could mean 'sacred to Wotan-Jupiter', but both inscription and translation are contested. Some scholars deny any association between the Goths and *Wodanaz/Woden.[39] They emphasize the alleged spread of the cult of Mercury eastwards from Gaul, but question the idea that it ever reached the East Germanic Goths: Richard North has cited the characteristic absence of weapon-deposits in Gothic graves in support of the thesis that Woden was unknown to the Goths.[40] However, there may be other reasons behind Gothic reluctance to deposit weapons, such as cost or inheritance customs, so it is difficult to say whether or not he was worshipped by the Goths. Almost equally problematic is the question of whether they venerated Thunor. The custom of taking the 'day of Jove' as a holiday might suggest that there had been a tradition of honouring Thunor on this day, amongst Visigoths, Sueves or both: but we cannot be sure that this was the case. Even where the major gods are concerned, there may have been distinct variations in the pantheon between different groups and peoples and there is no written source which tells us anything about the gods worshipped by the Burgundes. However, we are a little better informed about the Lombards and our information not only names their deities but also seems to fit a cognitive template.

One of intuitions that might develop in relation to the mental representation of a god too powerful to trouble himself with human concerns was that of the resourceful wife or consort goddess who might intervene on behalf of humans with her husband. The nineteenth-century British traveller, Mary Kingsley, noted of the great West African Nzame (Nzambi Mpungu) that he had such a consort, Nzambi:

Nzambi Mpungu takes, as is usual with his class, next to no interest in human affairs – legal or individual. Occasionally you come across long conversations between him and his consort Nzambi who is always on the worry about earthly affairs. His share in them is coldly cynical, often marked by sound sense, a sort of, 'If they will do it, whatever does it matter to me?' Now and again he will grant grand things as a gift to her, but by no means always.[41]

Thus there is an intermediary between the remote and indifferent god and humanity below. We can see an analogous situation in the Lombard *Origo*, which appears to contain a multiplicity of representations and intuitions of gods telescoped into the story of the naming of the Lombards. Frea is cast in the position of the goddess wife, who intercedes with her husband Godan or Woden. Here, Godan himself appears to display some of the characteristics of a supreme deity, not entirely interested in human affairs: but this may be a survival from an earlier version of the legend in which *Tiwaz or Tiw, the sky god had played the part now taken by Godan (something also suggested by the references to sunrise). In the *Origo* story there is also an intimation that Frea might have played a particularly significant role in the life of Lombard women: one of the figures who appeals to her is female and she instructs the women of the Winniles to play a decisive role in tricking Woden. But the legend also suggests that she was an important figure in the lives of the Lombards in general; and we also know that in her later Scandinavian persona, Freyja, she was venerated by men and women alike.[42]

The work of anthropologists and ethnographers also suggests what is confirmed by a cognitive approach to religion: that people may intuit lower levels of supernatural beings below major gods and goddesses. Though their powers may seem to be much lesser and more localized than those of the principal deities, they are highly relevant to practical concerns.[43] Describing West African religions, Mary Kingsley outlined numerous levels of divinities and supernatural beings below the creator god Nzame:

There are the great creating spirits like Nzambi Mpungu: beneath him are a class of great nature spirits: beneath them is another class of nature spirits, which may be influenced by the class of spirits that live in human beings: equal to these human spirits are a great class of spirits, the Mionde: beneath these there are an immense number of different sorts of spirits, who may be influenced by all the grades of spirits above them; men may use them, or the spirits which are above men may use them, either to guard against, or to injure, others of their own class, or those below them.[44]

One such group may be the ancestors. Jordanes claims that the Goths had venerated their ancestors as demi-gods or *Anses*: is this any more reliable than his view of 'Mars'? His work, based on Cassiodorus' lost Gothic history is heavily biased towards Theoderic's dynasty, the Amals, constructing seventeen generations between the mythical Gapt, its founder and Theoderic's successor. Had his source, Cassiodorus, matched the number of generations from Aeneas to Romulus to give his patrons equal status to that of the Roman emperors?[45] This seems quite probable, as we cannot trace the Amal line further back than the fifth century (see Chapter 4). Even so, the focus on family and ancestors reveals a general Gothic preoccupation; and ancestor veneration would be in keeping with what we know of Gothic and Germanic burial customs in general (see Chapter 6).

We also have intriguing evidence of a lesser Lombard divinity. The *Life of Saint Barbatus*, composed by a Beneventan cleric in the ninth or early tenth century, describes the effigy of a snake-god, venerated amongst the Lombards of Benevento in the 660s.[46] Discussion of this passage in the *Life* has traditionally focused on the identity of the snake deity: it has been identified variously as a Germanic divinity; or a local one, originally venerated by the Marsi, an Italian people credited with the ability to charm poisonous snakes; or a relic of the cult of the eastern goddess Isis (there was an earlier temple dedicated to her in Benevento); or, and least convincingly, a manifestation of the cult of Woden.[47] Whichever is the case, the viper would go on to enjoy a long association with Benevento.[48] What is of interest here is the way in which it was venerated. According to the *Life*, it was the object of a cult amongst the Lombards, even though they were technically baptized Christians: Barbatus had to wean them away from its worship as well as from another non-Christian rite (see below), by presenting the Christian God as a god of war and the Virgin Mary as the protector of the city when it was besieged by the Eastern Emperor, Constans II. Even though the Emperor lifted the siege, Duke Romuald and his immediate followers soon resumed the cult of the viper in secret: this was detected by Barbatus, who persuaded Romuald's wife to hand over the simulacrum to him so that he could destroy it.

Though located in the Christian Lombard duchy of Benevento in the 660s, this narrative can be interpreted from a cognitive perspective to tell us something about the pre-Christian beliefs of the Lombards. In this period, Benevento was 'semi-detached' from the Lombard state in northern Italy; even there (see Chapter 4), Catholic Christianity had only recently become the official creed of its rulers.[49] The Beneventan Lombards' beliefs involved a syncretism in which the Christian God was acknowledged while another minor power – the snake divinity – had a regular cult, suggesting that it was thought more likely to help in certain circumstances. Barbatus had to interfere twice in an endeavour to make the Lombards understand that the Christian God was a deity to whom they could pray and who would intervene in their favour. His first attempt failed: the *Life* suggests that he introduced the cults of the Virgin and St Michael, whose shrine at Monte Gargano would become a Lombard 'national' shrine.[50] But at this stage, the Lombards were still not persuaded that the Christian God could see into their hearts, as Barbatus claimed He could.[51] It is plausible that the Lombards, viewing the Virgin and the archangel as representatives of a lower level of divinity accepted them as such, at the same time continuing to venerate a subsidiary deity of their own, the viper. Only when Barbatus took the radical step of destroying the simulacrum was he able to focus their attention more successfully on the Christian God as sole god.

Philological studies are beginning to reveal more of the existence of these intermediate or lower-level supernatural beings. Germanic soldiers in some areas of the second and third-century Roman Empire venerated a number of female deities. Along with the Alaisiagae, mentioned above and Ahuecannae, dedicatory inscriptions have been found to individual divinities such as Hariasa and Harimella. There are also dedications to groups of three female beings known as *matronae* or *matres*, 'ladies' or 'mothers'. The categories of goddesses and *matronae/matres* overlapped to some extent: Philip Shaw has recently argued strongly in favour of both being the objects of small-scale local cults, identified with social groups or geographical areas or features. He suggests that the *matres* were 'mothers' associated with kin-groups.[52] The creation of votive inscriptions dedicated to them by Germanic troops serving in the Roman armies suggests their veneration by Germanic groups outside the imperial borders. This seems to be borne out by one inscription from

Cologne, referring to the *matres Germanis Suebis*. This designation, apparently indicating connections with the *Suebi* east of the Rhine, provides a clue to the beliefs of the Sueves in the era before they crossed into the Empire in large numbers in the early fifth century. The names of other groups of *matronae* – Aumenahenae, Nersihenae and Renahenae – suggest that they were tutelary beings, watching over or personifying rivers.[53] The idea of relatively small-scale local cults is an attractive one: Shaw is careful to note that the 'kin-groups' involved were not necessarily biologically defined.[54] A cult centred on one group or one relatively restricted geographical area could provide a means of binding families or individuals of different biological origin into a more cohesive social whole. The veneration of *matres* may have been widespread amongst the earlier western Germanic peoples and spread to Anglo-Saxon England. In his work *On Time*, the Anglo-Saxon monk Bede (d. 735) refers to the celebration of a winter solstice festival known as *Modranecht*: this is usually understood as the 'night of the mothers.'[55]

Another and more startling outcome to emerge from a consideration of Shaw's onomastic archaeology is the possibility that we might find evidence of a goddess venerated by the Goths in the unlikely context of Bede's work. The same chapter of *On Time* refers to a month known by the Anglo-Saxons as *Hredmonath*, 'named for the goddess Hreda.'[56] The identity and even the existence of this goddess are highly controversial topics amongst philologists. But if she did exist, then her name is associated in two late Anglo-Saxon poems, *Widsith* and *Elene* with the Goths, there referred to as *Hreðgotan*.[57] Might this late and much-debated evidence indicate that the pagan Goths had once worshipped a female divinity named Hreda or Hreða? At the moment, we can only say that this is a possibility.

Belief in a powerful but indifferent creator was not only accompanied by the intuition of less powerful but more approachable deities and divinities associated with kin-groups or localities, but also by intuitions of a multiplicity of lesser supernatural beings. Cognitive theory shows that some lesser supernatural beings could have had limited powers and very specific attributes – like the Maya 'Masters of the Forest', who know everything about the forest, but nothing about events or things outside it.[58] They could have been understood as living close to humans and affecting various aspects of daily life. In Anglo-Saxon England, for example, there were *ælfe*, beings whose name has come into modern English as elves. These are not the diminutive persons of modern books and film but tall, fair creatures who might injure humans and were

> invisible or hard-to-see creatures who shot their victims with some kind of arrow or spear, thus inflicting a wound or inducing a disease with no other apparent cause (elfshot). They appear to be lesser spirits than the Æsir deities, but with similar armaments in spears and arrows... .[59]

More recently, English *ælfe* have been diagnosed as other-worldly, human-like beings, dangerously seductive and, by the eleventh century, female.[60] Whether *ælfe* had a direct equivalent amongst the continental Germanic peoples at an earlier date is unclear. The only evidence offered by Wilhelm Boudriot in his *Altgermanische Religion* is reference to what he calls 'forest demons' and 'imps' (*Schraten, Kobolden*) in a much later work, the eleventh-century handbook of penance known as the *Corrector*. The passage in question actually asks:

> Hast thou made little, boys' size bows and boy's shoes, and cast them into thy barn so that satyrs or *pilosi* (literally, hairy ones) might sport with them, in order that they might bring to them the goods of others so that thou shouldst become richer?[61]

The same work refers to belief in *sylvaticas* – 'women of the forests', beings that assume bodily form, have sex with humans and then vanish and who sound rather like the later English *aelfe*; and also to 'unclean spirits', at their most harmful before cockcrow.[62] This would suggest belief in some lesser supernatural beings that interacted with humans for good (the satyrs and *pilosi* might be persuaded to benefit one individual by stealing from others, while the *sylvaticas* offered the prospect of sexual pleasure) or evil. They may not have been popularly called by the Latinate names given to them in the penitential handbook, which look like clerical attempts at assigning identities to them. Martin of Braga's work *On the Castigation of Rustics* composed in sixth-century Gallaecia gives classical names to what look like beings of this type, closely identified with natural features. By addressing his sermon to 'rustics', he suggests that 'Lamiae in the rivers, Nymphs in springs, Dianas in woods' were part of peasant intuitions.[63] But we cannot prove that they did not become part of those of the Suevic incomers to Gallaecia as well and that similar beliefs about beings who live in or close to rivers, springs and woods, did not spread amongst other Germanic settlers elsewhere in western Europe (see Chapter 5 below). As we have just seen, some *matronae* names from the earlier period derived from rivers and springs, indicating the propensity to venerate such features and to associate them with tutelary beings. Spirits of place, intuited by natives and incomers alike, may have played an important role in indigenizing settling Germanic groups.

Similar intuitions of divinity may also have done a good deal to integrate the Huns who threw in their lot with the Burgundians after the death of Attila in the mid-fifth century at a stage when the Burgundians were not all Christians. Modern scholars identify the Hunnic belief system with Tengrism, in which there is also a creator sky god and in which Heaven, Earth and the spirits of nature, as well as the ancestors, provide and care for human beings.[64]

Rituals

Our evidence for the rituals of the Germanic peoples is also fragmentary, but is capable of interpretation through a cognitive approach.

Tacitus claimed that the Germanic tribes, at the end of the first century, all venerated Nerthus (whom he identifies as the earth goddess, *Terra Mater*):

> There is a sacred grove on an island in the Ocean, in which there is a conse-crated chariot, draped with a cloth, which the priest alone may touch. He perceives the goddess in the innermost shrine and with great reverence escorts her in her chariot, which is drawn by female cattle. There are days of rejoicing then and the countryside celebrates the festival, wherever she deigns to visit and to accept hospitality. No-one goes to war, no-one takes up arms, all objects of iron are locked away, then and only then do they experience peace and quiet, only then do they prize them, until the goddess has had her fill of human society and the priest brings her back to her temple. Afterwards, the chariot, the cloth and, if one may believe it, the deity herself are washed in a hidden lake. The slaves who perform the office are immediately afterwards swallowed up in the same lake ...[65]

A ritual with similar basic characteristics is found in accounts of the pagan Tervingi, one of the groups that formed the Goths. During the persecution of Christians in Gothia in 369–72, by rulers who identified Christianity with

Romanization, those suspected of being Christians were ordered to show their loyalty by worshipping and making sacrifice to a traditional *xoanon*, placed on a wagon and drawn to their dwellings.[66] E. A. Thompson claims that the *xoanon*, or statue, was 'a wooden post like the Saxon Irminsul of a later time' and was normally wheeled about to ensure the fertility of fields and animals.[67] The sacrifice involved a ritual meal of food offered to the 'idol', which, according to Herwig Wolfram, was associated with the ancestors.[68] In his work *The Glory of the Confessors*, Gregory of Tours claims that in the past an effigy of the goddess Berecynthia was drawn through the fields on a wagon.[69] Berecynthia was an eastern goddess and Gregory sets his narrative in fourth-century century Gaul, before the arrival of the Franks. But as his purpose is to demonstrate the ineffectiveness of paganism in the face of Christianity, he may be combining elements drawn from a variety of paganisms to make his point: one of these elements may be a dim awareness of earlier Frankish fertility rites. Richard North points out the proximity of the shore-dwelling Ingvaeones to the tribes who worshipped Nerthus and also to the wagon-tour made by the god Freyr in later Norse mythology.[70]

Tacitus also claims that the Semnones, 'the most ancient and most noble of the Sueves' performed a ritual of human sacrifice:

> At a fixed time deputations from all the peoples who share the same origin meet in a wood sanctified by their forefathers' auguries and by ancient dread. A human victim is slaughtered on behalf of all present to celebrate the gruesome opening of the barbarous ritual … This whole superstition is based on the belief that from this wood the people derives its origin and the god who reigns over all dwells there …[71]

There were other noteworthy features of the ritual:

> Another form of reverence marks the grove as well: no one enters it unless bound with a chain, as an inferior being, outwardly acknowledging the power of the divinity. If they happen to fall down, they are not permitted to get up on their feet again: they roll out along the ground.[72]

This part of Tactitus' account is highly suggestive of one of the basic purposes of the ritual. The contrived circumstances of the Semnones' entry into the grove abolished everyday assumptions about the free status of the participants, as well as inhibiting the instinct to help one another. Coupled with the fact of human sacrifice, the experience of entering the grove was deliberately disorientating and awe-inspiring. Such experiences have been characterized by the cognitive anthropologist Harvey Whitehouse as imprinting vivid 'flashbulb memories' which recur with increasing vividness later in life.[73] These strategies create an internal cohesiveness amongst participants, who are in this case linked as a group, not just by ties of kin, but also by participation in the rite. Pascal Boyer also indicates the ways in which other elaborate and disorientating rituals, such as rites of initiation, can alter social relations between the participants.[74] The males of the Semnones were formed into a cohort by this experience, which would have cemented their identity as free warriors.

Rituals of human sacrifice amongst the Germanic peoples were probably a thing of the past as they came into more extensive contact with the Roman Empire. Wolfram reminds us that in the fourth-century battle 'At the Willows',

> the Tervingi also bound themselves on oath 'according to their custom' to come to one another's aid.[75]

We have evidence of a ritual designed to promote group solidarity amongst the warriors of Lombard Benevento in the seventh century. The evidence again comes from the *Life of Saint Barbatus*:

> Not far from the walls of Benevento … they venerated a sacred tree. They hung an animal skin from it, and all present, turning their backs to the tree, galloped very fast on horseback, digging their spurs into their horses, in order to overtake each other; and in this race, they threw their spears back over their shoulders at the skin. And thus they speared a smallish part of it to eat superstitiously. And because they fulfilled foolish vows there, because of this practice, they gave the place the name, by which it is still known, of 'the vow'.[76]

Scholars have attempted to link this ritual with a god, pointing out the connection between the Lombards and Woden and the association of his later Scandinavian personification, Odin, with hanging and hanged sacrifices.[77] But the most important aspect of this ritual may not have been any religious dimension but its social consequences. The race forged a bond between mounted warriors, who thus became members of a cohort created initially by a ritualized trial of skill. This also involved, in the way that such extraordinary bonding rituals do, a reversal of a normal situation and an added handicap or danger in that the race was *away* from the tree, rather than, as one might expect towards it, and the spears were thrown behind the riders, *manibus retroversis*.[78] Further ties were established between the group members by the ritualized communal consumption of consecrated food, in the shape of part of the animal hide or, more likely, the flesh adhering to it, which may also have been thought to impart strength, skill or bravery in hunt or battle. The importance of this bonding ritual is underlined by the fact that a Lombard law code of the 640s from the northern kingdom lays down penalties for abandoning a comrade in battle.[79] This was part of a 'Romanizing' policy by the northern ruler, Rothari, who was attempting, as far as he could, to move away from old-style Lombard kingship (see Chapter 4): his penalization of those who failed to help their fellows indicates how important traditional rituals were in creating solidarity amongst a warrior group.

Where ritual is concerned, Pascal Boyer has pointed to the way in which divinities tend to be added to the original rite:

> you can understand what gods are doing in ritual … once you realise they are an add-on to human activities that do not really require them.[80]

Even the rituals generally associated with fertility and good harvests had an important social dimension. Tacitus noted that the arrival of Nerthus was an occasion of festivities:

> There are days of rejoicing then and the countryside celebrates the festival, wherever she deigns to visit and accept hospitality …[81]

According to some scholars, this was really an occasion on which sacral kings, Nerthus in mortal form, toured the regions in spring and early summer, 'sexually coercing' women as they made their progress.[82] But the festivities themselves may have been what mattered. Charlemagne's biographer Einhard paints the last Merovingian king as a degenerate, wheeled about in an ox-cart, 'in rustic style'.[83] Rather than accept that there was a Merovingian tradition of 'sacral kingship' stretching back to the fifth century, we might, following Boyer, think that the divinity or person associated with the ritual was ultimately less important than the ritual itself; and perhaps also that a king whose political role had been taken over by his mayor of the palace, might have spent his time travelling from place to place presiding over traditional festivities.

There is no written evidence about the nature of any pagan religious practitioners apart from the priest and attendants mentioned in Tacitus' late first-century account of Nerthus' travels. They are not mentioned in later descriptions of similar rituals, but this does not mean they had ceased to exist. Looking at the early religion of the Tervingi, Herwig Wolfram thought that each tribal community would have had its own priests and priest-esses, associated with the 'idols' borne on wagons.[84] He also referred to the legendary *halirunnae*, women 'who engaged in magic with the world of the dead' allegedly expelled from the Goths by their migration leader, Filimer, and to the 'cannabis-saunas' of the ancient Scythians and Thracians.[85] This led him to reflect on the possible absorption of shamanistic elements into Gothic religion at an early stage.

We cannot tell whether shamanism was definitely a part of Gothic religion, but it is likely to have been associated with some of the rituals of the Lombards. While the idea that Goths venerated *Wodanaz or Woden has been challenged and we cannot be sure about Sueves, Burgundians or the Franks, as we have seen, there is a definite association between the Lombards and Woden. Woden's cult in Anglo-Saxon England was associated with shamanism and may have had this dimension on the continent as well. None of the priests of the pagan Germanic peoples, shamans or otherwise, would have been priests in the sense of Christian priests, a guild of professionals created by training. Instead, they would have been marked out in some way as being 'special', as in the case of Coifi, whom the Venerable Bede described as the 'chief priest' of King Eadwine of the Northumbrians and whose name indicates that he was born with an amniotic caul on his head.[86]

Ex-votos and 'abductive reasoning'

Gregory of Tours provides a brief but valuable description of a Frankish shrine (*fanum*) at Cologne in the earlier part of the sixth century. This had been destroyed by the Christian priest Gallus (his own uncle) and was a structure or place where 'pagans' had worshipped representations of gods (*simulacra*) and where they placed 'wooden models of parts of the human body whenever some part of their body was touched by pain.'[87] The dedication of such objects to the gods in return for healing, good harvest or prosperity must have been one of the most common rituals of Germanic paganism. Boyer has described the cognitive process behind such dedications as 'abductive reasoning'. A vow to make a dedication is followed by a cure, good harvest, or prosperity – therefore the being or force represented by the shrine is responsible for the result and the vow must be 'paid' or fulfilled.[88]

We catch some glimpses of such shrines in written sources of the sixth and seventh centuries, which, like Gregory's account, relate to their destruction and disappearance. One gives a valuable clue as to their differing types. An edict of the Frankish Christian King Childebert, ordering their removal, made a clear distinction between *simulacra constructa* and *idola daemoni dedicata ab hominibus factum* [sic]. The 'simulacra' are effigies, representations of deities, whereas the 'idols' must have been something different, either a minimally worked stone or other natural feature – or the natural feature itself.[89] In 597, Pope Gregory I admonished the Frankish Queen Brunichildis, who was acting as regent for her grandsons in Austrasia and Burgundy, to prevent her technically Christian people from (amongst other things) sacrificing to 'idols'.[90] The term 'idol' is specifically applied to natural features by the ninth-century Italian writer Andreas Agnellus who refers, in connection with a sixth-century ecclesiastical foundation at Comacchio north of Ravenna, to the nearby 'idols' of *Ignis* (fire) and *Baias* (springs).[91]

The singling out of natural features as the focus of ritual practices is something that transcends notions of culture. A recent work on the sacred tree describes this as 'a near-universal symbol in pre-modern cultures' with a

> particular and recognisable manifestation within the Indo-European cultural matrix, yielding rich ancient and medieval case-studies.[92]

Stones have also been – and still are – the objects of reverence in a wide variety of societies, religions and settings and across several continents, from Phoenician betyls, to the menhirs of Brittany, to the Ka'ba at Mecca.[93] In the Pyrenees, some inscriptions have been found in which 'sacred' trees are addressed – as 'beech' and 'six trees' – without any reference to any intermediary tutelary deity.[94] The Romans hung cloths called *vittae* (woollen ribbons, often translated as 'fillets') from trees.[95] Rags tied to the branches of trees considered special can still be observed in modern-day Turkey. Springs and wells were revered all over Europe; as were some lakes and, amongst the Celts in particular, rivers.[96]

'Nonreflective' belief in the special properties of natural features lay at the heart of much Germanic religious practice, just as it did elsewhere. The identification of particular trees, groves (as in Tacitus' account of the Semnones), stones, springs or lakes as sacred or efficacious is based on a complex mental process. It is easy to fall into the temptation of thinking that, in the case of trees, this was due simply to their unusual size or age (though the sacred oak of Geismar, felled by St Boniface in the eighth century was of 'extraordinary size');[97] or the odd configuration of a stone; or the healthy properties of spring water. Stones with holes or hollows in them were frequently perceived as having curative properties, in which the ill were placed to regain their strength.[98] Or the rainwater gathering in hollows of stones perceived as special could be used in cures.[99] But not every curiously shaped stone can have been regarded as 'special', not all aged or exceptionally tall trees venerated and not all springs with pure water regarded as sacred. The special tree, or grove, or stone, or spring, or lake, is one considered to have a certain essence that makes it special. The identification of the essence is also a product of Boyer's 'abductive reasoning': certain typical effects are observed; only a special tree/grove/stone/spring/lake would produce these effects; hence, it is concluded, it *is* special.[100] And once this perception is established, it can be associated with a tutelary divinity, lesser or greater, from river-*matrona* to Thunor.

If many of the details of Germanic paganism are lost to us, a cognitive approach helps us make sense of a very limited quantity of information drawn from disparate and often difficult sources. The crucial factor is that the religions of the Germanic peoples were based on intuitions or 'nonreflective' belief: there were no written doctrines or ritual instruction. The primary purpose of the rituals actually known to us may have been military or social, though they acquired an additional religious dimension. Religion in general was based on a sense of how gods, spirits or natural features felt to be imbued with special power affected the lives of peoples or individuals. Stones, springs, trees and lakes were thought to be able to cure sickness in people or animals or help guarantee a good harvest; people were surrounded by minor supernatural beings who might, if propitiated, help them. There were different levels of divinity, represented as having different ranges of power and activity; and the most powerful god of all, who had created the earth and sky, was generally far removed from the trials and tribulations of ordinary mortals.

Constructing 'Arianism'

One of the most noticeable features of the conversion of the European Germanic peoples to Christianity is the way in which they became 'Arians'. It is usually said that only the Franks went directly from paganism to Catholicism. The reality is slightly more complex: a Sueve ruler converted to Catholicism before 'Arianism' was imposed on the Sueves from outside, while Lombard 'Arianism' may in reality have been a syncretistic Christianity. 'Arianism', nevertheless, represented a stage in the religious history of the Visigoths, Ostrogoths, Burgundians and Sueves.

A term increasingly, and more correctly, used instead of 'Arianism' is Homoianism, indicating that this was a Christianity based on a view of the Trinity affirming that the Son is 'like' (*homoios*) the Father.[1] Homoianism is now understood as a theology that emerged in the decades of debate following the Council of Nicæa in 325 and for a number of years, beginning in 360, a Homoian creed was the official Symbol of the Empire. There is a general assumption that it had been adopted by Gothic groups because it was the religion of the Emperors at the period when some of the Tervingi on the Danube frontier first began to accept Christianity (soon after 369) and when groups of Tervingi and Greuthungi entered the Empire in 376. In fact, there is considerable evidence to suggest that Homoianism – itself a slightly misleading term – was actually an 'entry-level' version of Christianity, created by bishops and missionaries on the Danube frontier in a drive to Christianize the Goths.

Why 'Arianism'?

In the early years of the fourth century, a presbyter of Alexandria in Egypt named Arius advanced a Christian theology that differentiated sharply between the persons of the Trinity and suggested that Christ's divinity was of a lesser order than that of the Father. This provoked immense controversy and had long-lasting repercussions. Its most important short-term consequence was the production of the Nicene Creed in 325, at the first ecumenical council to be held by the Christian Church. The Nicene Creed outlawed the theology of Arius: it declared that the Son was

> begotten as the only Son out of the Father, that is, out of the substance of the Father, God from God, light from light, true God from true God, begotten not made, *homoousios* [i.e. of the same substance] with the Father ... and in the Holy Spirit.[2]

However, far from putting a decisive end to the matter, the production of the Nicene Creed would instead turn out to be the prelude to decades of argument among bishops and theologians over a universally acceptable model of the Trinity. Only in 381, when the Creed of Nicæa-Constantinople was proclaimed as the official Trinitarian theology of the Empire, was some sort of agreement finally achieved.

In theological terms, Homoianism emerged in the decades of debate and dispute following the Council of Nicæa. Nicæa had not achieved anything like agreement on fundamental questions of the relationship between the members of the Trinity. Both Arius and the Emperor Constantine died in the late 330s, and Constantius II (Eastern Emperor 337–50, sole ruler 350–61) embarked on a quest to produce a creed acceptable throughout the entire Roman Empire. Constantius' efforts resulted in a succession of councils and creedal statements: Serdica 343 (where individual Eastern and Western Councils of bishops issued separate documents); Antioch 345 (the 'Macrostich' or 'Long-liner' Creed); Sirmium 347/8; Sirmium 351 (the 'First Sirmian Creed'); and the Councils of Arles (353) and Milan (355). As council after council was held, numerous theological positions were advanced, only to be cut down in debate. One of the principal targets which emerged was the 'Sabellian' or Modal theology of Bishop Marcellus of Ancyra, who regarded the Son as undivided and un-separated from the Father.[3] And, at the opposite end of the spectrum, any suggestion that the Son was subordinate to the Father was likely to be labelled 'Arianism'.

The Nicene Creed had condemned

> those who say ... the Son of God is of another *hypostasis* or *ousia* [than God the Father] ...[4]

Ousia means 'substance' and is in origin a Greek philosophical concept. It is not applied to God in the Bible.[5] In the 350s, Homoians claimed that the Son was *like* the Father, not identical with Him and they voiced very strong objections to *ousia* terminology:

> The word *ousia* because it when it was naively inserted by our fathers though not familiar to the masses, it caused disturbance, and because the Scriptures do not contain it, we have decided it should be removed, and there should be absolutely no mention of *ousia* in relation to God for the future, because the Scriptures make no mention at all of the *ousia* of the Father and the Son.[6]

In the years 357–8, the Emperor Constantius organized several councils and gatherings in an effort to thrash out an acceptable formula. There were now three principal points of view: the *homoousians* who followed Nicæa; a newer grouping which had formed around the eastern bishop Basil of Ancyra and who argued for the idea that Father and Son, were *homoiousios* – 'of *like* substance';[7] and the Homoians. In 359, he went on to assemble two further councils: a gathering of perhaps as many as four hundred western bishops at *Ariminun* (Rimini) in the West was paralleled by a second smaller council of about 160 eastern bishops which began at Seleucia later in the year.[8] Constantius may have realized that it might be a good idea to keep easterners and westerners apart: he certainly told the western bishops not to make any decisions regarding the East.[9] After considerable argument and politicking – there would be later references to the 'fraud of Rimini' – combined with imperial pressure, the substantial minority who at first accepted the arguments of the Homoian party at Rimini turned into a majority. Further manoeuvres disabled opposition among eastern bishops and in Constantinople in 360 a creed, asserting that the Son was 'like' the Father – 'according to Scripture' and which also forbade all mention of *ousia* – was proclaimed.[10]

In his polemic *Against the Luciferians*, composed two decades later, Jerome would claim, with typical hyperbole that 'The entire world groaned and was amazed to find itself Arian.'[11] But though the label stuck for centuries, the Homoians had no connection with Arius. Nor was their theology the same as his: while they resolutely rejected the term *ousia* or substance in relation to God, Arius had himself used it.[12] The problem was that over the decades of dispute and creed-making any theology suggesting a distance or separation between Father and Son ran the risk of being branded as 'Arian' and this is precisely what happened to the Homoians, as early as the 340s. As Maurice Wiles has pointed out, the label 'Arian' rapidly turned into an invaluable polemical tool in theological controversy and the dead Arius became not so much a whipping-boy as a whip.[13] The pejorative term 'Arianism' has obscured the origins of Homoian Christianity, which lay not just in the doctrinal debates following Nicaea, but in attempts to Christianize the Goths on the Danube frontier.

Who were the Homoians?

The two names constantly associated with Homoian theology at the ecclesiastical councils of the late 350s are those of two bishops from the Danubian region, Ursacius of Singidunum (modern Belgrade, Serbia) and Valens of Mursa (modern Osijek, Croatia). There seems to be no evidence of any direct connection between them and Arius himself: their theology was not the same as his, except in the general sense of also being subordinationist.[14] It is true that in 343, the so-called 'Western Creed of Serdica' singled them out as vipers hatched from the 'Arian asp'. But this encyclical provides an early example of the polemical use of the term 'Arian': in the words of one scholar, it 'defined Arianism so broadly that every easterner who had ever heard of Origen was considered Arian.[15] At the Councils of Milan of 345 and 347, Ursacius and Valens were invited to condemn 'the heretic Arius and his accomplices' in order to exonerate themselves of earlier charges and readily did so.[16]

The alleged influence of Ursacius and Valens over the Emperor Constantius II in theological controversies together with their apparent inseparability has led to their being characterized as mere 'court bishops' or as 'the Rosencrantz and Guildenstern of the Arian controversy'.[17] Yet Valens in particular emerges as a force to be reckoned with. There are indications of a rift between Constantius and Valens when the latter mutinied at signing the so-called 'Dated Creed' of 359, which put forward a formula which seemed to back Homoianism, but which also included a clause – 'like in all respects' – that neutralized this position. Although he had been one of the bishops present at the meeting at Sirmium where it had originally been drawn up, Valens was now evidently reluctant to give formal assent to a compromise with Homoiousian theology, protesting that he had been compelled to sign by the Emperor and adding a rider to his subscription indicating his reluctance.[18] Events do not confirm the accusation that the two bishops were mere careerists.[19] Overall, the Illyrican bishops emerge through numerous changes and reverses, as tenacious proponents of a doctrine which maintained a strict separation of the persons of the Trinity and eschewed discussion of 'substance', a theology which they promoted for nearly two decades until it prevailed at Rimini and became the creed of the Empire at Constantinople in 360.[20]

Amongst the signatories at the Council of Constantinople in 360 was Ulfila, bishop to the Goths. Ulfila, the descendant of Anatolian Christians captured by Goths, had been consecrated bishop amongst Christians in Gothic territories in 341.[21] In 348, he led a group of Gothic Christians across the Danube to settle in the Roman province of Moesia Secunda, near Nicopolis.[22] It is likely that Ulfila, whose original ministry was probably to people who were, like himself, descendants of Christian captives, was expelled with his followers from the Gothic lands in 347 because Tervingi leaders had begun to perceive him as an instrument of Roman hegemony. The conjunction of Ulfila's status as a towering figure in the history of conversion with his unacceptable theology has exercised writers from the late antiquity to the present day. The fifth-century ecclesiastical historians Theodoret and Sozomen both struggled to explain this great teacher's embarrassing espousal of 'heresy' by suggesting that he had been hoodwinked and also that he was not a declared opponent of the Nicene Creed.[23] One modern commentator thinks that his support for 'anti-*ousian*' theology was given reluctantly and voices doubts that he was a 'positive homoean' (i.e. Homoian).[24] But after Ulfila's death in 383, his pupil Auxentius of Durostorum wrote a eulogy of his master, suggesting that Ulfila had demonstrated an energetic aversion to any discussion of *ousia* and had taught a marked degree of differentiation between the persons of the Trinity.[25] According to Auxentius, Ulfila

> strove to destroy the sect of homo[io]usians ... and deplored and shunned the error and impiety of the homoeusians [i.e. homoiousians] ...[26]

Auxentius also gives details of Ulfila's Trinitarian theology, in which the three persons were conceptualized as having different functions or dispositions and being active in different spheres:

> the Father is for his part the creator of the creator while the Son is creator of all creation; and that the Father is God of the Lord, while the Son is God of the created universe …
>
> … the Holy Spirit our advocate can be called neither God nor Lord, but received its being from God through the Lord … neither originator nor creator, but illuminator, sanctifier, teacher and leader, helper and petitioner and confirmer, minister of Christ and distributor of acts of grace …[27]

Here we have a view of divinity in which God the Father created the Son and is the object of the Son's veneration, while the Spirit, at a lower level, interacts with humans in many ways. It was a view later outlined by a Homoian bishop, Palladius of Ratiaria, who told his interrogator Ambrose of Milan at the Synod of Aquileia in 381 that:

> the Father sends the Son, and the Son sends the Paraclete, the Father delivers the Son to suffering and the Holy Spirit in the function of a servant everywhere proclaims the Son, and again the Son glorifies the Father and the Paraclete Spirit the Son … the Father redeems the church by the suffering of the Son, the Holy Spirit gathers and teaches the church redeemed by Christ's blood by his superintendence, in fact he appoint bishops in it for the honour of his Lord and orders ministries and distributes grace …[28]

The evidence relating to Ulfila and Palladius gives further explanation of the structured and subordinationist view of the Trinity promoted by Ursacius and Valens and reveals Ulfila's commitment to it.[29] It is certainly difficult to accept the characterization of Ulfila – an ecclesiastical leader who understood Gothic, Greek and Latin, the driving force behind a translation of the Bible into Gothic and the leader of sections of the Gothic peoples into the Empire – as a gullible pawn, tricked into acquiescing in Homoian doctrine. Instead, it is possible to read Homoianism as a theology which maintained a distinctive trajectory over several decades and in which Ulfila appears very much at home. As Maurice Wiles has observed,

> as far as the positive nature of Ulfila's own faith is concerned there is no reason to doubt that throughout his career it was of an Homoian character.[30]

In addition to demonstrating a level of theological coherence, Homoianism also displays a distinctively regional character. Its western cradle and principal axis lay in the Balkans, a region under pressure from the Tervingi Goths since the previous century.[31] Between the 330s and the 360s, the Empire's policy in the area had been 'the economic, military and political linkage of the Tervingi to the Roman state'.[32] Ursacius' and Valens' dioceses were both situated on the Empire's Danubian frontier. Homoian theology was also supported by others from the same area: by Germinius of Sirmium, metropolitan of Moesia Prima; and also by Palladius, Bishop of Ratiaria in Dacia Ripensis, who would stand up to Ambrose of Milan in 381 at the Council of Aquileia. Ursacius and Valens both appear to have died in the 370s: we do not know who succeeded Valens, but Ursacius' successor was Secundianus, another Homoian attacked by Ambrose at the Council of Aquileia. In the 380s, we find a Homoian bishop, Julianus Valens, based at Poetovio in Pannonia Superior.[33] Not all Illyrican bishops were Homoians and not all Homoians were Illyrican: two Iberian bishops, the centenarian Ossius of Cordoba, a veteran of the Council of Nicæa (and opponent of Arius) and Potamius of Lisbon, briefly lent their support.[34] Nevertheless, the principal concentration of Homoian bishops lay in the region of the Danube and the north-eastern frontier of the Western Empire, while five church councils of this period (347/8, 351, 357, and two in 358) took place in Sirmium.

In Homoianism, therefore, we have a consistent theology which first emerges in one particular region.[35] Was there a connection between the drawing of the Tervingi Goths on the Danube frontier into closer relations with the Empire and imperial backing for Homoian theology? The Sirmian Creed of 357 contains important clues that pastoral considerations underlay its formulation. The three Illyrican bishops definitely associated with it – Ursacius, Valens and Germinius of Sirmium – stated that

> some, or many, are concerned about substance (*substantia*) which is called *usia* in Greek, that is, to speak more explicitly *homoousion* or *homoiousion* as it is called, there should be no mention of it whatever.[36]

This point was further expanded in 359–60:

> The word *ousia* because when it was naively inserted by the fathers, though not familiar to the masses, caused disturbance …[37]

From these explicit expressions of concern about *reactions* to the Nicene Creed, the bishops appear to have thought that the introduction of the idea of shared substance was confusing to a mass audience. At the very least, all this looks like an attempt to keep the extremely complex theology of a triune God as simple as possible for a population which on the fourth-century Danubian border would include potential converts from a variety of polytheisms: local cults and Roman paganism, possibly Gnostic beliefs as well, but most importantly, from a political point of view, the religion of the Tervingi Goths. But Homoianism was more than a theology constructed for negative reasons. Applying insights drawn from the cognitive study of belief, it appears that teaching the Trinity in the Homoian way might have offered very positive advantages in a conversion situation.

R. P. C. Hanson memorably summed up a Homoian account of the Trinity as consisting of

> a high God who does not mingle with human affairs, a lesser God who does and a third – what?[38]

The Spirit, he suggested elsewhere, was conceptualized by Homoians as a 'superior angel'.[39] The doctrine of a tiered version of the Christian Trinity, with its different levels of activity and relationships with humans bears a striking structural resemblance to the non-Christian intuitions of divinity of the Germanic peoples discussed in the previous chapter: a relatively remote creator God, an intermediary level of divinity which had greater interaction with humans, and a lower one still, in which spirits or lesser beings were also active on earth. Given the fact that Christianization was a very important facet of imperial policy towards the Goths in the period when Homoianism emerged and also the strikingly close association between Homoianism and the Danubian border, it seems likely to have originated in efforts to convert the Goths (and incidentally other polytheists in the region) by attempting to map intuitions of various levels of divinity amongst the gods and spirits of polytheistic religion on to the doctrine of the Christian Trinity.

Daniel Williams has noted the extraordinary nature of Constantius II's involvement with ecclesiastical councils between 357 and 360.[40] A large part of his motive for involvement must have originated in his desire to be a successful Christian emperor and to achieve an Empire-wide religious settlement. But his other concern was the security of the Danube frontier. This was a problem throughout his reign, but was becoming acute in the later 350s. Chroniclers indicate that he fought a war against the Goths in the early or middle years of the 340s, while a Sirmian inscription of 352 gives him the title *Gohticus* (sic) *Maximus*.[41] Between October 357 and the autumn of 359 the Emperor returned to the region, spending his time in Sirmium, Mursa, or elsewhere on the frontier. In April 358, according to Ammianus Marcellinus, he invaded the territory of the Sarmatians: he campaigned against both them and the Limigantes, defeating the latter near Acimincum, in 359. At this stage, the over-stretched Empire was also under threat from the Sassanids in the East. After the Battle of Mursa in 351, according to E. A. Thompson, the Empire's shortage of manpower was such that imperial policy was to attempt to preserve the peace with Persia by any means.[42] Given these problems it is not difficult to see why Constantius would have come increasingly to favour the Homoian point of view. So when a large number of the bishops at the Council of Rimini at first wrote to the Emperor loudly proclaiming their hostility to Ursacius, Valens and the manoeuvres of the Homoians, while affirming their own loyalty to the Nicene Creed, Constantius replied by teaching them a lesson in the strategic realities facing the Empire. He refused to meet a delegation they sent. He explained that he had not the leisure to meet it as he was undertaking an expedition against the barbarians. Part of the pressure put on this majority delegation by his Praetorian Prefect is likely to have involved a spelling out of the political and military necessity of adopting the Homoian creed to maintain the security of the frontier that the Emperor was – at that very moment – defending.[43]

Gothic Homoianism as minority belief

The fifth-century ecclesiastical historian Socrates describes the entry into the Empire of a large group of Tervingi under the leadership of Alavivus and Fritigern in 376. He claims that these groups took the 'Arian' – that is to say Homoian – faith of the Illyrican-born Emperor Valens (Eastern Emperor 364–78) out of gratitude.[44] But there are likely to have been conversions before this in the period when Homoianism was advanced as 'entry-level'

Christianity for the Goths as well as a viable creed for the Empire. The entire length of the Danube frontier had been open for trade between 332 and 367 and as Peter Heather has indicated, 'before the reign of Valens, the Goths and the Tervingi had long been exposed to Christianity'.[45] Even after Ulfila's expulsion from Gothia in the 340s, contacts between Christians north and south of the Danube remained close: the *Passion* of the Gothic martyr Saba mentions a Gothic Christian priest called Sansalas 'who was able to drift across the frontier at will'.[46] Although he had spent only seven years in the Gothic lands and had been based in Moesia since the 340s, Ulfila may have been in touch with the Tervingi across the Danube, as he was able to act as intermediary in the negotiations for their settlement in imperial territory.[47] His great work, probably carried out in collaboration with Goths who accompanied him into Moesia, was the creation of a Gothic alphabet and the translation of the Bible into Gothic. Heather suggests that he might have seen this work as preparation for the resumption of his mission;[48] but it could be the case that parts of this translation, which must have taken many years to complete, were used on both sides of the Danube, before the Tervingi crossed into the Empire in 376. We know that some of the Tervingi had already adopted Homoian Christianity, evidently in sufficient numbers for the authorities to persecute them as crypto-Romans in 369. After this, Fritigern sought imperial help during an internal power struggle and accepted Christianity: Schäferdiek considers that a 'rudimentary church organisation' was established amongst the Goths.[49] The pagan historian Eunapius certainly claims that when the tribes entered the Empire they brought their church organisation with them; but he also considers that it was a sham:

> For countless tribes had crossed into the Empire and more followed since there was no-one to prevent them ... Each tribe had brought along from home its ancestral objects of worship together with their priests and priestesses, but they kept a deep and impenetrable silence upon these things and spoke not a word about their mysteries. What they revealed was a fiction and sham designed to fool their enemies. They all claimed to be Christians and some of their number they disguised as bishops and dressed them up in that respected garb ... They also had with them some of the tribe of so-called monks whom they had decked out in imitation of the monks amongst their enemies ... The barbarians used these devices to deceive the Romans, since they shrewdly observed that these things were respected among them, while the rest of the time, under deepest

secrecy, they worshipped the holy objects of their native rites with noble and guileless intent.[50]

Eunapius was no friend to Christianity and so may not be reliable. On the other hand he could be representing a situation where a mix of pagan and Christian Goths had entered imperial territory.

However, at the point where Homoian Christian Goths had entered the Empire, Homoianism was already being sidelined. Constantius' death in late 361 and the accession of his cousin Julian allowed Hilary of Poitiers and other pro-Nicenes a breathing space in which they could re-group and build support. Basil of Cæsarea's pro-Nicene influence was tolerated by the Homoian but pragmatic Emperor Valens (364–78).[51] The eventual result of these and other developments was the official promulgation in 381 of the Creed of Constantinople, an amplification of the Nicene Creed.[52] After this point Homoianism would be increasingly marginalized, identified with Goths and other 'barbarians'. Another ominous event in 381 was the summoning of the Council of Aquileia where Ambrose of Milan stage-managed the condemnation of the Illyrican bishops Palladius and Secundianus for 'Arianism' – their denials of any connection with Arius were of no help. There have been suggestions that even after this attack on Homoianism it took some time for Nicene Christianity to establish itself in Mursa and Singidunum, the cradle of Homoianism.[53] The truth is that we have very little evidence and Homoianism seems unlikely to have recovered from such a major body-blow. Ulfila arrived in Constantinople in 383 in an unsuccessful attempt to persuade the Emperor Theodosius that his support for the rival Homoousian doctrine was a mistake.[54] He had no success and seems to have died in the same year. The 381 Council of Constantinople made some degree of separate provision – though it does not specify exactly in what respect – for the recently-converted: 'The Churches of God which are among the barbarians must be administered according to the usage of the Fathers which has prevailed'.[55] But this special treatment only serves to emphasize that Homoianism was becoming increasingly identified with 'barbarians'. The Theodosian Code also legislated against 'Arians': though as Liebeschuetz has pointed out, contrary to what a reader of its provisions might expect, Arians continued to live and worship in Constantinople in considerable numbers. It may even be the case that they managed 'to retain the support of perhaps a majority of the capital's Christians for two decades'.[56] But it is also the case that they fragmented into factions, divided over the issue of whether God could have been 'the Father' before the Son had come into existence. Deprived of churches in the city, they set up their own outside the walls, though at one stage a Gothic general demanded a church in the city itself.[57] There were many Gothic soldiers stationed at Constantinople and it is symbolic of the increasing identification between Goths and Homoianism, that the division between the two groups of 'Arians' was eventually ended by the Gothic general Plinthas in 419.[58]

The diffusion of Homoian Christianity amongst the 'barbarian' peoples

Ironically, Homoianism appears to have been transmitted amongst the Germanic peoples just after the point when it fell out of favour as an imperial creed. Its progress in the West can only be inferred, but the most important vector in its dissemination seems to have been the ethnogenesis of the Goths and the movement of Gothic groups into and across Western Europe. In the East, the policy of peaceful Romanization of the Goths had come to an end in the reign of Valens (ironically, an emperor of Illyrian origin and a Homoian himself). In 378 he was killed at the Battle of Adrianople, where the Goths inflicted a massive defeat on the Empire. After this, the Goths retreated into Thrace, which they pillaged along with Macedonia and Greece. When the 381 Council of Constantinople made some degree of separate provision for the Goths, it seems to have signaled a return to the older policy of Romanization and pacification. In 382, Tervingi Goths were granted land to farm and allowed to maintain their own laws, an agreement which allowed them 'considerable communal autonomy' in return for military service to the Roman state.[59] This would not apply to other Gothic groups attempting to enter the Empire at a slightly later date: Greuthungi under Odotheus who tried to cross the Danube were crushed in battle and made to serve either in the imperial armies or as agricultural labourers and were subject to Roman law.[60]

The Goths who had settled in the province of Moesia II – Tervingi along some Greuthungi – revolted in 388 and in 395. Under the leadership of Alaric, they devastated Greece before withdrawing to Epirus. Alaric was declared *magister militum per Illyricum*, took control of the region, moving on to Italy after the overthrow of the Gothic general Gainas in 400 (an event which would lead to the massacre of 7,000 of Constantinople's Gothic inhabitants). He led his forces to Italy where they fused with the followers of a Gothic leader called Radagaisus, who had originally moved to Italy as a result of renewed Hunnic pressure. Under Alaric, they sacked Rome in 410, remaining under the control of a single leader, first Wallia, then Theoderic I (418–51), whose extremely long reign consolidated the rule of a single dynasty over the people that would become known as the Visigoths.[61] They were enrolled in imperial service and used against the Vandals and Alans in Baetica and Lusitania, the southernmost provinces of Roman Iberia. They were then withdrawn and settled in south-west Gaul, between Bordeaux and Toulouse, by Constantius III: this area effectively became a Gothic kingdom, federated to Rome in 439. They temporarily invaded Spain, defeating the Sueves in 456 and were granted Narbonne and Septimania in south-east Gaul to add to their territories in 462. By the 490s, Visigoths were settling in Spain, following their earlier destabi-lisation of the Sueve kingdom (which nevertheless survived). After a major defeat at the hands of the Franks under Clovis in 507, although a remnant of Gothic Gaul still continued to exist in Septimania, the main Visigoth terri-tories were now to be found in Spain.

The genesis of the Ostrogoths is almost equally complicated. Renewed pressure from the Huns in the early fifth century brought six or seven Gothic groups north of the Danube under their domination. The historian Jordanes writing in the sixth century would claim that one of these, led by the Amal family, would survive to emerge as the Ostrogoths. In reality, rather than seeing a uniquely prestigious Amal dynasty c. 450, 'we should envisage a series of competing Goths with their own dynastic lines', united partly by military action, partly by marriages, under the leadership of Valamer and able to throw off Hunnic hegemony. This may all have happened before the death of Attila the Hun in 453 – but could equally have taken place shortly afterwards.[62] These Goths had probably been settled by the Huns in the former Roman province of Pannonia; between the 450s and 470s they were to prove particularly aggressive neighbours of the Romans. Theoderic, the future Ostrogoth leader would spend ten years as child and youth as a hostage in Constantinople under the terms of a treaty by which the Romans paid the Goths three hundred pounds of gold annually.[63] Jordanes claims that the Pannonian Goths were victorious over Sciri, Sarmatians, Gepids and Rugians. After 473, their leaders also maintained 'intense rivalry' with the Goths of Thrace, who were recognized as federates of the Roman state and enjoyed a privileged position as a result.[64] After a period of conflict and shifting alliances, Theoderic the Amal would emerge as leader of both Pannonian and Thracian Goths and in the 480s, they would enter Italy. At this stage, they are known to historians as Ostrogoths.

The lengthy process by which 'Goths' emerge from groupings of Tervingi, Greuthungi and others who joined with them and the constant dissolution and formation of alliances are further complicated by the distances they travelled. The groups that formed the Visigoths came together in the Balkans and Italy, before settling in southern Gaul and then beginning to move into Spain. It seems difficult to believe that a 'rudimentary' Homoian Church could have survived these vicissitudes: yet this is what seems to have happened. Visigothic Homoianism was sufficiently strong for it to be transmitted it to other Germanic peoples.

The easiest case to trace is that of the Sueves. In 409–10 they had penetrated Spain along with the Alans and Vandals, settling in the north-west of the Iberian peninsula.[65] It is popularly assumed that the first Germanic leader to convert to Catholicism without passing through an 'Arian' stage was Clovis, leader of the Franks. However, the credit for this should actually go to the fifth-century Sueve leader, Rechiar (448–56). Hydatius, Bishop of Chaves, suggests that Rechiar overcame competitors in his own family and also that he was a Catholic before he became leader.[66] He must have seen Catholic Christianity as a means of distinguishing himself either from family rivals or the Hasding Vandals, who had vied with the Sueves for power in Gallaecia before crossing into North Africa in 429. From his base in Gallaecia, Rechiar harassed other Iberian provinces, only to find himself in turn attacked by the Visigoths of Toulouse, who had initially attempted to bring him into their orbit through marriage. In 456, he was defeated and subsequently executed, by his own brother-in-law. This marked the beginning of a long period of Visigothic hegemony over the Sueves. After their ruler Remismund (464–9) was married to another Visigothic princess, Theoderic II (453–66) sent a cleric named by Hydatius as Ajax and described by him as *senior Arrianus*, to convert the Sueves, who are likely to have mostly been pagan before his arrival.[67]

The process by which the Vandals adopted Homoianism is obscure but it seems more than likely that the Goths played a role in this, even if we cannot establish whether it was initially a means of establishing hegemony over them. It is assumed that they came into contact with Visigothic Homoianism as they passed into the Iberian peninsula, before crossing into Africa (and thus out of the areas covered in this book) to establish a powerful Vandal monarchy.[68]

Equally obscure is the date and means of the conversion of the Burgundians to Homoianism. Schäferdiek suggests this was passed on through links with the 'Visigoth' Athanaric, as stated by the sixth-century historian of the Franks, Gregory of Tours:

> The king of the Burgundes was called Gundioc: he was of the family of King Athanaric, who persecuted the Christians ...[69]

But this looks like a none-too-subtle attempt by the fiercely anti-'Arian' Gregory to discredit Gundioc (d. 473) by associating him with the Tervingi leader Athanaric who had persecuted Christians in the fourth century.[70] Alternative explanations of Burgundian 'Arianism' focus on Gundioc's marriage with the sister of the Suevic-Visigothic Homoian general Ricimer who controlled Italy in the name of a succession of puppet emperors between 456 and 472. The neighbouring Aquitainian Visigothic kingdom has been suggested as another possible source of Burgundian 'Arianism'.[71]

History actually records not one but two Burgundian conversions to Christianity. The Spanish author Orosius asserted that the Burgundians converted to Catholicism in the second decade of the fifth century. This flies in the face of other evidence and has been questioned by historians.[72] But the ecclesiastical historian Socrates, writing in the eastern half of the Empire, gives a more circumstantial version of events:

> There is a barbarous nation dwelling beyond the Rhine, denominated Burgundians; they lead a peaceful life; for being almost all artisans, they support themselves by the exercise of their trades. The Huns, by making continual irruptions on this people, devastated their country, and often destroyed great numbers of them. In this perplexity, therefore, the Burgundians resolved to have recourse not to any human being, but to commit themselves to the protection of some god: and having seriously considered that the God of the Romans mightily defended those that feared him, they all with common consent embraced the

faith of Christ. Going therefore to one of the cities of Gaul, they requested the bishop to grant them Christian baptism: who ordering them to fast seven days, and having meanwhile instructed them in the elementary principles of the faith, on the eighth day baptized and dismissed them.[73]

The Burgundians succeeded in their aim:

Accordingly becoming confident thenceforth, they marched against their invaders; nor were they disappointed in their hope. For the king of the Huns, Uptar by name, having died in the night from the effects of a surfeit, the Burgundians attacked that people then without a commander-in-chief; and although they were few in numbers and their opponents very many, they obtained a complete victory; for the Burgundians were altogether but three thousand men and destroyed no less than ten thousand of the enemy.[74]

This would seem to fit well with our information about the events of the late 420s, when we know of a Hunnic leader named Octar or Optar, the uncle of Attila.[75] But in what sense we should understand 'conversion' is open to question. Socrates writes of Burgundians 'embracing the faith of Christ': but this is the perspective of a Christian author, who may have been using the figure of three thousand Pentecostal conversions described in Acts.[76] Warriors were involved and their 'conversion' can be interpreted as a decision to add Christ to the existing pantheon of gods in the hope that he might be more effective in military affairs than the deity who currently oversaw such matters. The probably syncretistic nature of this understanding is underlined by the very brief period of instruction in the basics of Christianity by the unnamed Catholic bishop – possibly Severus of Trier.[77] He could have viewed this baptism either as representing the first stages of a conversion process or perhaps just as an expedient to get rid of a group of armed barbarians. Either way, there is no reference in the written sources to any follow-up and no firm evidence that any Burgundian outside the group of warriors that went on to defeat the Huns was baptized at this stage. But while highly successful against Octar in the later 420s, in 436/7 the Burgundian army was destroyed by the Roman general Aëtius and his Hunnic allies, thus putting a brutal end to what has become known as the 'First Burgundian Kingdom'. Subsequently, around 443, Aëtius settled the surviving Burgundians in Sapaudia as federates.

It has been conjectured that the surviving Burgundians could even have moved into the province of Sequania immediately after the disaster of 436/7, before being transferred to Sapaudia in 443.[78] In 455, their leader Gundioc was able to negotiate with the Gallo-Roman senators for an increased share of territory in Gaul and 457, he took up residence either in a villa at *Ambariacum* (Ambérieux-en-Bugey) or the city of Lyon (*Lugdunum*). As well as Sapaudia, the Burgundes controlled not only Lyon, but also Die and Vienne (annexed in 455) further south – in other words the south of the province of Lugdunensis Prima, plus Greater Sequania and part of the Viennensis. Under Gundioc's son Gundobad, greater Burgundy stretched from Besançon to Arles and from the Loire to the Alps. The numbers of Burgundians who lived amongst the Gallo-Roman populations of these regions may have been low to begin with, growing with the passage of time and also with the absorption of individuals from other population groups. One of the most significant discoveries of recent years has been the number of individuals in Burgundian cemeteries with intentional skull deformations or Mongoloid tooth characteristics.[79] This may indicate the incorporation of individuals or groups from the Hunnic armies which disappear from the historical record shortly after the death of Attila in 453.

Burgundian implantation looks to have been unevenly spread across a wide territory. A large amount of archaeological evidence has been discovered in a 50-kilometre radius around Geneva, the original nucleus of the kingdom; in its westward extension, there are limited but extremely important finds in the Ain valley. Almost all of the remaining archaeological evidence comes from the modern French Côte-d'Or *département*, where it appears to be principally concentrated on a northwest-southeast axis. The settlement of Burgundians in the northwest around Dijon was designed to protect Gallo-Roman inhabitants against attacks by the Franks and Alamans: but they also colonized the Saône basin, the lower Doubs valley and the Rhône valley between Martigny and Valence. One Italian source suggests that the Visigoth 'Theoderic' had been involved in the settlement of the Burgundians in Gaul. It also mentions Gundioc, implying that the Theoderic in question was Theoderic II, attempting to exert a degree of political domination over the Burgundians (as he also did in the case of the Sueves).[80] Such hegemony, as with the Sueves, is likely to have included the imposition of Homoianism. G. W. S. Friedrichsen, who studied the Gothic Gospels, noted a connection between the famous *Codex Argenteus* and a Biblical manuscript from Lyon.[81] Although Lyon has revealed little in the way of archaeological evidence from the period of Burgundian domination, it was politically important; and as it was situated in the western part of Burgundian territory, may have been the first port of call for Visigothic clerics from Aquitaine who arrived to spread the Homoian faith. Despite this, there are suggestions of a more durable Homoian minority in the eastern regions around Lake Geneva, while in more westerly areas Homoians would increasingly be outnumbered by Catholics.

Homoian Church organization

One of the greatest frustrations experienced in the study of Homoian Christianty is our almost total lack of evidence about its organisation and personnel. The ecclesiastical historians Sozomen and Olympiodorus mention a bishop (*episcopos*) associated with Alaric and Athaulf and we also find a bishop named Maximinus who accompanied Count Sigisvult's army into North Africa in the 420.[82] It is assumed that both Sigisvult and Maximinus were Goths. Maximinus would famously get the better of Augustine of Hippo in theological debate over the Trinity – Augustine allowed himself to be trapped into appearing to compare God to a dog.[83] Later, Maximinus would compose a commentary on the anti-Homoian 381 Council of Aquileia.[84]

While there is a general assumption that armies and peoples on the move had at least a bishop, this is largely speculation. Once they had settled in Iberia, Gaul and Italy references to Homoian clergy mostly use the term *sacerdotes*, which unhelpfully can mean either priests or bishops.[85] One of the insoluble puzzles has been the ethnic background of the *senior* 'Arian' Ajax, sent by the Visigothic ruler of Aquitaine to convert the Sueves. Our only source, Hydatius, bishop of Chaves, describes him as *natione Galata*: was he a Galatian, a Gaul, or even a Gallaecian?[86] In the Burgundian kingdom, the Catholic Bishop Avitus of Vienne referred to the Homoian King Gundobad's *sacerdotes* or *seductores* (seducers), the latter term perhaps implying the presence of foreign, Visigothic clergy.[87] Gregory of Tours would claim that Gundobad murdered his brother Godegisel, along with the latter's 'Arian bishop' in a 'church of the heretics' at Vienne.[88] In Italy, Andreas Agnellus, a valuable, if late, source for the history of Ravenna, tells us that in the twenty-fourth year of the rule of Theoderic (i.e. 518) a bishop with the Gothic name of Unimundus 'built from its foundations' a church (with episcopal residence) outside the walls of Ravenna.[89] The only evidence for the clergy associated with a Homoian cathedral comes from Ravenna in 551, but rather than from Unimundus' church, it refers to a cathedral built inside the walls by Theoderic himself. There were priests, deacons, doorkeepers and several cleric-ascetics as well as two scribes.[90] Here we appear to have evidence of a cathedral with a scriptorium and, apparently, some sort of religious community attached to it.[91] It is our only piece of evidence for a Homoian Gothic ascetic community. In Visigothic Aquitaine, King Euric (466–84) refused to allow Catholic sees to be filled in a period of political tension, but there is no suggestion that they were taken over by Homoian bishops.[92] A network of bishops associated with specific cities on the model of the Catholic Church appears in the 580s in Spain – but this was a royal creation in very special circumstances (see Chapter 4). It is not clear that there were any Homoian bishops in the central Meseta region where many of the Visigoths settled, except (probably) for a bishop at King Leovigild's capital of Toledo.[93]

The reality was that the Germanic peoples were a minority elite distributed – unevenly – among Gallo-Roman, Italo-Roman or Hispano-Roman populations. While Ostrogothic Ravenna saw the creation of a number of Homoian ecclesiastical buildings and Theoderic the Great may also have been responsible for the creation of Sancta Anastasia as well as a church dedicated to the Saviour in Verona, in other Italian cities Homoians appropriated Catholic churches for their use.[94] The latter pattern probably prevailed elsewhere. The church of La Daurade at Toulouse, demolished in 1762, may have been given a new decorative scheme in the Visigothic period.[95] After the Visigothic defeat at Vouillé the Council of Orléans of 511 decreed the re-consecration of 'heretical' churches, leaving it unclear just how many of these had actually been built by Homoians and how many taken over from Catholics.[96] In Burgundy, the Catholic Bishop Avitus of Vienne refers to churches built by King Gundobad for the 'heretics' and also to Catholic ecclesiastical buildings seized by them.[97]

Homoian teaching

Ulfila had aimed to capture intuitions of divinity by teaching a Trinity in terms which non-Christians could understand. While we regard him as Homoian, it might be more accurate to say that he was 'anti-*ousian*'. The most consistent feature of Homoian theology was not necessarily its insistence that the Son was 'like' the Father, even if Valens of Mursa had valiantly resisted the alternative 'like in all respects' (*per omnia*). Germinius of Sirmium, one of the original Homoian bishops at Rimini, had annoyed Ursacius and Valens by going over to the latter formulation about 366. But Germinius never abandoned opposition to *ousia* language.[98] The idea that the Son and Father should not be confused was at the heart of the idea of teaching Christianity to the Goths, because Ulfila could see that any suggestion of a confusion of beings ran counter to widespread intuitions of how supernatural beings worked. Thus as Auxentius of Durostorum pointed out:

> he [i.e. Ulfila] defended not comparable things [*comparatas res*] but different dispositions [*differentes adfectus*] …[99]

Over the course of the fifth century, the basic Homoian approach to the Trinity may have helped the absorption of non-Christian groups into Germanic communities and coalitions: the people of Hunnic descent buried in Burgundian cemeteries are likely to have become Homoian Christians. But Ulfila's intention was to move people beyond what we might describe as 'entry-level Christianity'. It was his mission to teach people Christian doctrine and before the formulation of the Homoian creed, he had already embarked on his major life's work, the translation of the Bible into Gothic.

Philostorgius tells us that Ulfila translated

> all the books of Scriptures … with the exception, that is, of Kings. This was because these books contain the history of wars, while the Gothic people, being lovers of war, were in need of something to restrain their passion for fighting rather than to incite them to it …[100]

This censorship – if, indeed, it ever existed – did not necessarily last as the Goths entered the Empire and their clerics and scribes came into contact with other versions of the Bible and Latin Homoian texts (see below). But there is no suggestion that Ulfila and his school of translators ever altered the Bible to produce a more 'Homoian' reading of the relationship between the three persons of the Trinity.

Gothic scripture

Around 403, two Goths, Sunnias and Fretela wrote to Jerome asking him about the differences between the Greek version of the Psalms and the Latin version – the so-called Roman psalter – which he had made c. 383. We have Jerome's reply to the 178 points about which they asked. Jerome indicates that they have been working from the Septuagint or 'common' Greek version, whereas he has been using the best critical text given by Origen – hence the discrepancies. But he expresses his delight that the Scriptures are being studied amongst the Goths.[101]

Scriptural study continued as the Goths settled in various parts of Europe. They had clerics who were evidently sufficiently expert to be able to consult the Latin versions of the Bible used in the localities where they settled. Collectively, these versions are designated the *Vetus Latina*, a term which covers a plethora of translations from the Bible; some are extensive, giving versions of the Gospels, while others consisted of excerpts or now survive only as fragments. These pre-dated Jerome's Vulgate, which was intended to replace variants with a single stylistically consistent version of the Bible, but it took centuries before this was used throughout the whole of Europe. It appears that when the Goths settled in Aquitaine and perhaps also in Spain, their clerics and scribes compared the Latin versions of scripture they found there with the Ulfilan translation. What the Ulfilan school of translators originally produced appears to have been a highly literal word for word translation and a very simple rendering of the text.[102] This had been made from the Greek (and which was in some respects cumbersomely literal, even reproducing Greek particles). Visigothic translators checked the *Vetus Latina* texts they came across and amended their Gothic text accordingly. This may also have happened in Burgundy as one of the *Vetus Latina* texts consulted may have come from Lyon.[103] Where the Visigoths and Burgundians (and also the Vandals of North Africa) were concerned, the Gothic Bible was subject to revision and alteration.

Very little indeed survives of the Gothic Bible: one estimate is that in print it would amount to fewer than 280 pages, virtually all of it drawn from the New Testament. Only sixty lines remain of the Old Testament in Gothic, fragments of the books of Ezra and Nehemiah. The most famous and by far the most extensive surviving Gothic Biblical text is the magnificent *Codex Argenteus* now in Uppsala University Library. It is a deluxe codex containing the four Gospels, written in silver and gold letters on purple vellum, generally thought to have been created in the reign of Theoderic the Amal, Ostrogothic ruler of Italy 493–526. It is not a complete manuscript: we now have 188 leaves (187 in Uppsala, the other in Speyer) out of – probably – an original total of 336. It follows the traditional order in which the Gospels were organized: that is, Matthew, John, Luke, Mark.[104] In 551, in the final years of the Gothic kingdom in Italy, we can see the personnel of the clerical-scribal community that had produced the *Codex Argenteus* in a papyrus charter, signed by the clerics and scribes of the Gothic cathedral. It disposed of a piece of marsh-land and was signed by nineteen individuals who subscribed in both Latin and Gothic. Most have Gothic names and even those with Latin ones may have been of Gothic origin. In all, there were priests, deacons, doorkeepers and several clerics-ascetics as well as two scribes. One of the latter was the *bokareis* Wiljarith, one of the two creators of the *Codex Argenteus*: by 551, he was no longer able to see properly and had to sign the document with a cross.[105]

The level of expertise that went into creating this magnificent codex indicates considerable experience in the production of Bibles. Its letters are very regularly written in a script resembling that of contemporary Latin Uncial manuscripts and the amount of parchment needed to produce the codex has been calculated precisely. It was written by two scribes: one copied Matthew and John, the other Luke and Mark. It has punctuation, headings, titles, Eusebian canon tables (which indicate where the gospels agree with or diverge from each other) and the Eusebian sections are indicated clearly throughout. Though a prestige object, it is also a work designed for consultation and use: there are fifteen instances of marginal glossing in Gothic, where someone has commented on a phrase in the body of the text. Some earlier marginal glosses even found their way into the main body of the text, where they sit alongside the phrases they are commenting on.[106]

Scholars have traced the relationship between the *Argenteus* and earlier *Vetus Latina* versions of the Gospels from northern Italy, dating from the fourth and fifth centuries, as well as with the original translations made by the Ulfilan school. It is also related to an earlier *Vetus Latina* version originating either in Visigothic Gaul or northern Italy. As we have seen, there are also affinities with a Lyon manuscript: does the latter imply contact with Gospels used by the Burgundians? Most intriguing of all is its relationship with African texts. Was this a result of connections with Visigothic Spain or contacts with the 'Arian' Vandals, who had settled in Africa in the 420s?[107] The surviving Gothic fragments of the New Testament Epistles also indicate that they had originally been translated from the Greek and subsequently Latinized: the Latinized renderings derive from the *Vetus Latina*, Augustine and Ambrosiaster and it is thought that these changes were probably made in Italy. One commentator has suggested that this points to the Romanization of the Goths in Italy.[108]

A Gospel manuscript preserved at Brescia, the *Codex Brixianus* has been recognized as the Latin part of a bilingual Latin-Gothic translation, of which the Gothic part is now missing. In both *Brixianus* and *Argenteus* the Eusebian canon tables occur on every page, not just at the beginning of each Gospel as is more common in other famous Latin Gospels, thus facilitating consultation and study. In addition, the composers of the preface to the Brescian Gospels not only announce that they are working partly from a Greek version of the Gospels, but also refer to what they call *vulthres*. These are annotations inserted in the (now lost) Gothic part of the Gospels indicating places where the translators had encountered discrepancies between Greek and Latin versions and were, in effect, resolving them. The annotations were intended to indicate how this has been done and the preface states that

> no-one should on these grounds be in any doubt that the true sense of the original text has been determined by careful consideration in accordance with the meaning of the translated language.[109]

The evidence from the Ostrogothic kingdom c. 500 all points in the direction of an energetic continuation of the Ulfilan tradition of the Gothic vernacular Bible, with new versions produced by clerics educated in both Latin and Greek. Yet there may be signs that this activity was changing orientation and becoming increasingly inward looking. Scholars consider that, though it still preserves signs of being influenced by Latin Gospels, the Latin of the *Brixianus* has actually been influenced by Gothic readings. It is also the case that there is less Latin influence on the Gothic versions of Matthew and John in the *Argenteus* than is apparent in Luke (where the text is particularly affected by Latin readings) and Mark. Had there been a purist reaction in favour of Ulfila's original text when the *Brixianus* was copied? Were Matthew and John in the *Argenteus* copied from a less Latinized 'Ostrogothic' original than Luke and Mark, the latter based on 'Visigothic' texts which had been much more extensively amended by reference to Latin versions?[110] This is speculation, but may suggest that, in Ostrogothic Italy in the early part of the sixth century, Gothic Biblical studies were becoming less receptive to outside influences than before. While the *Codex Argenteus* shows that considerable effort had been made over the years to render Scripture comprehensible, with Gothic words found or created for ideas and things – army, schism ('speaking amiss') holocaust ('all burnt'), *denarius* (the Roman coin) and sponge, there are also many instances where unfamiliar Greek or Latin expressions and concepts – among them angel, Paraclete, *evangelium* (gospel), *drachma* (the Greek coin), olive oil, mustard and scorpion – have remained un-translated since the days of Ulfila, and are merely transliterated.

Italian Gothic Homoianism – the only Homoianism we know about in any degree of detail – exhibits other conservative traits. The surviving eight leaves of *Skeireins*, a Gothic commentary on the Gospel of John – a manuscript that was scraped (almost) clean and re-used for Catholic texts later in the sixth century – tell us that it still maintained a strict separation between the persons of the Trinity. It emphasized Christ's descent from Heaven and taught that He was not the same as the Father and should be similarly, but not equally, honoured. It stuck to the idea, championed by Ulfila and Auxentius, that God the Father and God the Son had different functions:

> For not only the change of name signifies the difference of the two Persons, but much more the evidence of function signifies the One as verily judging no man but granting the authority of judgement to the Son.[111]

This might have been useful in converting any pagan associates who had entered Italy with the Goths; but then it goes on to condemn Sabellius and Marcellus who 'dared to say that the Father and Son are One'.[112] That a commentary apparently composed in the sixth century should refer to third and fourth century theologians suggests that it was targeted at literate clerics and that this theology was unlikely to mean much to a popular audience.

In addition to the *Skeireins*, a number of Homoian Latin sermons and homilies survive in a Verona manuscript from the late fifth or early sixth centuries. This provides further testimony to the scribal and linguistic expertise of its compilers as well as their access to earlier texts. The sermons for feast days contain Homoian teaching, presented in an un-aggressive manner, while a set of Gospel homilies contains nothing that is un-orthodox. These writings were sufficiently anodyne for them to pass, until 1922, as the work of the Catholic bishop Maximus of Turin. But were they used by Gothic clergy as they stand, in Latin, for a Gothic audience? Further questions are raised by two texts in the collection opposing Judaism and paganism, which were clearly composed at an earlier period by Latin Homoians. *Against the Pagans* denounces the deities of the Roman pantheon. Some of its themes – particularly the arguments that when pagans acknowledge a *summum deum* they are, in fact, demonstrating an awareness of the Christian God; or its arguments against the worship of idols; or its Old Testament-based case proving that God does intervene in human affairs – might have been useful if Gothic clergy had set out to convert any pagans who had entered Italy with them from the Balkans, but again the question of language arises.[113] This text might also suggest that, even if, as the historian Philostorgius alleged, Ulfila did not translate the books of Kings, they were now known in a sixth-century Italian Homoian context.[114] But we have no way of telling whether these works were ever actually put to use in terms of making further converts amongst any Germanic or Hunnic pagans who had entered Italy along with the Goths.

Homoian-Catholic debates

If there are any among the barbarians who seem in their books to possess the Sacred Scriptures less interpolated and torn to pieces than the rest, still the corruptions in their texts are due to the tradition of their first teachers, whose disciples hold rather to their tradition than to the Scripture itself. For they do not abide by the instructions of the true law, but by the interpolations of an evil and distorted interpretation.

The barbarians, indeed, lacking the Roman training or any other sort of civilized education, knowing nothing whatever unless they have heard it from their teachers, follow blindly what they hear. Such men, completely ignorant of literature and wisdom, are sure to learn the mysteries of the divine law through instruction rather than reading, and to retain their masters' doctrines rather than the law itself. Thus the interpretation and doctrine of their teachers have usurped the authority of the law among them, since they know only what they are taught.[115]

These are the words of Salvian, a fifth-century Roman, writing in southern Gaul in the 440s. Like Augustine in his *City of God* and Orosius in his *Seven Books of Histories Against the Barbarians*, Salvian sought to explain the disasters befalling the Roman Empire. In his work *On the Government of God* (more correctly, *On the Present Judgment*) he places the blame on the iniquities of the Romans, whose behaviour he contrasts unfavourably with that of the 'barbarians'. But even while he credits the Christian Goths and Vandals with some redeeming qualities, he also condemns them as heretics. This, he affirms, is not their fault: they have been misled by their teachers who have either foisted corrupt texts of the Bible on them, or simply taught heretical doctrine by rote, rather than allowing their people any access to Biblical texts. Salvian's stance reflects the marginalization of Homoianism and the way in which the activity of Biblical translation, envisaged by Ulfila as one of the fundamentals of Gothic Christianization, was presented as cutting Homoians off from mainstream Christianity.

By the sixth century any Hoimoian-Catholic dialogue seems to have consisted of debates revolving around Biblical texts relating to the Trinity, with opinions polarized and neither side prepared to concede. In Burgundy, the Catholic Bishop Avitus of Vienne reported to Sigismund, Catholic son of the Homoian ruler Gundobad about his debates with his father's *sacerdotes*. His letter reveals that Gundobad himself had

ordered me to send him an annotated and ordered list of all the passages from our scriptures that I had cited in response to questions at the time of the debate and indeed add any others, if they occurred to me.[116]

Another letter alleges that Gundobad's *sacerdotes* had attempted to 'prove' from a Biblical text that the Holy Spirit was one of God's creatures and therefore could not be God: the text in question says that, in making man, God 'inspired into him an active soul and breathed into him a living spirit'. Avitus' response implies that Gundobad's priests were confused: 'God', he writes 'is not supposed to have blown to add a spirit to a being that was already alive'. Discussion of this passage takes the debate into new areas, but this was exceptional.[117] It also suggests a lack of theological understanding on the part of Gundobad's advisers.

As Avitus' letter suggests, the norm was for both sides to line up a number of well-tried scriptural passages and then argue over them. As represented by the Catholic Bishop Gregory of Tours, Visigothic Homoians refused to recite the Catholic version of the *Gloria*, basing their case on scriptural texts such as John 14.28: 'My Father is greater than I'; or I Timothy 1.17: "Now unto the King eternal, immortal, invisible, the only God, be honour and glory for ever through Jesus Christ our Lord' and argued that the Son, who was sent, could not be equal to the Father who sent Him.[118] Gregory depicts himself countering the text from John with eleven different Biblical citations and demonstrating that the Homoian interpretation of the Pauline text was superficial. By the early seventh century, the Catholic Visigothic king Sisebut was able to reel off, in a letter sent between 616 and 621 to the Lombard queen-regent Theodelinda, a catena of Homoian citations:

'The Father', they say, 'is greater than I' [Jn. 14.28] and: 'He who sent me gave me a command' [Jn. 12.49] and: 'I did not come on my own but he sent me' [Jn. 8.42] and again 'I did not come to do my will' [Jn. 6.38] and again: 'As my Father said to me, so I speak' [Jn. 12.50] and: 'What he gave me, I have kept and everything he gave me no one takes from me'; after which they throw in: 'I shall ask my Father' [Jn. 14.16] and 'he will show me more than twelve thousand legions of angels' [Mt. 26.53] and: 'If this cup can pass away, unless I drink it, and if it can be let this cup pass from me: not as I wish but as you wish' [Mt. 26.42, 39] and they add: And what is pleasing to him I always do and 'To sit at my right or left, it is not for me to give you' [Mt. 20.23]; senselessly they add: 'And he gave him the name which is above every name and he exalted his boy' [Phil. 2.9] and the lord your God blessed you and roused him from the dead and made him sit at his right hand and many similar things which the most correct faith takes in such a way that it knows what is suitable to deity what to humanity ...[119]

He then gives a list of Catholic counter-citations:

> Therefore where God the Son is shown equal to God the Father, we have collected select pieces of flowers from the treasures of holy law and we have offered the collected gifts of the eternal king drawing them under one. For the Son says to the Father: All my things are yours; and again the evangelist: 'making himself equal to God' [Jn. 5.18] with all power and 'I and the Father are one' [Jn. 10.30] and in the following: 'that they may be one in us as I and you are one' [Jn. 17.21] and: 'Did you not believe that I am in the Father and the Father in me?' [Jn. 14.10] and 'My Father works and I work' [Jn. 5.17] and 'As the Father raises the dead and gives them life, so the Son gives life to those he wishes' [Jn. 5.21] and: 'Who saw me saw the Father' [Jn. 14.9] and: 'Who hates me, hates my Father' [Jn. 15.23] and 'Glorify your Son so your Son may glorify you' [Jn. 17.1] and 'I shall glorify on earth and manifest your name to men' [Jn. 17.4,6]. Let all intention of sophistry be at rest, let them accept this previous statement of John and defend it, retelling the most sacred words in this manner: 'In the beginning was the word and the word was with God and God was the word' [Jn. 1.1]. Let them cease, therefore, to make the statement of the mad with the tongue of powerful speech, which panting they try to separate the Son, substance of the Father, from the Holy Spirit which lives and reigns equal in unity of power with the Father and the Son.[120]

Sisebut was evidently able to refer to records of debates between Homoians and Catholics that had taken place in Spain before the Visigothic monarchy abandoned Homoianism in 589. It seems that these, like the equivalent debates elsewhere, were unproductive ritualized confrontations in which neither side had any intention of backing down.

The contest over relics

Although it had originally been devised as a means of appealing to intuitions of divinity and to 'nonreflective' belief in supernatural beings, the marginalization of Homoian Christianity seems to have led to its increasing sterility and fossilization. Homoians also appear to have been increasingly cut off from one of the most potent means of appealing to intuitive and 'nonreflective' belief: the cult of saints and relics (see Chapter 5). The issue of control of and access to these would become a problem for the Homoian Churches.

The Goths venerated their own martyrs. The most notable of these is St Saba, tortured and put to death by pagan Gothic leaders in a period of anti-Christian reaction: his *Passion* was written in Greek in the form of a letter from Christians in Gothia to the churches in Cappadocia and, although Saba is likely to have been a Homoian, his relics were transferred to Cappadocia. The martyrdom, deposition and – apparently – the relic-cult of other Gothic martyrs, is also recorded. More reliably, a fragment of a sixth-century calendar from Ostrogothic Italy combines the commemoration of Gothic martyrs with those of the Emperor Constantius, a Homoian bishop, and the apostles Philip and Andrew. A reference to 'old women' martyred at Beroea in Thrace may reflect a cult taken up originally by the Thracian Goths.[121]

The set of homilies for feast days copied in Verona in the sixth century from an earlier Latin work, contains brief sermons for the major feasts of the Christian calendar, as well as for St John's day, the *Passions* of Peter and Paul, St Cyprian, St Stephen's day and no less than three for the day on which all martyrs are celebrated.[122] Although we do not know whether these homilies were ever read out in public in sixth-century Verona, their calendar looks like a development of the calendar used in fourth-century Milan, so possibly gives some indication of the feast-days celebrated in Verona by Homoian churches in the early sixth century.[123] But the dedications of Homoian churches to the Saviour or to his Resurrection, as in Theoderic's Ravenna, might indicate that they did not actually contain the relics of saints. It is notable that when a number of Theoderic the Great's churches in Ravenna were 'reconciled' by the Catholic Bishop Agnellus (577–70), they were re-dedicated to Saints Martin, Eusebius, Theodore and George.[124] It is likely that relics were placed in them at this point. Pope Gregory I followed a similar procedure with two former Gothic churches in Rome, where the relics were carefully chosen to convey anti-'Arian' and anti-Gothic messages. The first church, previously dedicated to the Saviour, was re-dedicated to the virgin martyr St Agnes of Catania, who had been invoked to help the Byzantine side in the struggle to recover Sicily from the Goths in the 530s. The other was endowed with the relics of St Severinus, Catholic apostle of Noricum.[125] While it is possible that Italian Homoians had control of relics in churches that they had taken over from Catholics (see pp. 73–4 below) this situation is likely to have changed after the Justinianic reconquest of Italy. In 563–5, the Catholic Bishop Nicetius of Trier derisively represented 'Arians' in Italy 'furtively' venerating the relics of the apostles and lurking outside the basilicas housing the relics of SS Peter, Paul and John in Rome:

> They consult about celebrating Masses there, but they do not dare ... because they are clearly not the disciples of the Lord Peter and they are proved to be enemies of Christ ...[126]

This was written in the decade or so after the final defeat of the Goths in Italy, when Goths may have been ejected from any churches with relics that they had formerly held and now could only attempt to gain occasional entry to the major shrines. Nicetius' letter was addressed to Chlodosuintha, the Frankish Catholic wife of Alboin, the Lombard leader who was still at this stage a pagan. He must have been contemplating conversion as had sent some of his followers to visit the Roman basilicas, outside which, according to Nicetius, Gothic Homoian churchmen gathered 'furtively, as dogs'. Nicetius grandiloquently invited her husband to send his *fideles* instead to the shrine of St Martin at Tours

> where every day the blind receive their sight, the deaf their hearing and the dumb their speech. What shall I say of lepers, or of many others who, no matter with what sickness they are afflicted, are healed there year after year ...[127]

Nicetius' triumphalism underlines the difference between the Frankish Church, where the cult of relics played a major part in Christianizing 'nonreflective' belief (see Chapter 5 below) and Homoian Christianity in Italy which may never have a enjoyed an extensive cult of relics and was now effectively excluded from it.

In Visigothic Spain under the Homoian King Leovigild (569–86), control of relics was recognized as a major priority. The Catholic (and violently anti-'Arian') *Lives of the Fathers of Merida*, composed in the seventh century, underlines the tension over relics when it makes the 'Arian' bishop of Merida, Sunna, appropriate a number of Catholic churches and attempt to take control of the basilica housing the relics of the virgin martyr Eulalia. A debate is arranged between Sunna and his Catholic opposite number, Bishop Masona, to decide possession. Thwarted in debate, Sunna then attempts to remove Eulalia's tunic to the 'basilica dedicated to the Arian depravity' in Leovigild's capital of Toledo.[128] Gregory of Tours claims that when Leovigild wanted to win Catholics over he went to pray at Catholic churches, particularly those containing the tombs of martyrs.[129] In 592, three years after Catholicism was declared the official religion of the Visigothic state, the Council of Zaragoza decreed that 'Arian' relics should be tested by fire to see whether they were genuine or not.[130] This gives an interesting perspective on the use of relics: it looks as if the major items (as in the case of the tunic of Eulalia at Merida) were in Catholic hands, but that Homoians had tried to supplement them with items which were less well known – or were perhaps of more dubious provenance, as there does not seem to have been any concern about reaction to this ordeal of relics. To what extent new churches had been built or older ones, already housing relics, were taken over is not clear.

In Burgundy, it is noticeable that Sigismund, king from 516–24 and a convert to Catholicism even before his accession, sent to Rome for relics: references in the homilies of Bishop Avitus of Vienne to churches dedicated to St Peter could indicate that he obtained and distributed Petrine relics. This looks like an attempt to strengthen the position of Catholicism in Burgundy. Sigismund's request also serves to underline the point that Catholics had a potential source of relics in the pope, an option completely unavailable to Homoians. In 515, even before he succeeded his father, he founded the monastery of Agaune. This was already a place where groups of ascetic laypeople – the texts suggest women – had tended the relics of St Maurice and the soldier-martyrs of the Theban legion; his sisters founded monasteries dedicated to other members of the same group. At Agaune, Sigismund replaced the women by monks, organized into squadrons or *turmae* named for the monasteries from which they were drawn, who chanted the psalms in continual relays. This represented a fusion of established Catholic monastic elements with the practice of continual psalmody pioneered by the Akoimetoi or 'Sleepless Ones' of Constantinople. Sigismund could have learned about them as a result of his diplomatic missions to the eastern emperor.[131]

Was there a drift towards Catholicism in the Germanic kingdoms?

A letter of Pope Vigilius to Profuturus of Braga in 538 and the canons of the Council of Epaone (517) both indicate that Catholics had converted to Homoianism in Gallaecia and Burgundy, but we have no details as to numbers or dates. It would seem reasonable to assume that political and social issues lay behind these conversions. In point of fact, it was easier for a Homoian to become Catholic than the other way round: as Vigilius' letter to Profuturus indicates, 'Arians' re-baptized Catholics to convert them to their faith. A Homoian becoming a Catholic, however was only 'chrismated', anointed with unction.[132] In 538, Profuturus was apparently in a position to be able to re-admit Catholics who had accepted a second baptism and Vigilius advised that they be reconciled by a laying-on of hands as was done when penitents were reconciled. There are also indications of conversions to Catholicism in Visigothic Spain.[133]

The Council of Epaone was more rigorous in its attitude towards Catholics who had gone 'Arian', prescribing two years' penance before they could be readmitted to Catholic communion.[134] Nevertheless, the fact that the issue was mentioned at all indicates that some degree of movement back to Catholicism was anticipated now that the Burgundian ruler, Sigismund, was a Catholic. In one of his letters to the pope, Avitus of Vienne affirmed that Sigismund's conversion, which is believed to have taken place c. 502, had encouraged Burgundians to become Catholics even though his father King Gundobad was still a Homoian.[135] Epigraphic evidence might suggest that a drift towards Catholicism had begun even earlier (see Chapter 6, pp. 149–50 below). One feature of the Burgundian ruling dynasty that has attracted the attention of numerous commentators is the religion of its female members. The wife of Chilperic I, Gundobad's own wife Caretena, his brother Godegisel's wife Theodelinda, and Chilperic II's wife and daughters were all Catholics.[136] (The wives of Gundioc and Sigismund, both the daughters of Homoian leaders in Italy, were not, however, forced to convert and probably brought their own chaplains or bishops with them.)

John Moorhead suggests that Ostrogothic Italy saw 'a steady flow from Arianism to Catholicism.' Procopius represents Gothic envoys telling Justinian's general Belisarius that under their rule, no Roman had changed their creed, whereas Goths had become Catholic and not been penalized. This seems to have been true of Theoderic's reign at least. We have the names of some converts to Catholicism, most of them, apparently, women.[137] In Gallaecia, while we have no information about individual Sueves, the Catholic Church appears to have been gaining in strength at the point of Vigilius' response to Profuturus: his answers deal with the restoration of church buildings and the celebration of Easter, the formulas for baptising and reciting the *Gloria*, as well the problems presented by 'Arians' and the native heresy of Priscillianism.

Homoianism had been designed as a way of making Christianity appealing to polytheists. Yet however successful as 'entry-level' form of Christianity it may have been, it was not necessarily well equipped for survival. It captured intuitions of divinity and translated them into Christian terms: but the great achievement of the creation of a Bible in the Gothic language only served, in the long run, to isolate the Homoian churches. The remarkable level of study and activity sustained by Gothic clerics and scribes and the nature of debates over the Trinity between Homoians and Catholics reveal that, as a minority and marginalized religion, Homoianism began to ossify into a 'doctrinal' religion, focused on Scripture and creed. Its access to more intuitive elements, in the shape of relic cults was limited and we can identify a number of Germanic Catholics. While some individuals had accepted re-baptism as Homoians for political reasons, we learn of their existence at the point where they were reneging on that decision and Catholic bishops were envisaging their possible re-admission to the Catholic Church. It is difficult to escape the impression that amongst some sectors of the population, a gradual drift towards Catholicism, the majority religion, was taking place.

4

Approaching the Macrocosm

While the sources suggest that some of the Germanic peoples were drifting into the Catholicism of the peoples amongst whom they settled, the story of their rulers is a different one. 'Arianism' – Homoianism – remained the official creed of a number of rulers and peoples into the sixth and seventh centuries, prompting suggestions that 'Arianism' was something of a mark of national identity.[1] This not only contradicts the evidence for a drift into Catholicism, but also masks the real nature of the problem. Work on a different era and region has the potential to cast some light on the situation. In the 1970s, the Africanist Robin Horton coined the idea that West African rulers, coming into contact with Islam and Christianity and faced with a dilemma – conversion or not – were in effect caught between the macrocosm of the great world religions, with their wider network of relationships and affiliations on one hand and the microcosm of their traditional religions, intimately connected to existing politics and alliances on the other.[2] For the rulers of the Sueves, Ostrogoths and Visigoths, Burgundians, Franks and Lombards the macrocosm was the Roman Empire. From a modern perspective, this was the Late Roman Empire, already waning in power: the last western Roman emperor would be deposed by Odoacer, the commander of the Italian armies, in 476. But even if 'the Fall of Rome was not an intellectual fiction unnoticed by contemporaries,'[3] from the Germanic leaders' point of view, an emperor ruled in Constantinople and the Empire continued to be the most powerful and prestigious institution in existence. 'Barbarian' leaders still attempted to buy into the discourse of Empire or to define themselves in relation to it. A very important part of that discourse consisted of the practise of orthodox Christianity and thus Catholicism was part and parcel of the macrocosm to which they aspired. Catholicism also had the very powerful attraction of adding practical as well as prestige value to rulership: it consolidated relations with the networks of bishops, key figures in the territories over which they ruled. For leaders, the path to underpinning their rule lay in the acquisition of *Romanitas* and Catholicism. But they had to attempt to balance this, not always successfully, against the needs of the political-military microcosm from which they had sprung.

Goths and Burgundians

While Homoianism had become in effect the Christianity of the Goths, there are numerous signs that by the sixth century, Gothic leaders were anxious to escape the restrictions it placed on them. This is particularly evident in Ostrogothic Italy under Theoderic the Great. Of all the 'barbarian' leaders discussed in this chapter, Theoderic (453?–526) had the greatest personal experience of the Roman macrocosm. He had spent his formative years in Constantinople, sent there as a hostage after his people had devastated Illyricum, as part of a peace-settlement with the Emperor Leo, arriving as a child of eight.[4] The sixth century chronicler Jordanes wrote in *De origine actibusque Getarum* c. 550/1 that Theoderic was a fine child who gained the imperial favour.[5] Later Byzantine chroniclers would claim that he received a good education while resident in the palace. His ten years in the imperial city must have done much to shape his ideas and aspirations: the power of the largest city in the Roman world to impress 'barbarians' is well known and Rome's successor state, the Byzantine Empire, would capitalize on this for centuries. While he was at this youthful stage 'a smallish fish in a large and murky pond', and while he would not hesitate to threaten the Empire when engaged on building his own power, once settled in Italy and proclaimed as *rex* by his warriors, his aim seems to have been to achieve recognition from Constantinople of the 'virtual parity' of his status with the emperor.[6]

According to Jordanes, Theoderic returned from Constantinople at the age of eighteen to his own people, embarking on a military career that led him through the Balkans. He first of all led his father Theodemer's followers in a campaign in which they defeated the Sarmatians and captured Singidunum: he and Theodemer then moved east. The emperor granted them seven towns in Macedonia and when his father died, Theoderic took his armies to lower Moesia. A period of conflict with the Empire and the leader of the Thracian Goths, Theoderic 'the Squinter', followed and after both he and his son died, the Thracian Goths united under Theoderic's leadership. In 483 he made peace with the Empire and became *magister militum* and consul for the year 484: Jordanes states that he visited Constantinople again to be invested with these honours. Theoderic's relationship with the Emperor Zeno was still a tense one: in 486 he devastated Thrace and advanced on Constantinople, only withdrawing after his conditions, which included a substantial payment, had been met. In 488, he appears to have agreed with Zeno to go to Italy to attack its current ruler, Odoacer. Probably towards the end of 488, he descended on Italy at the head of an army of Goths and their associates. For several years he and Odoacer each controlled their own zones of the peninsula. But in 493, Theoderic defeated and killed Odoacer and became the *de facto* ruler of Roman Italy.[7]

Theoderic created alliances in the Germanic world through the traditional means of marriage. He himself had married Audofleda, the sister of the Frankish ruler Clovis; his sister Theodegotha was married to the Visigothic king, Alaric; his daughter Ostrogotho-Areagni married Sigismund, son of the Burgundian ruler Gundobad; while a third daughter Amalafrida became the wife of the Vandal king Thrasemund.[8] His niece Amalaberga married the ruler of the Thuringians.[9] He nevertheless threw out many hints of his desire to enter the macrocosm. He did nothing to censor the theological writings of his adviser Boethius, who, around 520, composed works on the Trinity that constituted a technical attack on Homoianism: these formed part of a theological and philosophical dialogue with a cleric who, not long after, became Pope John I.[10] In the earlier part of his reign, Theoderic even issued an edict ordering that gold and silver be removed from graves in territories which were not under the direct control of any lord: precious metals, he declared, were of use to the living rather than the dead, though the ashes of the dead were not to be disturbed. Interments, he pronounced, should be protected by a building: sepulchres should be adorned by columns or marble.[11] While he does not attempt to interfere with traditional Gothic mourning and inhumation rites and while the graves he has in mind may have been ancient burial mounds, Theoderic is nevertheless indicating that he does not subscribe to the belief system underpinning the rituals of his own people. His magnificent mausoleum stands outside the walls of Ravenna near a cemetery that contained Gothic furnished inhumations, but its references are imperial and therefore, by implication, thoroughly Christian, even Catholic.

It is clear that Theoderic, as ruler of Italy, for many years oriented himself towards the Roman world. Up to about 519, his advisers had constructed a discourse of *civilitas* as a means of addressing the Italo-Roman population (and perhaps partly as a means of justifying the Gothic appropriation of large amounts of Italian land). This discourse represented the Goths as the armed wing of the Roman state, while the Italo-Romans stood for law and civil life (and paid taxes). Theoderic also maintained a highly respectful demeanour towards the Catholic Church. The major theological disputes of the period were Christological rather than Trinitarian in character, so there was no occasion for his personal beliefs to be put under the spotlight. He was asked by the Catholic bishops to arbitrate in the disputed papal election of 498 and again in its aftermath in 502: his intervention in the first case was not only by invitation but also comparatively 'low-key' and in the second he left decisions up to the episcopate.[12] During the synod of 499, he was acclaimed by the assembled bishops ('Hearken, O Christ! Life to Theoderic!') no fewer than thirty times.[13] During the period of Gothic rule, Catholic churches and bishops carried on as normal and the Catholic bishops of Ravenna – one of Theoderic's three 'capitals' and the one where he constructed his most famous monuments, including both his own mausoleum and several churches – themselves initiated or contributed to ambitious building projects. These took the shape of a baptistery in Classe, the port city; an episcopal residence, known as the *Tricollis*; the church that eventually became San Vitale; as well as the church of Sant' Apollinare in Classe, founded by the financier Julianus Argentarius.[14] Some of these were begun in Theoderic's own reign. This evidence would suggest that for a considerable period, the Catholic hierarchy flourished under his rule.

Ravenna, however, is also the site of Theoderic's most famous monuments. Some are still standing, including his own mausoleum; the so-called 'Arian Baptistery'; and the church now known as Sant' Apollinare Nuovo, originally dedicated to Christ and erected beside his (now destroyed) palace. In the baptistery and Sant' Apollinare, some of the original spectacular mosaic decoration remains. Theoderic also ordered the creation of a cathedral (now Santo Spirito), which is less well known, as none of its early decoration survives. In addition, he seems to have been responsible for the creation of another 'church of the Goths', inside the city, pulled down by the Venetians in the later Middle Ages, though some of its columns, bearing Theoderic's monogram, were re-used. Originally, 'Arian' churches seem to have been placed outside the city itself. One was in Classe; one in the suburb of Caesarea; and two were just outside the city walls, in a location known as the *Campus Coriandri*. These last two both had an episcopal residence attached. One, according to Andreas Agnellus, had been constructed by a bishop with the Gothic name of Unimundus in 518. The richness of the surviving decoration of Theoderic's intra-mural churches indicates that both baptistery and the palace church, were, as we might expect, true prestige projects, while the ground plan of his cathedral has imperial echoes as it mimics the proportions of the church of St John Stoudios in Constantinople. What is striking about what remains of the decoration of Theoderic's baptistery, though, is its similarity to that of the Catholic baptistery built by Bishop Neon in the fifth century. Scholars have eagerly scanned the two sets of iconography for differences, but the consensus of opinion seems now to be that they are minor and that there is nothing to indicate theological divergence. When the palace church was 'reconciled', that is re-dedicated by Bishop Agnellus later in the sixth century, he excised representations of Theoderic and his circle (though scholars argue that one portrait of Theoderic, labelled as 'Justinian', survived), leaving the upper two registers of decoration in the nave more or less intact and adding a third, lower, register of his own. There was nothing theologically contentious about the upper two cycles of mosaics in the nave, and it seems very unlikely that there was anything problematic about the iconography of the art in the apse. This apse collapsed in an earthquake in the ninth century, but we can assume that it contained a representation of Christ to whom the church was originally dedicated. Technically 'Arian', Theoderic's cathedral, baptistery and palace church were constructed not to declare his opposition to Catholicism but rather to display his own power and elevate his prestige in the eyes of Italo-Romans, Catholics and the Empire.[15]

The leaders of the Burgundes had probably accepted Homoianism from the Aquitainian Visigoths. Insofar as we can establish a chronology for this event, it is most likely to have occurred in the reign of Gundioc (d. 473). Gundioc's successor Gundobad (c. 473/4–516) was clearly intent on entering and playing a part in the Roman macrocosm. His father and uncle had both been awarded the title of *magister militum*; he himself had become *magister militum* in Italy. In 472, he was created *patricius*, backing an imperial candidate and only returning to Burgundy on the death of his uncle, Chilperic I.

Gundobad was a new kind of Burgundian ruler. He violently abandoned the custom of shared rule of the Burgundian territories: he murdered his brother Chilperic II and his sister-in-law, forcing his nieces Chrona and Clothild to flee from Lyon. His brother Godegisel continued to rule Sapaudia for a time; but the rivalry between the two came to a head around 500 CE. Gregory of Tours gives a lengthy account of the struggle between the two brothers, which ended with Godegisel and his 'Arian bishop' being cornered and killed in a church in Vienne.[16] Gundobad also revealed his political ambitions when he married his son Sigismund to the daughter of Theoderic the Ostrogoth.

Gundobad thus emerges as a very ambitious king, not content with the custom of sharing rule with a family member and extremely eager to increase his own prestige. A Latin inscription in Geneva records his extension of the royal residence at his own expense.[17] His marriage of his son to the daughter of the king of Italy, who technically ruled on behalf of the emperor, represents an attempt to re-assert himself in the world of imperial politics which he had first known as *magister militum*. The correspondence of Burgundy's leading Catholic churchman, Avitus, bishop of Vienne from c. 494 to c. 518 reveals that Gundobad's aspirations were accompanied by a strong interest in Catholicism. He consulted Avitus on points of doctrine and we have Avitus' replies – though unfortunately, no way of dating any of Avitus' letters with absolute confidence. In one, Avitus responded to queries about the efficaciousness of deathbed penance, trying to reassure the king that it might not be in vain. In another he gave an explication of a Biblical passage:

> For the law shall go forth of Zion, and the word of the Lord from Jerusalem.
> And he shall judge among many peoples and rebuke strong nations afar off; and
> they shall beat their swords into ploughshares, and their spears into pruning-
> hooks; nation shall not lift a sword against nation, neither shall they learn war
> any more. But they shall sit every man under his fig tree; and none shall make
> them afraid.[18]

The tenor of the prophecy, with its themes of war and peace, law and the extension of power over more than one people is of obvious interest to an ambitious ruler. Avitus, however, wrote back impatiently, offering only a short and probably, from Gundobad's point of view, not very satisfactory explication.

A feature of the Burgundian ruling dynasty that overtly signalled a lack of hostility towards Catholicism was the Catholicism of its female members. The wife of Chilperic I, Gundobad's own wife, his brother Godegisel's wife, as well as Chilperic II's wife and daughters, were all Catholics.[19] And although Gundobad never himself became a Catholic, his son Sigismund, whom he associated with himself in kingship, took this step as early as 502. Sigismund's wife, however, was a Homoian and may have brought her own chaplain or bishop with her from Italy.

Thus in their different ways, the Ostrogoth and Burgundian leaders appeared to orientate themselves towards Catholicism, the natural accompaniment of their aspirations to *Romanitas* and their involvement with the Empire. Yet neither actually became Catholic. Theoderic and Gundobad both appear to have been restrained from taking this step.

Theoderic's political orientation would change radically in the last years of his life. In the last six or seven years of his reign, the discourse of *civilitas*, employed when dealing with Romans, disappeared. Instead he began to resort to the terminology he had formerly reserved for other rulers of the Germanic microcosm, emphasising the superiority of the Gothic *gens* through its prowess in war. Theoderic's change of direction seem to have been created by a perception of his insecurity as ruler of his own people, an insecurity rooted in the fact that he had no adult male heir to succeed him. His initial solution seems to have been that Eutharic, the Visigoth husband of his daughter Amalasuentha would be his successor, but Eutharic died some time around 522. Members of other families may have already begun to imagine that they themselves could rule over the Goths. As Peter Heather observes:

> Any Italian Goth aged 50 or above will have remembered Theoderic's real origins and the struggles which established his rule, despite his later, imperial, pretensions.[20]

Heather has made a convincing case for the limitations imposed on Theoderic's power by 'distance, numbers, alternative memories and traditions'.[21] The

Goths were widely dispersed: the main areas of Gothic settlement in Italy were in the areas of present-day Friuli, Trentino and Veneto; the areas to the west of Ravenna and along the Adriatic coast between modern Romagna and the Marche; and northern Piceno and Sannio. Goths were to be found in the cities of Milan, Tortona, Trento, Aquileia, Rome and even Naples and some other southern cities as well.[22] The scattered nature of this settlement meant that Theoderic had three 'capitals': Pavia, Verona and Ravenna. But other Goths were settled at isolated defensive points, living as nuclei of warriors and families, having limited contact with the native population.[23] A classic example of such an isolated settlement is Monte Barro in modern Lombardy where Goths lived in a 'highly defensible' location – if 'in some style'.[24] Amongst the archaeological finds from this site were a hanging crown, a symbol of authority: this may be a sign that that some groups had their own internal hierarchies and traditions which they maintained on the lands that they were either given when they entered Italy, or were able to purchase as a result of payments in cash.[25] Although Theoderic had appointed officials in the countryside and gave out cash payments (donatives) in return for military service at annual assemblies, to all intents and purposes many of these groups were beyond his control.[26] One surviving document demonstrates that Theoderic could only confirm the choice of a local leader made by the Goths of Rieti and Nursia.[27] Another, the papyrus of 551 signed by Wiljarith and the clerics of Ravenna's 'Arian' cathedral, refers to 'the law of the Goths', presenting the 'law' as specific to certain places – in this case Nervi and L' Aquila – suggesting a particularism which outlived Theoderic.[28]

In the earlier part of his reign, Theoderic relied on land, or donatives, or other forms of patronage to keep the Goths happy. He occasionally executed individuals who posed a threat to his authority. As time wore on, he appears to have realized that he needed to address the problem of the Goths more fully and this need became more urgent after Eutharic's death when it was vital that he avoided being seen as a 'lame duck king'.[29] Part of his programme of dealing with the Goths consisted of setting his Italo-Roman adviser Cassiodorus the task of creating the impression of a unique Gothic ruling dynasty: Cassiodorus produced a genealogy tracing the Amals back sixteen generations. Theoderic's other tactic was, apparently, to emphasize his Homoianism. In this, he appears to have been playing something of a double game: just before his death, he approved the choice of a new pope, an act very much in line with his earlier policy of calculatedly deferential involvement in Catholic affairs.

Exactly what he did to present himself as a Homoian is obscured far more than illuminated by the two principal sources for his last years: the second part of the chronicle known as the *Anonymus Valesianus;* and the *Liber Pontificalis* entry for the pontificate of John I (523–6). Introducing his narration of the later years of Theoderic's reign, the *Anonymus* is apocalyptic in tone:

> Shortly after that the devil found an opportunity to steal for his own a man who was ruling the state well and without complaint. For presently Theoderic gave orders that an oratory of St. Stephen, that is, a high altar, beside the springs in a suburb of the city of Verona, should be destroyed. He also forbade any Roman to carry arms, except a small pen-knife. Also a poor woman of the Gothic race, lying in a colonnade not far from the palace at Ravenna, gave birth to four snakes; two of these in the sight of the people were carried up on clouds from west to east and then fell into the sea; the two others, which had but a single head, were taken away. A star with a train of fire appeared, of the kind called a comet, and shone for fifteen days. There were frequent earthquakes.[30]

These sources portray Theoderic as a rabid 'Arian', who demanded that Emperor Justin re-open 'Arian' churches in the eastern part of the Empire and planned the closure of all Catholic churches in Italy. The *Anonymus* also suggested he was in league with the Jews, a caricature of Theoderic's policy towards this minority, which appears enlightened – for the age. Both sources construct alleged Catholic martyrs; either Theoderic's Italo-Roman adviser Boethius, whom he executed for conspiring with the Emperor Justin; or Pope John I, ailing when he is sent on a mission to Constantinople, and who dies as a result of being imprisoned and maltreated on his return. What actually happened is not entirely clear. The chronology of events such as the execution of Boethius is uncertain and Theoderic's alleged threat to close Catholic churches looks like a wild exaggeration.

Both works were composed after Theoderic's death and the beginning of the Justianianic war to recover Italy from the Goths and their accounts are biased and highly schematic. But it appears to be the case that, in the last years of his reign, Theoderic had attempted to present himself as an ardent Homoian. The one stridently anti-Catholic homily in the Verona collection of

Homoian texts may date from this period.[31] In this persona, it is possible that he did ask for the re-opening of old 'Arian' churches outside Constantinople and perhaps took over some Italian Catholic churches for the use of the Goths. Ostrogothic Ravenna saw the creation of a number of Homoian ecclesiastical buildings and Theoderic may also have been responsible for the foundation of Sancta Anastasia and a church dedicated to the Saviour in Verona, but in other cities Catholic churches were appropriated for Homoian use.[32] It is not clear to what extent these takeovers had occurred when the Goths first settled in Italy, or whether they were characteristic of the latter part of Theoderic's reign. It might have been a combination of the two, with some churches being used by the Goths from the outset, followed by Theoderic's later attempting to increase the number of churches in Gothic hands.

As well as using Homoianism as a political expression of Gothic solidarity, Theoderic may also have viewed it as a potential means of converting pagans. In his *Book of the Pontiffs of the Church of Ravenna*, the ninth-century chronicler Andreas Agnellus records the Emperor Justinian's grant to his namesake Bishop Agnellus (557–70) of

> all the property of the Goths, not only in the cities but also in the suburban villas and hamlets and in their temples and altars, slaves and handmaids, whatever could pertain to their jurisdiction or to the rite of pagans …[33]

This seems to suggest that as late as 557–65, there were still visible remnants of non-Christian religious structures or sites associated with the Goths. Many or all of the people who used them may have belonged to other ethnic groups who joined with the Goths in the Balkans or even after they had entered Italy. Some could have been of Alan or Hunnic origin, such as the man aged over fifty buried at Collegno who had an intentionally deformed skull and leg-bones showing evidence of long periods of time spent in the saddle. A child buried in the same group of interments has a similarly deformed skull, indicating a continuation of traditional practices, so it is not unreasonable to hypothesize the possible continuation of traditional religious practices as well. Theoderic may have believed that that Homoianism could be used to convert non-Christians who had entered Italy along with the Goths – as it was originally designed to do – and thus into closer relations with him. The *Codex Argenteus* might even have been created as part of this policy. However, the increasingly doctrinal and conservative nature of Ostrogothic Homoianism raises questions about how effective such a policy would have been – and perhaps accounts for the continued existence of non-Christian cult sites. After Theoderic's death, the tensions between 'Romanizing' elements, represented by his daughter Amalasuentha and the Gothic nobility continued. With no male heir, she tried to secure her position: first through the murder of three opponents, then, when her husband died, through the elevation of her cousin Theodahad to the throne. She herself was murdered in turn. By this time, the East Roman Emperor, Justinian, had decided to recover Italy and launched a war of re-conquest which, by the 550s, had put an end to Gothic control of Italy.[34]

The information we have about the forces inhibiting Gundobad suggest that he too was held back by fear of the political consequences of his conversion, wishing to become a Catholic, but worried about reactions if he did so. Gregory of Tours portrays Gundobad as covertly desiring to become a Catholic and asking Avitus of Vienne to arrange for him to be anointed with the chrism in secret. He makes Avitus admonish the king to have the courage of his convictions:

> You are a king and you need not fear to be taken in charge by anyone: yet you are afraid of your subjects and you do not dare to confess in public your belief in the Creator of all things.[35]

Whether Avitus ever expressed such a direct view is unknown. His letters certainly demonstrate that he expended a considerable amount of energy in trying to persuade Gundobad to convert. When writing to Gundobad, Avitus is always careful to stress the king's piety, even his 'orthodoxy' and 'Catholic understanding'. He criticizes the king's *sacerdotes* (priests or bishops) for both their translations and their readings of Biblical texts.[36] He is careful never to call Gundobad 'Arian' to his face, perhaps anticipating a denial of any connection with Arius, though he does not hesitate to use the term behind his back to his Catholic convert son Sigismund. He attempts to explain some of the basics of the Trinity to Gundobad: the Son is equal with the Father;[37] the Holy Spirit proceeds, eternally, from the Father and Son;[38] the Trinity is necessary, was adumbrated in the Old Testament and is united.[39] In arguing for the unity of substance in the Trinity, Avitus at one point reveals that he is dealing with a variety of Homoianism that took the separation between the three persons so far as to postulate three separate substances.[40] His letters to Sigismund refer to debates between himself and Gundobad's *sacerdotes* (whom he calls 'seducers' and 'sectaries') and to treatises that he himself had composed.

All of this indicates not only a high level of activity on Avitus' part but also on that of the rival Homoians. When Avitus writes to the Catholic Sigismund, he mentions an 'annual contagion at which our opponents are assembled' and also alludes to an earlier gathering at Geneva which had caused anxiety.[41] This has been interpreted as evidence of an annual synod and of a well-organized Homoian church – though there may be other explanations.[42]

A key to achieving some understanding of the situation may be the letter in which Avitus indicates the existence of private Homoian churches. After the accession of the Catholic Sigismund, Victorinus, bishop of Grenoble, had written to ask Avitus whether these could be put to the service of the Catholic religion, once their founders had converted to Catholicism. Avitus expresses an extraordinary aversion to the idea. He first of all muddies the issue by extending Victorinus' original question to cover churches set up by Gunobad 'for the heretics'. Should these also be turned over to Catholic use? No: Catholics should not lay themselves open to the 'calumnies of heretics and pagans', who will accuse them of oppression. The next ruler may not be a Catholic. A foreign power may retaliate for this treatment of 'his priests' in Burgundian lands by taking measures against Catholic priests in his territories. He seems to be suggesting that the takeover of churches previously set up for Gundobad's wife Ostrogotho-Areagni could provoke her father Theoderic the Amal into reprisals against Catholics in Italy. Avitus in fact distinguished between churches (*ecclesiae*) as opposed to the heretics' little basilicas, which he calls 'basilicules', or oratories. Far from being eager to take over the heretical 'basilicules', Avitus expresses the hope that they will, eventually, be left to rot. However: a Catholic church which had originally been *appropriated* by heretics is not judged to be polluted in the same way as a 'basilicule' actually *built* by heretics – so it may be re-possessed. This crucial distinction is repeated in Canon 33 of the Council of Epaone of 517.[43]

Avitus deploys a large amount of rhetoric to suggest that his objections were based on the idea of ritual pollution: 'polluted things pollute what touches them rather than being purified by the contact.' He introduces Old Testament texts that refer to sacrifice and to the pollution of consecrated bread:

> And Haggai said, 'If a polluted man touch any one of those things, will it not be polluted?' And the priests said, 'It will be polluted'.[44]

Even chalices and patens associated with such altars are too contaminated for use in a Catholic church. But was this rhetoric poured out in an attempt to avoid admitting that Homoianism had been entrenched in private churches and oratories on landed estates that the Church was afraid to enter?

It is possible that the majority of Burgundian Homoians were warriors, some of them even descended from remnants of the Hunnic armies, who had been converted from paganism by Visigothic and then Burgundian Homoian *sacerdotes*. Homoianism could plausibly have been presented to them as not only corresponding to their intuitions of divinity, but also as an alternative to Catholicism, a creed associated with the disastrous end of the 'First Burgundian Kingdom' and as such unsuitable for warriors. The exact mechanisms of Burgundian settlement on Gallo-Roman territory are unknown: were they given land, taxes or some combination of the two?[45] Could Burgundian warriors have been summoned to an annual gathering, similar to those at which Ostrogothic men of military age paraded and received their donatives? If so, this might explain Avitus' comment to Sigismund about an 'annual contagion at which our opponents are assembled'.

It is clear that, in the year after the accession of the Catholic Sigismund, Homoianism still existed. The Council of Epaone of 517 reveals that, although the synod was attended by twenty-five Catholic bishops, presided over by Avitus himself, the Catholic Church was not either as powerful or as united as it might have been. Epaone itself was not an episcopal city, but a parish located somewhere between Vienne and Valence: was the council held there because the bishops could not agree which city it was to be held in? One canon allowed laymen to summons priests, a practice which Avitus disagreed with, and his letters reveal problems within the episcopate.[46] Some canons suggest that churches had passed into private hands. 'Arian' basilicas and oratories are to be left alone. Catholics who have 'lapsed' and accepted Arian baptism are given a reduced penance of two years. Deathbed conversions to Catholicism are valid, but should the individual make a recovery, they are to go to the

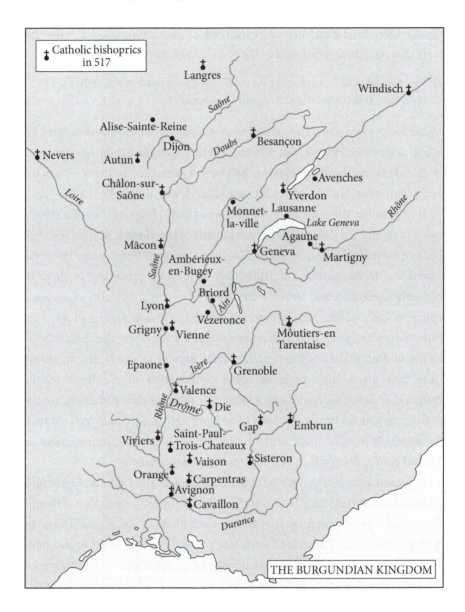

+ Catholic bishoprics
  in 517

Langres

Windisch +

Saône

Alise-Sainte-Reine

Besançon

Dijon   *Doubs*

+ Nevers

Autun +

Châlon-sur-
Saône

Loire

Avenches

Yverdon

Monnet- Lausanne
la-ville   *Lake Geneva*

Mâcon +

Agaune

Ambérieux-   Geneva   Martigny
en-Bugey

Saône

Briord

Lyon   *Ain*

Grigny   Vézeronce
        Vienne

Môutiers-en-
Tarentaise

Epaone   *Isère*

Grenoble

Valence

Rhône *Drôme* Die

Viviers

Gap   Embrun

Saint-Paul-
Trois-Chateaux

Vaison   Sisteron

Orange
Carpentras
Avignon
Cavaillon

Durance

THE BURGUNDIAN KINGDOM

bishop in order to be readmitted properly to the Catholic Church. There are 'Arian' clerics: Catholic priests are penalized for mixing with them.

All the indications point to a very real tension in the reigns of both Gundobad and Sigismund between their aspirations and the realities of power in Burgundy. Gundobad apparently did not dare become a Catholic: to do so would have exposed his aim to bypass or undercut the independence of his warrior class. He had probably moved too quickly in disposing of his brothers and the resentment felt by their supporters would have combined with a more general opposition to increased royal power in the aftermath of what Halsall describes as the war of 500.[47] He had no major territorial gains to offer his warriors by way of compensation: Burgundian participation in the defeat of the Visigoths in 507 brought only temporary advantages and the real beneficiary was the Ostrogoth Theoderic. So Homoianism survived as a symbol of their desire to check his power. It appears to have been sufficiently well-entrenched for the Gallo-Roman episcopate to have to deal with its existence in the year after his accession.

Sigismund's letters to the emperor in Constantinople reveal his overwhelming desire to be part of the Roman world, combining a subservient tone with insistent reference to a title he has received – presumably *magister militum per Gallias*.[48] His reign would come to an end during a Frankish invasion: the religious orientation of his successor, Gundomar, is unclear, but the Franks would finally destroy the Burgundian kingdom in 534.[49] A surprising number of warriors seem to have survived: in 539, a two thousand-strong Burgundian force was sent by the Frankish ruler Theudebert to aid the Ostrogoths in Italy against the Emperor Justinian.[50] Was this the remnants of a warrior landed class whose private 'basilicules' had been a source of such annoyance to Avitus?

The collapse of the Ostrogothic and Burgundian states in the wake of East Roman and Frankish invasions ends the traceable history of Homoianism in these areas. In both, however, the rapprochement of their rulers with Catholicism appears to have been inhibited by the structure of their societies and the resistance of military elements to any increase in royal power and control. In Visigothic Spain and Suevic Gallaecia, there are also signs that moves towards co-operation with, or control of, the Church were part of a drive towards consolidation of power by rulers and were not necessarily welcomed by their elites.

Sueves and Visigoths

Suevic rulers had quietly been attempting to shake off the Homoianism imposed on them by the Aquitanian Visigoths since at least the 530s. Suevic power from the late fifth century on was in effect confined to Gallaecia, while anarchy ruled in the rest of the Iberian peninsula. We know little about the details of their settlement there apart from the fact that Braga (*Bracara Augusta*) was their capital. It is not quite true, as one historian has claimed, that between the defeat of Rechiar by the Visigoths and the arrival of the Catholic missionary Martin of Braga c. 550, 'the Suevic kingdom enters a period of absolute historical darkness'.[51] In 538, Pope Vigilius replied to a number of queries from Bishop Profuturus of Braga, who had written to him in an attempt to put the Catholic Church in Gallaecia on a more secure footing after what had evidently been a very difficult period in which churches had been destroyed and relics removed (perhaps to places of safety). Amongst Profuturus' queries was one about the procedure to be followed for Catholics who had accepted rebaptism as 'Arians'. There also seems to have been confusion about the correct formula to use for the Trinity in baptism and in reciting the *Gloria*. In addition, Pope Vigilius decreed that baptism was to be performed by the ancient ritual of triple immersion (and this instruction would be repeated at the First Council of Braga in 561). A letter of St Martin of Braga contextualizes these prescriptions: in the Iberian peninsula, triple immersion was often rejected in favour of a single one because the 'Arians' used triple immersion.[52]

Vigilius' letter to Profuturus indicates the increasing confidence of the Catholic Church in Gallaecia and it is hard to imagine that Profuturus had approached the pope without the king's approval. Gregory of Tours claims that around 550, relics of St Martin of Tours, Francia's premier saint and alleged opponent of heresy, arrived in Gallaecia, at the same time as Martin, future bishop of Braga. We are told that Martin of Braga was Pannonian in origin, like Martin of Tours himself, but scholars have recently pointed to evidence of his western education and connections with Francia.[53] This would again suggest that the Sueve rulers were attempting to align themselves with Catholicism as a gesture of independence from the Visigothic state that was now their neighbour in the Iberian Peninsula. In 561, King Ariamir ordered the convening of the First Council of Braga, an assembly of Catholic bishops. This made no reference whatsoever to Homoianism, though the letter of Pope Vigilius to Profuturus of Braga was read out. The main doctrinal concern of the council was Gallaecia's older home-grown heresy, Priscillianism.[54] In

572, a Second Council of Braga took place: there were now two metropolitan bishops (Braga and Lugo) and thirteen bishops altogether, as opposed to the eight who had attended the previous council. Ariamir was now acting in concert with an expanding network of Catholic bishops.[55]

In 569, under King Theodemir, Catholicism was formally decreed as the religion of Suevic kingdom. The late sixth-century document known as the *Parrochiale Suevum* lists thirteen dioceses – one of them 'of the Bretons' or 'Britons' – and their dependent 'churches'. The churches reflect a mixture of ethnic group names (e.g. Equisis, Celesantes, Bibalos, Teporos, Geurros, Verecanos, Calapacois, Fraucellos, Pesicos) and Celtic place names (e.g. Carantoni, Brigantia, Tongobria, Turonio, Turedo, Senabria, Bergido, Senimure) as well as names of Hispano-Roman domains (e.g. Curmiano, Carisiano, Marciliana).[56] This suggests that the Sueve minority ruled over a territory that was exceptionally heterogeneous in terms both of ethnicities and also of the articulation of social and economic power, which appears to have been extremely devolved and fragmented. The development of the Catholic Church under royal patronage created a degree of centralization that might be thought to favour the ruling dynasty. In contrast to the Ostrogothic and Burgundian kingdoms, the Sueve rulers seem to have been allowed to encourage Catholicization and there is no evidence of attachment to a Homoian Church – on the contrary there may even be evidence of a drift back to Catholicism as early as the 530s. Yet at the same time, the chronicler John of Biclaro records the existence of factions within the Suevic kingdom. After the death of King Mir in the 580s, Audeca seized the kingship, married Mir's widow and had the heir Eboric tonsured as a monk.[57] This precipitated an invasion by Leovigild and the absorption of the Suevic kingdom into the Visigothic state (see below). Even after the removal of Audeca, another contender attempted to place himself at the head of the Sueves – only to be defeated in turn by Leovigild. The appearance of contenders for kingship among the Sueves at this stage may indicate the reasons why earlier monarchs had hoped to strengthen themselves by means of ecclesiastical support. But the Catholic Church in Gallaecia was still comparatively underdeveloped and the concerns expressed at length in the canons of the First Council of Braga about the survival of Priscillianism suggest that this may have been a real problem. After Leovigild's conquest of the region, however, the history of the Suevic Church merges with that of the Visigothic Church.

Visigothic rulers had begun to orientate themselves towards the macrocosm in the late fifth and early sixth century. In Aquitaine, both king and Catholic episcopate came to realize the political advantages of co-operation. At first we can detect tensions: under Euric (466–84) there were debates between Homoians and Catholics and in the 470s a number of Catholic bishops were exiled, among them Sidonius Apollinaris. This is likely to have been because of their political opposition to Visigothic rule.[58] But after a period in which Euric refused to allow episcopal elections, the situation seems to have relaxed. Alaric II (484–507)

> gave his approval for sees to be filled, considered himself a God-appointed monarch and called councils for the general health of the Church within his kingdom.[59]

When the Frankish ruler Clovis attempted to de-stabilize the Burgundian kingdom by promising to protect Catholic religious foundations, Alaric exiled Bishops Verus of Tours and Cæsarius of Arles, whose dioceses stretched into Frankish and Burgundian territory. But Cæsarius was soon recalled, presiding over the Council of Agde in 506. This issued forty-eight canons dealing with church organisation and discipline, which conclude by offering thanks first to God and then to 'our lord King Alaric'.[60] Just before the catastrophe of the Battle of Vouillé destroyed his kingdom, Alaric was planning 'an even grander synod, one that would convoke bishops from both Gaul and Spain'.[61]

Before 507, Visigoths had begun to move into Iberian peninsula in the wake of their destabilization of the Sueve kingdom, now largely confined to Gallaecia. They may never have constituted a large proportion of the Iberian population.[62] For much of the sixth century, there was no strong monarchy in Visigothic Spain and Septimania. For a time, these territories were controlled by Theoderic the Great, technically on behalf of his grandson. Theudis, originally Theoderic's general in Spain, became king in 531. His murder was followed by the rule of a series of short-lived elective kings, when 'the choice of monarchy was effectively in the hands of the nobility of the court'.[63] The monarchy appears stronger under Athanagild, who rebelled against Agila in 551 and ruled until 567, although his reign saw the invasion of the south by Byzantine forces. Consolidation of dynastic power really began in the reign of Leovigild (568–86), an energetic ruler, who aimed at nothing less than the creation of a united Spain under his rule. (This soon included Gothic Septimania, initially ruled for a few years by his brother Liuva, as well.) In the 570s, Leovigild expelled the Byzantine Empire from the foothold it had established in the south; he also vanquished the Basques and in the last years of his reign, the Sueves.

Leovigild aimed to create a new discourse of Visigothic kingship. He began the transformation of Toledo, his capital in the latter part of his reign, into the ceremonial centre of his kingdom and he established the new cities of Reccopolis and Victoriacum. The physical remains of a palace church survive in the ruins of the city of Reccopolis, founded in 578 and perhaps named after his son Reccared (alternatively it could have been Rex-opolis, king's city).[64] Its plan is unusual, somewhere between a basilica and a cruciform church and the side aisles are divided from the central one by walls. This is not thought

IBERIAN PENINSULA c. 570

SUEVIC KINGDOM

■ Eido da Renda
● Dume
● Braga

● Victoriacum

■ Herrera de Pisuerga

● Zaragoza

Duraton
■ ●Reccopolis

Tarragona

■ Alcalà de Henares

●Almódovar del
● Pinar
Toledo

Merida
● Lisbon ●

VISIGOTHS

SEPTIMANIA

BYZANTINE SPAIN

■ Cemeteries mentioned in
Chapter 6

to be indicative of liturgical differences between Homoians and Catholics so much as representing a stage in the evolution of Hispanic church architecture.[65] Leovigild surrounded his rule with trappings of *Romanitas*, using Late Roman regalia – crown, sceptre and throne – and issuing coinage with the bust of the king on both obverse and reverse.[66]

Under Leovigild's predecessors, relations between king and Catholic bishops had not been bad: under Theudis (531–48) a number of provincial synods had taken place.[67] The hiatus between two councils held in 546 and Toledo III in 589 may have in part been created by the very unsettled conditions in the peninsula before Leovigild's accession. The political importance of control of the church in his reign is foregrounded in the seventh-century text known as the *Lives of the Fathers of Merida*. It indicates possible Byzantine attempts to control the city through two Greek bishops who arrive from the east as well as struggles between Catholics on one hand and Leovigild and the 'Arians' on the other for ecclesiastical control of the most important city in Lusitania, highlighting their conflict over the basilica and relics of the virgin martyr Eulalia. The *Lives* give a highly biased picture of Leovigild's backing of his 'Arian' bishop Sunna and the exile of the Catholic Goth Masona, who had defiantly refused to hand over the relic of the virgin's tunic so that Leovigild could take it to his capital of Toledo.[68]

According to the *Lives*, Leovigild at one stage removed Masona and installed a more compliant Catholic bishop. He clearly appreciated the importance of control of the episcopate. But he was not prepared to turn Catholic to achieve this. The Catholic chronicler John of Biclaro noted that in 580

> King Leovigild assembled a synod of bishops of the Arian sect in the city of Toledo and amended the ancient heresy with a new error …[69]

The amendment proposed was that the Son's equality with the Father was admitted – though not that of the Spirit. (Technically this is the same as the Macedonian Christianity of the fourth century.[70]) The Homoian requirement that Catholics who converted to their creed be re-baptized was also dropped in favour of the imposition of hands and communion. These changes were clearly designed to persuade people that the gulf between Homoianism and Catholicism was not so great and to make conversion to the former much easier. One Catholic bishop, Vincent of Zaragoza, actually went over to the new religion. Gregory of Tours makes no mention of this apostasy, alleging instead that he had been told by Frankish envoys to Spain that

> Those Catholics who still exist in Spain keep their faith unimpaired. The King has a new trick by which he is doing his best to destroy it. In his cunning way he pretends to pray at the tombs of the martyrs and in the churches of our religion. Then he says, 'I accept without question that Christ is the Son of God and equal to the Father. What I cannot believe is that the Holy Ghost is God, for that is written in none of the Scriptures.'[71]

The description of Leovigild's behaviour suggests that he was deliberately attempting to minimize the differences between Homoians and Catholics and in another work Gregory claims he returned property looted from a Catholic monastery dedicated to St Martin. He even came to favour a Catholic holy man, Nanctus.[72] Roger Collins has suggested that the Visigothic elite associated itself with the Homoian hierarchy and that the latter was drawn from the ranks of the former: thus Leovigild was, according to this argument, afraid to antagonize the 'Arians'. However, we have no evidence for any extensive Homoian hierarchy before Leovigild's reign. Our information about them is drawn to some extent from the *Lives of the Fathers of Merida* and the *Chronicle* of John of Biclaro, but also from the proceedings of the church council that ended Homoianism. The 'Arians' were all bishops of major cities: none are associated with the important area of Gothic settlement in the Meseta, barring a putative Gothic bishop of Toledo (see below). Most of them had a Catholic opposite number, as Sunna had in Merida. It looks very much as if Leovigild desired to create a united church on his own terms, but realized he would have to placate his elite. Rather than openly going over to Catholicism, he tried to persuade Catholic bishops to become Homoians and when this manoeuvre failed went on to create what was probably an almost entirely new network of Visigothic Homoian bishops in his major cities in the 580s. In effect, he was allowing the Gothic elite a stake in the new Church which he hoped to forge to support his leadership, rewarding their representatives with positions of influence – and plausibly also with property confiscated from individuals and Catholic churches. At the same time, it looks as if some Catholic sees were deliberately kept vacant when their incumbents died: it has been calculated that in 589, over half the Spanish bishops had been in post for four years or fewer. However, while Leovigild's policy was undoubtedly a bold one, it failed. His son, Reccared, who succeeded him in 586 must have realized that his best chance of controlling the episcopate was to take the ultimate step of converting to Catholicism.[73] In 587, ten months after his accession, he did so, meeting with the newly created Homoian bishops and gaining the acquiescence of almost all of them. This was 'the real turning point' in the conversion of the Visigoths to Catholicism. In this year, he began to return the property confiscated by his father, and restored rights and legal privileges that had been removed from Catholics. Thus in 589, Catholicism was proclaimed as the official religion of Visigothic Spain. The Homoian bishops of Barcelona, Valencia, Palencia, Viseu, Tuy, Lugo, Oporto and Tortosa all proclaimed their renunciation of their former doctrine and were rewarded by being allowed to remain in place – even if there was a Catholic bishop in the same city. In the case of Elvira, there were two Catholic bishops, suggesting a situation on the lines of Merida, where Leovigild had at one stage replaced Masona with the more accommodating Catholic Nepopis.

Three Homoian prelates – Sunna of Merida, Athaloc of Narbonne (in Septimania) and Uldila, probably bishop of Toledo – did not sign in 589. All are on record as conspiring against Reccared along with a number of Visigothic counts, who had no doubt been the principal beneficiaries of Leovigild's confiscations, as Collins points out. In 588, Sunna plotted not only to murder the Catholic Bishop Masona of Merida but also to replace Reccared with a noble called Segga. The conspiracy was discovered and Sunna was offered the option to remain in office if he did penance, but he refused and left for Africa. After the Council of Toledo in 589, there were revolts: one was led by a noble named Argimund; another by Reccared's stepmother Goiswinth and Bishop Uldila of Toledo.[74] Significantly, one of Sunna's co-conspirators in 588 is named as Witteric, who is depicted in the *Lives of the Fathers of Merida* as betraying his fellow-conspirators. Whether this is true or not, Witteric would go on to kill Reccared's son Liuva and become king himself: the seventh-century writer of the *Lives* was evidently attuned to the divisions and tensions of the late sixth century.

The Third Council of Toledo prescribed the destruction of Homoian writings and our evidence for the clergy and rituals of this late stage of Homoian Christianity is minimal. Gregory of Tours represents Oppila, an envoy from Spain to the Franks in 584, as attending a Catholic mass at Easter with him, but refusing to receive communion or give the kiss of peace. When quizzed about this by Gregory, his objection seemed to be that the Catholic version of the *Gloria* included the Holy Spirit – although he also stated that he believed the three persons of the Trinity to be equal in power.[75] We can probably see here the way in which differences between Catholicism and Homoianism were becoming blurred for Spanish Visigoths, especially those closely connected with the court, as Leovigild manoeuvred for control of his Church. In terms of personnel, the only other evidence we have dates from three years after the official abolition of Homoianism. It is not until 592 that we find a provincial church council held at Zaragoza in the north east of Spain, where it is suggested there had been a significant concentration of Gothic settlement, deciding what was to be done with 'Arian' clergy.[76] The canons of the council allow them to become Catholics and to continue as priests, if chaste, suggesting the possibility that some Homian clergy were married.[77] The same council orders that 'Arian' relics are to be handed over and subjected to ordeal by fire. There are no other canons of provincial councils to tell us about the dismantling of the Homoian Church in Spain. It is tempting to conclude that it had appeared on an ad hoc basis as the Goths moved into Spain. The acts of the Third Council of Toledo represent Reccared as having desired the recitation of the Nicene-Constantinopolitan Creed by the faithful because it had played a key role in his conversion – but the conversion of the Visigothic monarchy to Catholicism was first and foremost a political event.

Clovis and the Franks

The Frankish leader Clovis (466–511) is viewed as unique among the leaders of the Germanic peoples in converting directly to Catholicism without any intermediate 'Arian' stage. As we have already seen, this is not quite correct. The Sueve Rechiar had converted to Catholicism, though the Visigoths swiftly imposed Homoianism on his people. Nevertheless, Clovis' decision to opt for Catholicism provides a valuable contrast with the behaviour of other rulers, in particular that of his contemporary the Burgundian Gundobad.

The fourth-century author Ammianus Marcellinus describes attacks on the Empire by a number of groups such as the Salii and Chatuarii; but he also records the Salii as settling within the imperial borders which they defended in 406 – albeit unsuccessfully – against Alans, Sueves and Vandals.[78] In this piecemeal process of absorption, some 'Franks' became high-ranking officers in the imperial army in the same way as other 'barbarians' such as Ricimer and Odoacer in Italy. Clovis' father, Childeric, was a Salian who served in the Roman military in the decade between 460 and 470: his power base appears to have been in the region of Tournai, where he was buried c. 481–2. In 486, Clovis attacked Soissons, the centre of the province of Belgica Secunda. After conquering this region, he also defeated the Thuringians and – temporarily – the Alamanni. The precise dating of these events has proved problematic. It is based on the notoriously contradictory chronology given by Gregory of Tours, writing roughly a century later. One aspect of Gregory's presentation of Clovis which has made historians cautious about it is its depiction of the way in which he first overcame external enemies and only subsequently went on to defeat internal enemies – Chararic, ruler of the Salian Franks, and his own kinsmen, the kings of Cologne and Cambrai. This looks like a reversal of the logical order of things, in which an aspirant dynast would begin by removing all internal competitors, before expanding into a wider sphere of operations to challenge external rivals.[79] But Gregory draws his discussion of Clovis' slaying of his kinsmen of Cambrai – and his narration of Clovis' career – to a close with the observation that:

> In the same way he encompassed the death of many other kings and blood-relations of his ... One day, when he had called a general assembly of his subjects, he is said to have made the following remark about the relations whom he had destroyed: 'How sad a thing it is that I live among strangers like some solitary pilgrim and that I have none of my own relations left to help me when disaster threatens!'. He said this, not because he grieved for their deaths, but because in his cunning way he hoped to find some relative in the land of the living whom he could kill.[80]

Even if he is often schematic and biased, Gregory's order of events in this case may not be as odd as it first appears: instead it may explain why Clovis, unlike Gundobad, was able to fast-track into the Catholic macrocosm.

From the moment he inherited his father's power-base, Clovis was already poised on the edge of this world. Childeric had maintained good relations with a Christian charismatic – St Genovefa of Paris – sparing prisoners

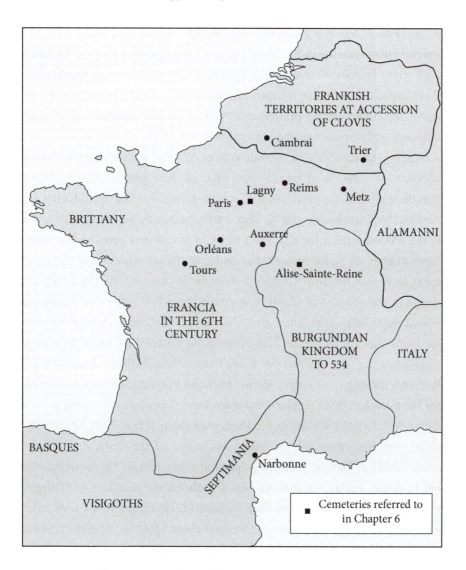

when she interceded for them. He also afforded his protection to Christian clergy.[81] When Clovis succeeded his father as ruler of Belgica Secunda, he received a letter from Bishop Remigius of Rheims, in which he was exhorted to encourage his people, relieve the afflicted, protect widows and encourage orphans; he should be a fount of justice and receive nothing from strangers or the poor. By emphasizing Christian values which harmonized with the 'barbarian' ideal of a strong, just and generous leader, Remigius was attempting to encourage Clovis' conversion: he not only urged him to defer to his bishops but also combined the familiar idea of reputation, vital to a warrior ruler, with the rather more unexpected suggestion that the Christian God might actually be watching over him. The *Life of Genovefa* would claim that Clovis, like his father, released prisoners on Genovefa's insistence: if true, this statement reflects his prudence as Paris, where she commanded immense influence and respect, became his 'capital'.[82]

Writing in the 560s to Chlodosuintha, Clovis' granddaughter, Bishop Nicetius of Trier highlighted the role of her grandmother Clothild (Crodechildis) in his conversion. Nicetius praises her for introducing her husband to Catholicism and he also credits St Martin of Tours with a role in the process, explaining that the astute Clovis had only promised to accept baptism after seeing for himself that claims of miraculous cures at the saint's tomb were not fiction.[83] However, there is no mention of the Martinian shrine in the account of Clovis' conversion given by Gregory of Tours: this is odd, especially as he knew that Clothild had retired to lead a religious life there after Clovis' death. Can Nicetius be trusted? We know he wanted Chlodosuintha, who was married to the Lombard ruler Alboin, to convert her husband, inviting her to persuade her husband to send his *fideles* to Tours to see the miracles which regularly occurred there (as opposed to going to Italy, where 'Arian' Goths wanted to win them over for their brand of Christianity), so he may have invented the Martinian aspect of the story. But Gregory confirms his picture of Clothild as playing a key part in the conversion of her husband, explaining that she was a Catholic, the daughter of Chilperic who was murdered by his brother Gundobad. He claims that Clovis often sent envoys to Burgundy and was thus told about Clothild, 'an elegant young woman and clever for her years'. Although he already had another wife and son, Clovis asked for her hand in marriage.[84] Doubts have been cast on many elements of this story – though not on the essentials of Clothild's Burgundian origins and Catholicism.[85]

Gregory represents Clothild as attempting to persuade Clovis to abandon his gods. It seems that Gregory knew little of the deities of the pagan Franks, as he makes her denounce the behaviour of the Roman gods in terms which he borrows from Cæsarius of Arles (see Chapter 5 below). Gregory also claims that Clothild had her firstborn baptized, because of her adherence to the Catholic faith. This child, Ingomer, died immediately while still 'in his white robes', suggesting that he was already ailing and that his mother had him baptized because she feared he was about to die. Gregory has Clovis reproach his wife for their son's death, which he blames on the baptism. The death of infants in such circumstances would create an unfortunate association between infant baptism and mortality. The Church would find such associations and apprehensions hard to shift.[86]

Gregory's presentation of Clovis' initial encounter with his wife's religion is one in which he views Christianity in terms of his traditions and intuitions. As such his response is negative. However, intuitions soon lead him to a more positive view. Gregory describes how Clovis is 'converted' during a battle often (wrongly?) identified as the Battle of Tolbiac (Zülpich):

> war broke out against the Alamanni ... It so turned out that when the two armies met on the battlefield there was great slaughter and the armies of Clovis were rapidly being annihilated. He raised his eyes to heaven when he saw this, felt compunction in his heart and was moved to tears. 'Jesus Christ', he said, 'you who Clothild maintains to be the Son of the living God, you who deign to give help to those in travail and victory to those who trust in you, in faith I beg the glory of your help. If you will give me victory over my enemies, and if I may have evidence of that miraculous power which the people dedicated to your name say that they have experienced, then I will believe in you and will be baptized in your name. I have called upon my own gods, but as I can see only too clearly, they have no intention of helping me. I therefore cannot believe that they possess any power, for they do not come to the assistance of those who trust in them. I now call upon you. I want to believe in you, but I must first be saved from my enemies.'[87]

According to Gregory, Clothild then arranged for Clovis to be baptized in secret by Remigius of Rheims, who urged him to 'forsake his idols, which were powerless to help him or anybody else.' Clovis maintained that he could not force his people to abandon their gods: but when he summoned an assembly to discuss the matter, before he even had a chance to speak, those present spontaneously and unanimously expressed their willingness to become Christians. Gregory describes a splendid ceremony in which Clovis was baptized:

> Like some new Constantine he stepped forward to the baptismal pool, ready to wash away the sores of his old leprosy and to be cleansed in flowing water from the sordid stains which he had borne so long.[88]

This image of the 'new Constantine' has been diagnosed by one commentator as a repetition of earlier pro-Merovingian propaganda dreamed up by Catholic bishops.[89] Yet despite the Catholic bias evident throughout Gregory's account of Clovis, historians also acknowledge that he was working partly from oral accounts passed down over the years.[90] Shorn of its Catholic rhetoric, Gregory's narrative is informed by a series of traditions that convincingly describe pagan responses to Christianity. Clovis' reaction to the death of his and Clothild's first son exhibits a view of baptism common among converting peoples.[91] The son's name is given as Ingomer, suggesting that that Clovis' original devotion was to Ingui – a god venerated by many of the Germanic peoples (see Chapter 2). Ingui appears, however, to have been associated with fertility and prosperity, so it is likely that before the battle which may or may not have been Tolbiac, he was not the only god invoked: Clovis may have prayed to or sacrificed to other divinities as well. It is plausible that, seeing his forces being wiped out, Clovis would have understood that the Germanic gods had rejected his prayers and offerings in favour of those of the Alamanni – and turned to the god of his wife for help. His initial acceptance of Christ emerges therefore not as the acceptance of doctrinal Christianity that Gregory would like us to believe in, but rather in terms of a traditional and intuitive understanding of divinity. Clovis added Christ to his pantheon, seeing him as the supernatural being who had showed him particular favour.

Gregory's descriptions of the secrecy surrounding Clovis' original plans for baptism and his declaration of his inability to force others to forsake their traditional gods plausibly convey his hesitation to declare himself openly as a follower of Christ. But his success against the Alamanni was accompanied by victory over the Visigoths at the Battle of Vouillé in 507, enabling him to expand Frankish rule over Aquitania and also to provide rewards for his warriors; he was particularly fortunate that an Ostrogothic counterattack would affect the Burgundians rather than the Franks. Bishop Avitus of Vienne sent a letter congratulating Clovis on his baptism, which, like all his letters, has come down to us without a date. Its most recent editors think that the evidence points to a date of composition in 508. This would suggest that it was a continued run of success and luck that enabled Clovis to 'come out' at this stage and opt for public baptism. We might treat Gregory's assertions that an entire assembly of Franks spontaneously declared that they would abandon their old gods or that more than three thousand of his warriors followed him to the baptismal pool with some scepticism – the figure of three thousand is Biblical and was used by Orosius in his account of the conversion of the Burgundian armies in the 420s. But some may have opted for baptism along with or soon after their leader; and at the very least, the Frankish warrior class would have viewed their leader's new deity as an effective war god who had brought their leader and themselves success and rewards. Clovis' success in war was so great that he had no need to appease his military – unlike Gundobad. In congratulating Clovis, Avitus of Vienne alluded to the latter (without actually mentioning him by name):

> Many in this very situation, seeking true belief, if they have moved to the suggestion, encouraged by priests or their friends, usually invoke the custom of their race and the rites of ancestral observance as stumbling-blocks. Thus, to their own detriment they prefer due reverence to salvation.[92]

Gundobad's career could be understood as the mirror image of that of Clovis. Despite the titles conferred on him by the emperor, he could not match Clovis' outstanding military success – the Burgundians had lost territory to the Ostrogoths. His prior elimination of members of his own family combined with this military setback would have created obligations and fostered resentments; in these circumstances an adherence to tradition would have been doubly necessary to secure the support of his warriors. Clovis, by contrast, was sustained by military triumphs achieved under the aegis of Christ, understood as bringer of success in war. Thus he could, as Gregory describes, spend his latter years in seeking out and destroying family rivals. Gregory depicts him as supremely confident, telling warriors of one dead rival that they should put themselves under his protection.[93] It could easily have gone otherwise. Like Theoderic's, his family had risen to power in the comparatively recent past; but unlike Theoderic he had male heirs to succeed him.

Is it possible that Clovis considered 'Arianism' before becoming Catholic and even went through an 'Arian' period himself?[94] One of his sisters, Albofled, was baptized along with or shortly after him, but a second sister Lantechild or Lenteild abandoned 'Arianism'. However in Clovis' own case, Avitus' letter mentions baptism rather than anointing with chrism (which was the ritual for those abjuring 'Arianism', like Lantechild) so there is no evidence for an 'Arian' stage. Nor can we say that there were major Homoian influences close to him. His sister may originally have accepted 'Arian' baptism because she was betrothed to, or married to, to an 'Arian', possibly a Burgundian.[95] Long before his baptism, Clovis had been advised of the possibilities of working with a Catholic episcopate by Remigius of Rheims. In 511, he convoked the Council of Orléans. In the preface to the conciliar acts, the bishops alluded to his care for the Catholic faith and depicted him as taking a pro-active role. It spelled out both Clovis' role in ecclesiastical governance and a new identity for the Gallic Church itself.[96] A number of the clauses deal with questions of property rights and questions of ecclesiastical sanctuary. Yet Clovis was also responsible for the setting down in writing of the first version of the *Lex Salica*, a legal compilation which underwrites many traditional, non-Christian practices: it protects the sacrificial pigs of his peoples and upholds the tradition of a naming-ceremony on the tenth day of an infant's life. It also lays down penalties for desecration of burials, particularly the robbing of grave-mounds.[97] The council underlines the way in which Clovis, who had accepted Christianity on his own, syncretistic terms clearly saw the advantages of control of, and collaboration with, the episcopate: 'the Gallo-Romans who really ran Gaul'.[98]

The Lombard rulers

The Lombards entered Italy from Pannonia in 568 under the leadership of Alboin, capturing the city of Cividale del Friuli in 569. This became the seat of the first of the Lombard duchies, ruled by Alboin's nephew Gisulf. They then conquered Vicenza, Verona, Brescia and Milan and, in 572, Pavia, which became their capital. They next moved south into Tuscany and even into central and southern Italy where they established the duchies of Spoleto and Benevento (which would soon become independent of the northern kingdom). The entire Lombard territory was divided into duchies centred on the main Italian cities, with the king's authority represented by officials known as *gastaldi*. Alboin and his successor Cleph were both murdered, and for nearly a decade there was no overall Lombard ruler until the prospect of an invasion by the Franks led to the election of Cleph's son Authari in 584.[99]

Before their arrival in Pannonia, the Lombards were probably largely pagan but they may have come into contact with Catholicism there. Procopius refers to them as 'Christians' at the time of their subjugation by the Heruli in the late fifth century. He believed them to be Catholics, just as he believed the Vandals of North Africa to be 'Arians'.[100] All this suggests that some of the Lombards had been converted by Catholic clergy long before they entered Italy.[101] Audoin, the Lombard ruler in 548, chose to present himself to the Emperor Justinian as Catholic. According to Procopius, when the Lombards appealed for imperial support against their rivals the Gepids, his envoys made their case to the Emperor Justinian with the statement that the Romans should favour them:

> seeing that we have been in agreement from the first as regards religion, they [i.e. the Romans] will stand in opposition to our opponents for the simple reason that they are Arians.[102]

The next leader, Alboin, never seems to have converted himself, but married a Frankish Catholic princess, Chlodosuintha. A letter sent by Bishop Nicetius of Trier to Chlodosuintha around 565 denounces the activities of 'Arian' missionaries at Alboin's court. But there is no evidence that Alboin became an 'Arian': indeed, Nicetius' letter also indicates that some of Alboin's *fideles* had been sent on pilgrimage to the papal basilicas of Rome, suggesting that Alboin was courting Catholicism.

There is also evidence that Authari, Alboin's successor, attempted to cultivate the popes. In a letter of June 597, Pope Gregory I complains of the Lombard conquest of Crotone in Italy the previous year and of their holding of captives for ransom. This section of the letter is not untypical of the concerns expressed by the pope about the Lombards elsewhere in his correspondence.[103] But from Gregory's correspondence it also emerges that Authari had tried to woo his predecessor Pope Pelagius by sending him a relic that had been sacrilegiously seized by a pagan Lombard together with a placatory gift. In a letter to the bishop of Auxerre of October 580, Pelagius had complained of 'insults' offered by idolatrous Lombards to the Catholic faith.[104] Although we cannot date Authari's gift, it may have been intended to counteract Pelagius' fears and to demonstrate that the Lombard leader did not countenance desecration of Christian relics – and indeed desired papal favour.

One of the most obvious signals of the Lombard rulers' wish to align with the Catholic macrocosm was through marriage to a Catholic princess, the Bavarian Theodelinda. Initially Authari's bride, on his death in 590 she became the wife of his successor, Agilulf (590–616).[105] Theodelinda founded and richly endowed the church of St John the Baptist at Monza, its dedication symbolic of a desire to integrate the Lombards into the Catholic world.[106] Papyri from Monza record that she obtained oil from the lamps which burned at the tombs of the Roman martyrs.[107] Agilulf's conclusion of a peace-treaty was accompanied by gifts to the pope, as Gregory noted in a letter of November–December 598: in this, he also praised the king for showing his love of God through his love of peace.[108] Agilulf had his daughter and son baptized as Catholics.[109]

The son, Adaloald was presented as king in the Roman circus at Milan in the presence of foreign ambassadors, in an imitation of imperial ceremonial.[110] Paul the Deacon records that, in addition to the church of St John, Theodelinda built a *palatium* at Monza: the images of figures on its walls which he describes suggest comparison with the Justinianic mosaics of Ravenna.[111] Her husbands' aspirations to *Romanitas* were also expressed in their use of Roman titles and forms: both Authari and Agilulf appropriated the Roman title *flavius*.[112]

While the Lombard rulers were eager to join the Catholic macrocosm, one major obstacle lay in their way: the Tricapitoline or Three Chapters Schism which had cut off relations between the bishops and clergy of Northern Italy and the popes since the 550s. While marriage to Theodelinda should have paid dividends in helping them achieve rapprochement with Catholicism, she and her ecclesiastical advisers were schismatics. As long as the breach in Catholicism was not healed, Agilulf remained sidelined. Pope Gregory I attempted to convince Theodelinda to end the schism, but without success. He wrote diplomatically to Agilulf at the conclusion of a peace-treaty in 598 about his love of God and his love of peace.[113] But after Gregory's death in 604, nothing happened until Irish monk Columbanus arrived in Italy in 612–13.

Columbanus was allowed to establish a monastery at Bobbio in the Appenines and, at the Lombard ruler's request, penned a letter to Boniface IV (608–15), requesting in the most forceful terms that the pope devote his energies to ending the schism. This request appears to have fallen on deaf ears. But the foundation of Bobbio gave successive Lombard rulers a link to the Catholic world. Adaloald was replaced after ten years by Arioald, duke of Turin, referred to as an 'Arian' by writers from Jonas of Bobbio onwards. In 628, Arioald not only refused to judge between the monastery and the Bishop of Tortona but even provided funds for Abbot Bertulf to go to Rome to plead Bobbio's case against the bishop with the pope – the outcome being the first ever papal grant of monastic exemption from episcopal authority.[114] Arioald maintained other links to Catholicism. His wife Gundiperga was Adaloald's sister, who had also received Catholic baptism. His successor, Rothari (638–52) is the only Lombard ruler labelled as 'Arian' by the eighth-century writer Paul the Deacon:

> he was brave and strong and followed the path of justice: he did not, however, hold the right line of Christian belief, but was stained by the infidelity of the Arian heresy ...[115]

But although 'Arian', Rothari married Arioald's widow Gundiperga and after his conquest of Liguria, husband and wife jointly requested Pope Theodore to uphold Honorius' exemption for Bobbio. Both Rothari and his son Rodoald gave privileges to the monastery.[116] Bobbio became a lifeline to Catholicism for the Lombard rulers.

Although Rothari, Arioald, Agilulf and Authari are usually labelled as 'Arian', it is less than clear that they were actually Homoians. A letter in which Gregory claimed that Authari had forbidden Catholic baptism of Lombard children in the Catholic faith and assuming that they must have been given 'Arian' baptism instead was written at the beginning of his pontificate, when he had little knowledge of the situation in the schismatic north. He may have mistakenly believed that there were still some Gothic Homoian clergy active in this region. What Authari was probably objecting to was infant baptism rather than Catholic baptism per se: converting peoples tended to associate infant baptism with infant mortality.[117] In his letter asking Pope Boniface to end the schism, Columbanus refers to the Lombards as 'Arian', but, significantly, describes Agilulf as a 'pagan king', *rex gentilis*. He does not seem in the letter to be aware of the major tenets of Homoianism – he mentions 'substance', not in the Trinitarian context of the fourth and fifth centuries, but as it was employed in Christological disputes in the sixth.[118] There is also a strong suggestion both in his letter and in the *Life of Columbanus*, composed in 642, that there were Lombards who were non-Christians and also that some

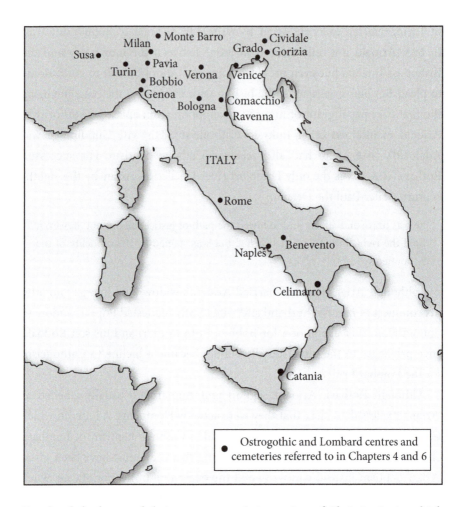

Lombards had created their own syncretistic version of Christianity in which non-Christian beliefs and rituals continued.

Our sources also suggest that Lombard 'Arianism' was an extremely limited phenomenon in terms of ecclesiastical hierarchy and organization. Jonas of Bobbio depicts a confrontation between Blidulf, a monk of Bobbio, and Arioald during the period when the latter was 'duke of the Lombards'. Blidulf denounces 'Arian' priests:

> Those whom you have hitherto called *sacerdotes* [priests or bishops] have deceitfully secured the title for themselves ...[119]

The existence of 'Arian' priests or bishops at Pavia is confirmed by Paul. Writing of the period of Rothari's rule, he states that:

In the city of Ticinum [Pavia] too there is shown down to the present time the place where the Arian bishop, who had his seat at the church of St. Eusebius, had a baptistery ...[120]

He names this individual as Anastasius. He also claims that there was a Catholic bishop at the same time in Pavia and that:

In this time there were two bishops throughout almost all the cities of the kingdom, one a Catholic and the other an Arian.[121]

However, this last statement has been greeted with universal disbelief. Historians have failed to find any evidence of this alleged parallel hierarchy.[122] Jonas' account seems to imply that at Pavia, there was a bishop appointed by the duke, while Catholics in the city were partly sustained by the support of Bobbio, but had no bishop of their own. Paul provides some confirmation for this picture when he notes that the 'Arian' bishop in Pavia,

Anastasius ... became converted to the Catholic faith and afterwards governed the church of Christ.[123]

On the basis of this evidence, the Lombard 'Arian' church under Arioald and Rothari appears to have consisted of a limited number of ducal or royal appointees, possibly only in Pavia itself. Anastasius appears to be a seventh-century 'Vicar of Bray', who has no difficulties in switching his affiliations as royal policies dictate.

The most convincing explanation of the Lombard rulers' 'Arianism' is that it was shorthand for a Christianity in which some non-Christian rituals and ceremonies of a military nature were performed by the ruler, dukes and warriors. The 'Arian' *sacerdotes* look like compliant clergy, prepared to turn a blind eye to these and equivalent practices. The case of the Lombards appears to parallel that of the Burgundians and Goths in many ways, with a drift towards Catholicism by some Lombards accompanied by an attachment on the part of dukes and warriors to traditional gods and rituals – but without any acquaintance with actual Homoianism, which had died out after the Gothic defeat. Agilulf, Adaloald, Arioald and Rothari all had to negotiate a path between their own aspirations on one hand and those of the aspirations and traditions of their dukes and their military on the other. According to Paul the Deacon, Agilulf had defeated or overthrown at least eight dukes.[124] But

Agilulf, though in reality keen to enter the macrocosm of the Catholic world, may not have wished to show himself too eager to make a move which would have aroused resentment. It is interesting that Columbanus' letter to Pope Boniface IV, in which he claimed to be writing at Agilulf's behest demanding that the pope end the Three Chapters Schism, accused the popes of favouring both Nestorius and Eutyches, theologians whose Christologies were diametrically opposed. There appears to have been no reply to Columbanus' hectoring letter. Perhaps a certain amount of disinformation about the papal position had been fed to Columbanus, whose inept approach has long puzzled historians.[125] At this particular juncture, while Agilulf may have wanted to look as if he was opening negotiations, he may not have wanted them to move too quickly.

Agilulf's son Adaloald lost his throne because he failed to maintain an equilibrium with his dukes. As regent in his minority, his mother Theodelinda had tolerated 'Arians'; but in 622 Adaloald issued diplomas for Bobbio.[126] Fredegar relates that he was removed four years later because he had become the puppet of a certain Eusebius, put twelve of his nobles to death and conspired to hand over the Lombard state to the Empire.[127] This account may be highly sensationalized, but it is suggestive of major splits in the Lombard kingdom and of a ruler seen by some Lombards as far too committed to the macrocosm. His successor Arioald had played the part of the enemy of Bobbio when a duke, but as we have seen also supported it once he became king. Arioald's successor Rothari was a highly successful ruler who expanded Lombard rule into Byzantine Liguria and much of Emilia and to achieve and consolidate this success, he clearly needed a secure basis in the microcosm. In 643, he issued his *Edict*, a compilation of Lombard law, something which Wickham describes as a 'very Germanic thing to do' – even if its setting down in writing reflects a continuation of the Romanizing developments of Agilulf's state.[128] Rothari's continuation of Arioald's policy of controlling a compliant bishop, Anastasius, at Pavia arguably represents a degree of overt commitment to Christianity at the same time as the maintenance of some traditional cults and rituals. What these were in the north of Italy we cannot say for certain, but they were likely to have been akin to, if not identical to, the warrior ritual performed in the southern Lombard duchy of Benevento later in the century (see pp. 25–6 above). Lombard 'Arianism' seems to have disappeared without trace, possibly because there had never been a real Homoian Church in Lombard Italy, but only pagans, Catholics and syncretistic Christians who still adhered to traditional non-Christian rites as well. In striking contrast to Visigothic Spain, where Catholicism was formally declared at the Third Council of Toledo in 589, there is no record of any synod or council summoned to affirm correct doctrine or anathematize heresy in the Lombard kingdom. The *Carmen de synodo Ticinensi* credits Aripert (653–61), with abolishing 'Arianism' – an event so insignificant that it merits only passing mention in a work composed to celebrate the final resolution of the Three Chapters Schism in 698.[129]

***

Piecing together the often obscure history of Germanic kings' moves towards the Catholic macrocosm, a number of themes emerge. Their ability to enter it depended on their military-political success, ability to reward warriors and the fathering of an adult male heir. Like Theoderic's, Clovis' family had risen to power very recently, but unlike Theoderic he achieved notable victories and could therefore reward his followers. He also had four male heirs, whereas Theoderic had none, allowing others to dream of becoming king themselves. Gundobad was not able to cash in on military success against the Visigoths and had probably created problems for himself by disposing of his brothers too early without being able to placate their followers. The need to move carefully is apparent in other cases: after officially declaring their Catholicism, the Sueve and Visigoth rulers both faced revolts and the situation was clearly very delicate in the case of the Lombard rulers. It was approximately three decades after the removal of Adaloald that a Lombard king felt secure enough to declare for Catholicism.

Another theme that emerges is the importance of control of or co-operation with the episcopate for the creation of a successful monarchy. The Visigothic rulers of Aquitaine tried to achieve this as far as they could. Gundobad maintained a relationship with Avitus. Clovis had been taught, well before he became a Christian, that co-operation with the Gallo-Roman bishops would underpin success as a ruler. For much of his reign, Theoderic deferred to the Italian episcopate and to the pope. The support of the Catholic Church appears to have played a major part in the rise of the Suevic monarchy and in its attempts to exert some control over the heterogeneous groups living in their kingdoms. Lombard rulers were to an extent frustrated in this by the Three Chapters Schism, but used Bobbio as a link to the pope. In Spain, Leovigild tried the radical but ultimately unsuccessful tactic of creating his own Homoian episcopate – many of whom survived to become Catholic bishops.

The question remains of the beliefs of those who opposed their rulers' Catholicization. In the case of the Lombards, it seems that traditional beliefs and rituals simply died out in the north as royal power grew, only surviving for while in the 'semi-detached' south until the Church decided to deal with them. The Gothic Homoian Church in Italy had gradually vanished from view during the Justinianic Reconquest. Homoian theology was modified by the Spanish king for his political ends in 580, indicating that 'Arianism' was now a matter of politics rather than of beliefs, a signal of attachment to the microcosm. Even if a handful of 'Arian' bishops refused to accept the new dispensation, theological differences between them and Catholics were virtually non-existent. We do not know very much about the revolts against the Sueve rulers – but what we do know does not reveal a religious dimension. The only real question-mark seems to hang over Burgundy, where a year after Gundobad's death there still seem to have been Homoian clergy, and where we cannot be absolutely sure that the ruler after the Catholic Sigismund was also a Catholic. The Frankish takeover would have eventually put an end to any organized Homoian Church. However, we might ask what precisely the Homoianism of Burgundian warriors had consisted of and whether – despite the existence of some private Homoian churches – the annual 'contagion' alluded to by Avitus involved some non-Christian military rituals on the lines of those of the Lombards. The nature of some of the archaeological finds from the eastern Burgundian region dating from the Frankish period suggests that for the layperson Homoianism might have not have meant much more than an intuitive understanding of the Christian God.

Bringing God to Mind

Beliefs, practices, testimonies, problems

One of the most contentious issues for historians of religion and in particular of Christianization in 'barbarian' Europe is that of non-Christian belief after the official acceptance of Catholic Christianity.[1] Not only is evidence for non-Christian practices gleaned from hostile testimonies, but many historians also believe that much of it derives ultimately from the sermons of Bishop Cæsarius of Arles (502–42). Thus its value has been questioned as evidence of anything that happened anywhere apart from southern Gaul in the first half of the sixth century:

> Practices first described in 6th-century sermons intended for the inhabitants of southern Gaul and northwestern Iberia were assembled, scissors-and-paste fashion, in sermons presumably delivered to the Alamannians and northern Franks of the 8th century and elements drawn from Caesarius of Arles turned up in 10th-century Anglo-Saxon texts.[2]

In the 1920s, Wilhelm Boudriot pointed out that conciliar legislation all too often repeated condemnations of practices voiced initially by Cæsarius.[3] Dieter Harmening also stressed his influence.[4] Asking whether *any* local observations were ever made by Christian writers for themselves, Ken Dowden observed that Boudriot took the view that they did not. Dowden himself contended that 'if an extreme position is to be adopted, that is the one', though he suggested we 'soften its hard lines a little'.[5] Others such as the Soviet historian Aron I. Gurevich, who believes in the 'stability of the vital phenomena' described in the literature and who thinks the literature can provide evidence of what he calls 'medieval popular culture' deem these evaluations too sweeping or pessimistic.[6] But not everyone has been convinced of this. Rudi Künzel even demanded that testimony be 'authenticated' before it can be accepted as valid description of an actual rite, rather than a copy of words from an earlier written source – as if this were really possible.[7] And both Valerie Flint and Yitzhak Hen raise again the problem of Cæsarius' denunciations. Flint writes of the 'long shadow' cast by Cæsarius.[8] Hen claimed that while Boudriot and Harmening 'somewhat exaggerated' the extent of his influence, we may nevertheless trace it in saints' *Lives*, such as the *Vita Eligii* and the *Vita Amandi*, in Martin of Braga's *On the Castigation of Rustics* and on later texts right up to the *Corrector*, a tenth-century work used by Burchard of Worms in his *Decretum*, completed in 1023.[9] Hen then goes on to assert, however, that the denunciations of 'paganism and superstitions' are 'a very small portion of a large body of material' and that Cæsarius had more to say about drunkenness.[10] Hen's purpose is to suggest that 'paganism and superstitions were marginal phenomena within the Merovingian cultural milieu'; that there was no 'specific religion' involved; and that Cæsarius, who often speaks rather vaguely about the perpetrators of the non-Christian rites, was really trying to reinforce Christian group identity and bind his flock to their bishop.[11] While agreeing that Cæsarius' strictures were frequently repeated, he refuses to endorse either the opinions of Boudriot and Harmening on one hand or of Jean-Claude Schmitt, who thinks that they are evidence for the continuation of such practices, on the other. Hen maintains that what we are dealing with is literary convention, but one which also reflects 'a certain reality which existed at the time of composition'.[12] He offers no way in which we might be able to distinguish one from the other.[13]

Underlying the concerns and objections voiced by so many scholars seems to be the idea that rituals cannot possibly have been the same – or similar – over several hundred years and across large areas of Europe. The cognitive study of ritual suggests the opposite: that there are common features to be found in rituals even in vastly different 'cultural' environments.[14] This may help us account for the repetition of prohibitions, which were effectively aimed against the continued survival of the same sorts of rituals and practices over a wide area and for centuries. It also suggests that they would not necessarily have been exclusive to either 'rustics' or townspeople, Romans or Germans, in our period: based on intuitions or 'nonreflective' belief, they would have been much more widespread.

Forbidden practices

What sort of practices were actually targeted by the Church in the sixth century? In Italy, the Three Chapters Schism and the Lombard conquest inhibited ecclesiastical legislation against non-Christian practice, though at the end of the century, we find Pope Gregory I (590–604) condemning 'idolatry' and 'tree-worshippers', as well as soothsayers and 'magicians' in letters to bishops in Sardinia, southern Italy and Sicily.[15] In Spain, the few councils summoned between the reign of Theudis and the 580s did not deal with such matters. The Third Council of Toledo (589), summoned to mark the passage of Visigothic Spain from 'Arianism' to Catholicism, referred to the development of the 'sacrilege of idolatry' throughout all of Spain and even asserted that 'idolatry' had spread throughout Gaul – by which it is possible it meant the Visigothic *Gallia Narbonensis* (Septimania) as well.[16] Most of our evidence comes from Francia (which now included Burgundy) and Suevic Gallaecia.

The canons of the Councils of Orléans of 533 and 541 condemned returning to the cult of, or offering food to, 'idols' or eating carrion (Orléans, 533) or continuing to sacrifice to 'demons' even after being warned by a priest (Orléans, 541). The Synod of Auxerre (585><92) and other Frankish councils of the second half of the sixth century prohibit auguries and divinations; rituals at stones, trees and fountains in 'places of the pagans'; and more specifically 'fulfilling vows' at sacred trees and springs. Auxerre specifies that people are not to make *sculptilia* (literally, engravings) or 'wooden feet or men', in other words, leave representative *ex voto* offerings there.

The same Frankish councils also complain that that some major Christian festivals were accompanied by celebrations of non-Christian origin. Auxerre tried to put a stop to private festivities in people's homes on the feast days of saints and to all-night revels, especially on the feast of St Martin.[17] It looks as if the Tourangeaux had a winter season in which they mixed Christian celebrations with those of a different kind. The Christian winter celebrations began with Martinmas on 11 November, going on to the Feast of the Nativity (25 December) and then Epiphany (6 January). But the latter were interrupted by the celebration of the Kalends of January, a non-Christian festivity strongly condemned by both Tours and Auxerre.[18] The Council of

Tours (567) deemed it a pagan rite, implying that it was a celebration of the Roman deity Janus, 'who was a pagan man and could not be a god': it asserts that no-one who believes in the Father, Son and Holy Spirit and also observes this piece of paganism can entirely be a Christian. Auxerre gave details of the disapproved behaviour in terms echoing those of the festal sermon collection of Cæsarius of Arles: 'making the stag or heifer' – that is, disguising oneself as an animal; and 'observing the diabolical *strenae*'. In Gallaecia, the canons added by Bishop Martin to the decisions of the Second Council of Braga (572) would forbid divinations and magic, pagan sacrifices or purifications, planting trees or crops according to observation of the moon or stars, observing the Kalends, and accompanying the use of medicinal herbs with 'incantations'.[19]

The first striking aspect of these prohibitions is their lack of connection to Germanic deities. At some point between 533 and 554, Childebert, King of Paris, made a clear distinction between *simulacra constructa* and *idola daemoni dedicata ab hominibus factum* [sic].[20] The *simulacra* were probably actual effigies: they disappear from legislation in a way that suggests they disappeared from the landscape. However, 'idols' seem to survive rather longer: we find a late reference to them at the Council of Clichy in 626/7, which prohibited eating food sacrificed to 'idols'.[21] Though clerics from all over Francia attended this council, it is likely that the ban had Austrasia, the eastern part of Francia, principally in mind. The penitential attributed to the Irish monk, Columbanus, who worked in this area two decades previously had laid down penances for eating food offered to 'idols'.[22] The canons of the Second Council of Braga (572) are prefaced by the injunction that the assembled bishops teach the faithful 'to flee the errors of idols or other crimes'.[23] Whether the 'idols' were anthropomorphic representations of gods and goddesses is to be doubted. Stephen McKenna and Michel Meslin associate 'idolatry' in Spain in the sixth century and up to the end of the seventh principally with the cult of trees, stones and springs.[24] Even when Spanish ecclesiastical councils of the late seventh century condemned 'idolatry' as well as the worship of stones, trees, and springs, the text of the condemnations suggests representations of animals. It is possible that they were similar to the posts with representations of animal heads we find in Anglo-Saxon England;[25] though the word used by the Spanish councils is *sculptilia*, engravings.[26] But Bernadette Filotas indicates the increasingly political dimension of these late seventh-century Spanish condemnations, which demonstrate a tendency to exaggerate and demonize disapproved practices, so they may have only been engraved stones.[27] The overwhelming impression is that the Church was dealing not with the worship of gods, but with the continuation of rituals based in 'abductive' reasoning and focusing on 'special' features of the landscape or powers associated with the natural world. The tree featuring in the seventh-century Beneventan Lombard ritual described above (see Chapter 2) was known as '*votum*' – the vow: that is, it was a tree felt to have special properties and was the object of offerings. In Italy, the laws issued for the Lombards by King Liutprand in 727 condemned, along with divination, the practice of 'sorcery' and incantation, any Lombard

who like a rustic prays to a tree as sacred or adores springs …[28]

The delinquent was to pay as composition half his price to the royal fisc. Bishop Gregory of Tours professed himself scandalized when Agilan, an 'Arian' envoy from the Visigothic ruler Leovigild told him that:

Indeed it is a proverbial saying with us that no harm is done when a man whose affairs take him past the altars of the Gentiles and the church of God pays respect to both.[29]

However, Gregory's writings reveal that he was conscious that such divided loyalties were possible amongst Catholics in Francia as well.

The other major target of the Church's wrath was the celebration of the Kalends of January. Rituals celebrating the New Year are found across different cultures from Europe to China. Many of the superstitions attached to the New Year in modern European culture also revolve around its setting the tone for the remainder of the year in terms of prosperity and the necessity of not allowing one's own resources to be depleted on this day. Back in Roman times, the *strenae* objected to by churchmen were branches of laurel or other evergreens, fixed to the doors of dwellings, along with lanterns; or presents of honey cakes, dried fruit or money.[30] These appear to parallel some of the features of the modern Christmas – evergreen tree, lights, cakes (with fruit) and presents – suggesting that these rituals may somehow in later times have been detached from New Year to be attached to the Christian festival a few days earlier. Whatever the truth of this last suggestion, there is no real problem in accepting the idea of widespread New Year celebrations in both Mediterranean and Germanic cultures across Late Antiquity and the Early

Middle Ages. It also seems reasonable to assume that the same basic intuition that the first day augured well or ill for the rest of the year underlay many of the rituals performed.

Linked with the Kalends celebrations is the intuition of the presence of the dead around this time of year. Carlo Ginzburg treats the animal disguises, the 'making the stag or heifer' referred to by both Cæsarius and the Synod of Auxerre, as a ritual correlative of the animal metamorphosis experienced during shamanic ecstasy and therefore as a sign of communication with the dead, the 'ambiguous dispensers of prosperity during the crucial period when the old year ends and the new begins'.[31] In sixth-century Tours on the feast of the Chair of St Peter (18 January), people left church only to go on to make offerings of 'things which had not decayed' to the dead and then to return home to eat food which had been 'offered to demons'.[32] Ginzburg has found evidence of these winter rituals over the centuries and not just in Western Europe but in central and eastern Europe as well.[33]

'Paganization' and 'demonization' of 'nonreflective' belief and practices

Our picture of the nature of the practices condemned by the Church has been muddied by its readiness to depict them as 'pagan' or associate them with 'demons' as some of the canons of the councils described above indicate. This was a key element in the tactics employed to deal with these beliefs by two eminent sixth-century bishops, Cæsarius of Arles and Martin of Braga.

Cæsarius attacked many common customs: the use of charms and amulets to encourage conception; divinations and auguries; and in one sermon, the re-opening or use of pagan shrines.[34] Even his festal sermons raised these concerns. An Easter sermon, which we might expect would be entirely given over to the theme of the Resurrection, contains warnings against amulets, soothsayers and magicians.[35] He devoted two sermons given on 1 January to attacking the celebrations of the Kalends of January on the grounds that Janus had been a dissolute pagan, elevated to the status of deity by 'foolish and ignorant men'. On the day dedicated to him, men wore animal-skins and took on the aspect of stags, or deer or sheep or other animals. Others dressed as women. People exchanged 'diabolical' gifts, or set tables with food as an indicator of banquets to be enjoyed in the year to come. By taking part in such rituals, Cæsarius warned, they were giving themselves over to demons.[36]

Cæsarius categorized other customs as 'pagan': only setting out on a journey on propitious days, honouring the sun, moon, Mars, Mercury, Jupiter, Saturn or Venus. He attacks the honouring of these classical gods – whom he characterizes as 'extremely based and wicked men' or in the case of Venus as a 'shameless harlot' – through the use of their names for days of the week:

> let us think that no day should have the name of demons and let us not observe what day we ought to set out on a journey.[37]

Cæsarius' nephew Cyprian, who composed his *Life*, tells us that his uncle made a collection of sixty-eight of his festal sermons – including the two on the Kalends – to be circulated for other preachers in Gaul.[38] So many of his favourite themes were deliberately drawn to the attention of clerics elsewhere.

They were further developed in Suevic Gallaecia, in Bishop Martin of Braga's work *On the Castigation of Rustics*, composed in the 570s. Links between Gallaecia and the Frankish Catholic Church had been established in the 550s as the Sueve monarchy attempted to shake itself free of the Homoian 'Arian' Christianity that was a symbol of Visigothic hegemony over their kingdom. Martin seems to have had links with Tours in particular and he may have come across Cæsarius' festal sermon collection as a result of this connection.[39] Martin, too, condemns the January Kalends celebrations: indeed, he was so opposed to these that he insisted, not just in the *Castigation* but in another of his works, that the first day of the year was not 1 January, but the spring equinox, 25 March, the day on which he maintained God had divided light from darkness.[40] He was arguing against popular consciousness, in which 1 January was seen not just as the New Year but also as a day with predictive value for the year to come. In sixth-century Gallaecia, it was apparently the practice to place bread and cloth in a cask or box: to the extent which it was either intact, or was nibbled or destroyed by these vermin, the rest of the year would be prosperous – or not. Martin denounced this practice:

> But in vain does wretched man make these calculations on the future so that if, in the beginning of the year, he is glutted and joyful in every way, so it will be the whole year through.[41]

Martin also suggests that the first day of each month was considered as having a similar divinatory aspect.[42] He denounces divinations and auguries and the burning of candles at stones, trees and springs, or at crossroads (*trivia*, 'where three ways meet'). He condemns the pouring of wine over a log in the hearth or the putting of bread in a spring and the custom of 'observing the foot'. He also castigates the way in which women invoke 'Minerva' in their weaving; the way in which weddings are held on Fridays (the 'day of Venus'); and – like Cæsarius – the way in which people aim to start their journeys on a propitious day. He deplores the tendencies to 'mutter spells over herbs and invoke the names of demons in incantations and many other things which it takes too long to say'; to see omens in birds and sneezes and to encourage 'incantations' invented by magicians and enchanters.[43]

On the Castigation of Rustics sets out a version of creation in which the Devil and 'his ministers, demons' are cast out of Heaven and arrive on earth, where they seduce humans into worshipping them. Martin identifies these demons as the gods and goddesses of the Roman pantheon, denouncing their adulteries, fornications, incest, strife and theft. Like Cæsarius he attacked the use of the names of the classical pantheon in the names for days of the week and seems to have succeeded in having this custom abolished: in Portugal, weekdays consist of 'Sabbath' (Saturday) and 'Lord's day' (Sunday), plus second to sixth days (Monday to Saturday). The canons added by Martin to the decisions of the Second Council of Braga forbid a range of 'pagan' customs: divinations and magic, pagan sacrifices or purifications, planting trees or crops according to observation of the moon or stars, observing the Kalends, accompanying the use of medicinal herbs with 'incantations'.[44]

A cognitive approach helps us understand the concerns and aims of both Cæsarius and Martin. It is not clear that the beliefs, practices and rituals they condemned really involved any deities whatsoever, whether Roman, Celtic or Germanic.[45] What they were attacking was non-Christian 'nonreflective' beliefs and practices based on them: the leaving of stones at crossroads to ensure good fortune (a practice he associates with Mercury); the automatic invocation of 'Minerva' (which female deity was really meant by this is unclear) by a woman taking up her weaving; or belief in sneezing being harmful (we still say 'bless you'). Martin was acutely sensitive to the way in which the thoughts of the Christian flock were being directed away from Christianity.

The celebration of the Kalends, the leaving of *ex–votos* on trees, at springs or in lakes, underlined an uncomfortable fact for Christian churchmen: the Christian God did not automatically come to mind for everyone where the crucial matters of health, prosperity and the future were concerned. Both Cæsarius and Martin were prepared to up the ante, attempting to intimidate their flocks by preaching that such habits of mind and deed were 'pagan', or 'demonic', or the 'work of the Devil'. *On the Castigation of Rustics* insists on the incompatibility of a whole range of beliefs and actions with the name of Christian: 'for one cannot worship God and the Devil at once'.[46] But it is noticeable that at the same time, the canny Martin prescribes no punishment or penance for these offences:

> Only make a pact in your heart with God, that from now onward you will no longer worship demons, nor adore anything except the God of Heaven …[47]

What he wants to achieve is nothing less than the breaking of non-Christian habits of mind. People should replace 'devilish' incantations with more powerful Christian ones – the creed, the sign of the cross, the Lord's Prayer. Martin recommends that the Christian should do no work on the Lord's Day (dominical observance was also a theme of church councils), perform good works – and that he should often visit the 'places of the saints'.[48]

Bringing God to mind

Martin of Braga advocates visits to the *loca sanctorum* as an alternative to the practices he condemns and demonizes. His contemporary, the Gallo-Roman bishop, Gregory of Tours composed two works – *The Glory of the Martyrs* and *The Glory of the Confessors*[49] – in which he sets out an explicit account of how shrines and relics functioned as the Christian substitute for the rocks, trees, lakes and springs and other locations considered to embody the power to heal and cure, to ensure good harvests, or to ward off misfortune. These two works have often been 'cherry-picked' by historians for evidence of Gregory's family affiliations and political role or for accounts of individual miracles.[50] They have up to now proved something of an enigma not just in the context of Gregory's corpus of writings but even within that of his 'eight books of miracles', his hagiographic output. Hen suggests that both 'were probably composed for reasons of utility' as the generally brief individual chapters would provide useful readings for saints' days.[51] Raymond Van Dam, who has translated the works into English also thinks that they contained sermon material and that 'most people would have heard rather than read these stories'.[52] Yet he still finds them faintly puzzling as collections: in a work devoted to the *Glory of the Martyrs*, it is more than a quarter of the way through that Gregory includes an account of the first Christian martyr, Stephen.[53] In a book about the miracles of confessors, Gregory 'never defined who confessors are' and cast his net rather widely, with stories concerning 'two lovers'; a hermit who died after falling out of an apple tree; and an old hermit who only had a wooden pot in which to cook his food.[54] Van Dam indicates a number of possible motivations for Gregory's approach, notably his desire in *Glory of the Martyrs* to offer a theology of martyrdom for ordinary believers, transposing it to the level of daily moral struggle.[55] But Giselle de Nie may be nearer the mark when she writes of Gregory's 'concrete and practical' piety.[56] Gregory was writing in the first place for a clerical audience, who would be able to read the entire work and then encourage their flocks, probably through the use of individual chapters as the bases for sermons, to cultivate the practice of shrine visitation, thus stimulating a 'nonreflective' level of belief that underpinned Christianity.

In *Glory of the Martyrs* and *Glory of the Confessors*, Gregory demonstrates an extraordinary sensitivity to the needs and intuitions that drew people to throw votive offerings into water, or to seek to predict the fortunes of the following year, or to touch objects believed to be invested with special powers in order to restore health. He outlines the power inherent in the relic and the way that this *virtus* can be transmitted from one object to another; he illustrates the role of relics and shrines in healing and curing the sick; and he encourages the process of discovery – or rediscovery – of the tombs of saints and martyrs which are the locus of this Christian *virtus*.

Gregory wants to leave his audience in no doubt whatsoever about the power of relics. The most precious relics he discusses are those of Christ's passion, brought from the Holy Land. These were greatly prized: one of Avitus of Vienne's letters is a request that the pope intercede on his behalf with the patriarch of Jerusalem for a fragment of the True Cross. It is not clear whether the patriarch obliged, though Avitus certainly received some relics.[57] Radegund, wife of the Merovingian ruler Chlothar I, and founder of a prestigious nunnery in Poitiers acquired fragments of the cross in 569.[58] Her community was dedicated to the Holy Cross and the poet Venantius Fortunatus who later became Bishop of Poitiers, composed three famous hymns – *Crux benedicta*, *Pange lingua* and *Vexilla* regis – for their *Adventus* ceremony.[59]

Gregory provides dramatic testimony to the power visibly and tangibly present in the relic of the cross kept in the nunnery church at Holy Cross:

> When visiting the tomb of St Hilary [at Poitiers], I happened out of respect to arrange a conversation with this queen [Radegund]. I entered the convent, greeted the queen, and bowed before the venerable cross and the holy relics of the saints. Then, at the conclusion of my prayer, I stood up. To my right was a burning lamp that I saw was overflowing with frequent drips. I call God as my witness, I thought that its container was broken, because placed beneath it was a vessel into which the overflowing oil dripped. I turned to the abbess [Agnes] and said: 'Is your thinking so irresponsible that you cannot provide an unbroken lamp ... but instead you use a cracked lamp from which the oil drips?' She replied: 'My lord, such is not the case; it is the power of the holy cross you are watching' ... I turned back to the lamp [that was now] heaving in great waves like a boiling pot, overflowing in swelling surges through that hour and (I believe in order to censure my incredulity) being more and more replenished, so that in the space of one hour the container produced more than four times the oil that it held.[60]

Later in *Glory of the Martyrs* Gregory alludes very briefly to the same phenomenon – oil bubbling and overflowing from lamps – at another church that also possesses relics of the cross.[61]

In the opening chapters of his work, Gregory sets out a theory of the power contained in these potent relics. He maintains that they were surrounded by their own force-field. The True Cross had been discovered by St Helena, the mother of the Emperor Constantine: Gregory claims that she cast one of its four nails into the Adriatic to calm the sea, which still remains calm at this very spot. Another two were put into the bridle of the emperor's horse 'so whatever hostile peoples resisted the emperor, they might more easily be dispersed by this power'. As for the fourth nail, some claim that it was placed in the diadem or helmet of a statue of Constantine in the city of Constantinople with the result that what one might call a helmet of salvation crowns the entire fortification over which it towers.[62]

Gregory's extended treatment of these topics suggests that that there may even have been a degree of scepticism about the power of the imported relics of the cross. He feels obliged to provide a careful account of the configuration of the cross to account for the four nails, suggesting that the number was somehow at odds with contemporary iconography.[63] Indeed, when he describes the overflowing lamp of the convent of the Holy Cross, he goes so far as to suggest that he himself had once been a sceptic:

> Often I heard how even the lamps that were lit in front of these relics bubbled up because of the divine power ... because of the foolishness of my closed mind, I was never motivated to believe these stories until that power which is at present being revealed reproved my slow-witted hesitation.[64]

Gregory tells another story relating to the cross, in which an individual presents him with a robe in which it had allegedly been wrapped. He portrays himself as expressing outright disbelief as to its authenticity. But having been given a provenance for the object, he dares to wash it and to allow people suffering from fevers to drink the water. When they are cured, he even cuts the robe up and begins to distribute it to monks as a 'blessing' (*pro benedictione*). The head of a religious community to whom he gives one of these 'blessings' returns two years later and swears under oath that it had healed twelve possessed people, three blind people, two paralytics and one mute. Gregory concludes that:

> The promise of the Lord convinces us trustfully to believe this story; for the Lord said: 'Believe that you will receive everything which you have asked in my name and they will come to you' [Mk 11.24].[65]

In this last case, Gregory is very obviously describing what cognitive theorists have labelled a 'CONTAINER schema': the essence of Christ has transferred itself to the cross, which has then transferred itself to the robe. This essence has survived the division of the robe and even transmitted itself into water:[66]

> Thus objects can wield ritual agency by virtue of being containers of a given essence.[67]

The assumed transmission of the essence of holiness into a cloth provided the basis of relics.[68] Gregory demonstrates the method by which such relics are created at St Peter's in Rome:

> if someone wishes to take a blessed relic [*beata pignora*], he weighs a little piece of cloth on a pair of scales and lowers it [into the tomb]; then he keeps vigils, fasts, and earnestly prays that the power of the apostle will assist his piety.[69]

And he makes the remarkable claim that the essence of divine power is so real that it may even be weighed:

> [What happens next] is extraordinary to report! If the man's faith is strong, when the piece of cloth is raised from the tomb it will be so soaked with divine power [*divina virtute*] that it will weigh much more than it weighed previously ...[70]

As well as illustrating the power of the cross, Gregory notes 'other items from the Lord's suffering', in particular the crown of thorns (which miraculously withers and regenerates), the column against which Christ was whipped, and the tomb where his body lay. The last two are themselves the sources of further contact relics. The faithful weave cords which they tie around the column and which they then keep as an apotropaic against various illnesses, while the earth from the tomb frequently exhibits a natural radiance: it is dug up and fashioned into tokens. Gregory claims that the sick often obtain cures as a result of these tokens – and also that they can ward off snakes. But, he asks,

> what do I rashly dare to say about them, since faith believes that everything the sacred body has touched is holy?[71]

There are many other instances in Gregory's work of the transmission of *virtus* through objects that have come into contact with the saints, such as the bed of Bishop Silvester of Châlon-sur-Saône which, after his death, was cut into tiny pieces by the faithful, who believed that it had the power to heal the sick.[72] Indentations in the stone in Rome on which Peter and Paul stood when they prayed against Simon Magus filled up with rainwater into which the *virtus* of the apostles passed, creating a medicinal liquid.[73] Gregory also recounts how people poured wine or cider into depressions in the top of a stone to which a martyr's feet had been fixed with molten lead, to produce similar curative substances.[74]

Gregory encourages his audience to seek out the tombs of saints, aiming to demonstrate that these centres of power are all around them. One of his major themes in *Glory of the Confessors* is that of the miraculous revelation or discovery of the concealed burial place of the saint. Sometimes this is the tomb of an early Christian as in the case of the accidently broken tomb in the church of St Venerandus in Clermont, which revealed the incorrupt body of a Christian virgin. Her sanctity is demonstrated not only by the state of her body, but also by the miracles that begin to occur there.[75] Other stories are suggestive of neglect and abandonment of tombs, perhaps as a result of war or invasion. In the case of Amarandus, a martyr of Albi, his resting-place was covered by brambles and concealed by thorn bushes for many years:

> But at the command of the Lord, it was revealed to the Christians, and the crypt
> in which he was buried was uncovered and shone forth. Then, because of the
> outbreak of hostility, the residents abandoned this place. [New] inhabitants
> came from far away and attempted to offer honour to the blessed martyr as if to
> their own guardian ...[76]

This story might be an invention as the crypt dedicated to Amarandus is at Vieux.[77] By contrast, the tomb of Stremonius, bishop of Clermont in the village of Issoire is ignored and no 'cult of respect' is offered because of what Gregory calls the 'coarse rusticity' of the villagers. Only a miraculous vision seen by Cautinus, a future bishop, but at the time a deacon living in the village, ensures its discovery.[78] Other tombs are indicated by the appearance of mysterious lights, or the presence of mysterious figures in white, chanting the Psalms. Gregory thus suggests that the discovery or revelation of the resting-places of yet more saints is possible.[79]

The saints signal their holy presence in a number of miraculous ways. For Gregory, light and fire are major indicators of the presence of sanctity: he believes that fire often appears from the relics of saints and that it contains a 'mystical sacrament' (*mysticum sacramentum*) which produces light without burning anyone and is visible only to 'just men'.[80] When Gregory visits the tomb of St Germanus of Auxerre, he becomes aware of the odour of sanctity, the fragrance of lilies and roses.[81] When the tomb of Bishop Melanius of Rennes catches fire, it remains essentially undamaged.[82] The tomb of Bishop Aravatius of Maastricht lies outdoors, its position and importance indicated by the way in which falling snow never collects on it. A meagre wooden oratory constructed over it collapses and eventually it is translated to a suitably spacious church, where numerous miracles take place.[83] Another theme which emerges from *Glory of the Confessors* is the need for the saint's resting-place to be accessible. In Limoges the tombs of two priests who were companions of its patron St Martial were mysteriously relocated overnight so that the faithful could gain easier access.[84] The tombs of two lovers who had maintained their chastity were miraculously moved together.[85] The tomb of St Venerandus at Clermont is designed with a small window through which the faithful put their heads when they pray to the saint.[86]

Gregory seems to be recommending to his clerical audience the promotion of the cult of hitherto obscure or forgotten holy men and women as local saints and also that they follow the already widespread policy of bringing the cult out of cemeteries and into churches. Cemeteries may have resembled traditional non-Christian sites too much for his liking: they were outdoors and were likely to have been the burial places of pagans as well as Christians. At one point, he even seems to suggest that relics were not to be the property of private individuals: he relates a miracle in which a tribune who surreptitiously hacked off a tiny part of the tomb of St Germanus of Auxerre, was rooted to the spot, unable to move until he agreed to place the relic in a church.[87] If this is indeed Gregory's message, it certainly signals a new departure for him, as he reveals that his own mother and father kept relics in a private chapel and had even worn them round their necks as apotropaics.[88] He himself kept relics in an oratory in his own residence – although when he installed the relics of the martyrs Saturninus and Julian and the blessed Illidius in this private chapel, he also demonstrated consciousness of the public importance of the relic:

> there were in attendance no small group of priests and deacons dressed in white robes, honoured citizens of the highest order, and a large group of people of the second rank.[89]

Gregory devotes much of *Glory of the Confessors* to demonstrations of the efficacy of the saint as healer. As we might expect, a large number of these involve healings and cures at the actual burial place of the saint itself. Others involve the dust or liquid obtained from their place of burial, or a cloth imbued with the essence of holiness. In some cases, he merely notes that people were cured of illnesses at a certain tomb.[90] On one occasion he provides personal testimony, explaining how he himself had been cured of terrible pains by moss from a saint's tomb.[91] Relief from chills and fevers, including quartan fever, is the most common theme.[92] Mutes, the blind, the possessed (*inergumini*), contracted and twisted limbs, paralysis and toothache are all relieved by the relics of the saints.[93] The 'groin plague' – bubonic plague – which made an appearance in Western Europe from the 540s onwards – is averted by the relics of St Remigius of Rheims and by those kept by his mother at home.[94] Gregory's lengthy testimonies to the efficacies of these cures were a reminder that Christianity could offer a powerful alternative to traditional non-Christian beliefs and practices.

One of the most striking chapters in Gregory's *Glory of the Martyrs* is the one in which he associates a martyr's shrine with a winter miracle predicting prosperity or hardship for the year to come. Gregory claims that at Merida in Lusitania on the feast-day of the martyr Eulalia in mid-December, trees blossom spontaneously, predicting a good harvest or outcome for the populace in their personal affairs. Should this miracle fail and the flowers bloom more slowly, then disaster threatens: though this may be averted, if the martyr allows herself to be placated by the tears of the people.[95] A predictive event linked to a winter festival strongly recalls the condemned belief in the Kalends of January as indicating the fortunes of the year to come. However, Gregory surrounds this Christian alternative with theologically 'correct' elements: it is the intervention of a Christian martyr that produces the miracle and she may also be entreated by a contrite people to soften her harsh decision. The occasion is one of episcopal blessings and religious processions, in marked contrast to the wild cavortings of people dressed as animals on the Kalends that churchmen so objected to.

This story illustrates the way in which, although Gregory is in effect proposing the direct substitution of Christian objects and ritual for non-Christian ones, he is careful to stress throughout both books that it is not the objects themselves which heal or predict: it is God working through them and they are effective only if faith is genuine. Thus when describing the fashioning of *beneficia*, in this case gold keys which people have made for unlocking the railings of the tomb of St Peter in Rome, and which absorb the saint's power to heal the sick, he concludes that 'An active faith overcomes all'.[96] The miraculous appearance of the star of Bethlehem in a well, where it can be seen moving from one side to the other, is granted only to those who are pure in heart.[97] Yet Gregory also narrates the story of Bishop Franco, a devotee of the confessor Mitrias of Aix, who was despoiled by an important man at the court of King Sigibert. On returning to Aix, Franco knelt in prayer before the confessor's tomb, recited a psalm and said:

> 'Most glorious saint, no more lights will be lit here, no more melodies of psalms will be sung, until you first avenge your servants and restore to the holy church the properties that have been violently taken from you'. Then he threw briers with sharp thorns on top of the tomb; after he left, he shut the doors and put other briers likewise in the entrance.[98]

This would become in time the ritual known to historians as 'humiliation of relics'. The cessation of liturgy and blocking of the church with thorns was directed not just at the perpetrator of an offence, but against the saint as well for allowing it to happen. It would become a tactic employed by numerous monastic communities up to the High Middle Ages, an act of coercion and of punishment directed at the saint himself.[99] It emphasized that there was a two-way bond between saint and community and that his compliance could be forced. This ritual of coercion demonstrates that even amongst the theologically literate classes it was not always clear where faith stopped and magical manipulation began. Jesper Sørensen has observed that:

> It is an open question whether participants in a given ritual using an object connected to a sacred agent will have any representation of that agent as the efficacious agent, or whether the object *in itself* will be ascribed such agency ...[100]

As reflected in both the canons of ecclesiastical councils and Gregory's two works, the tactics used by the Church alternated between condemnations of non-Christian 'nonreflective' belief and attempts to Christianize this through the development of the cult of the tombs and relics of saints. The diocese of Auxerre, for example, would see an extraordinary growth in the number of saints venerated in this period, particularly local saints. Hen has counted thirty of the latter in the time of Bishop Aunarius, who died in 605. A number of these new saints were celebrated in May and while Hen rejects the idea that this might have been a deliberate counter to traditional May celebrations, the way in which Gregory of Tours opposes the cult of saints to non-Christian beliefs and celebrations, combined with the Synod of Auxerre's strictures relating to these, might make us think otherwise.[101] Sometimes Christianity seems simply to have taken over traditionally venerated sites. In Visigothic Spain, some traditionally venerated springs and pools, such as those we now know as Santa Lucia de Trampal and Santa Eulalia de Boveda were turned into places of Christian worship (though it is difficult to trace the chronology of these transformations).[102] In Spain, there also appears to have been an attempt to counter the Kalends celebrations by prescribing a fast.[103] But as well as putting the strategies which we see advocated in Gregory's writings into action, the Church would also find new ways of creating Christian 'nonreflective' belief, through the administration of penance.

In 626/7, the Frankish ruler Clothar met at Clichy with his bishops and nobles 'for the good of the king and the health of the country'.[104] The bishops – drawn from all over France – noted that some of their flocks, probably in the eastern parts of Austrasia, were 'eating food with pagans' and should be admonished to abandon this error. If they did not amend their ways and continued to associate with 'idolaters and sacrificers' they were to perform a 'period of penance'.[105] The Irish monastic leader, Columbanus, who had arrived in Francia in the 590s and set up a group of three monasteries on the borders of Austrasia and Burgundy, similarly specified penances for those eating food sacrificed to idols:

> If any layman has eaten or drunk beside the temples, if he did it through ignorance, let him undertake forthwith never to do it again, and let him do penance on bread and water. But if he did it in derision, that is, after the priest has declared to him that this was sacrilege, and then he communicated at the table of demons, if it was only through the vice of greed that he did or repeated it, let him do penance for a hundred and twenty days on bread and water; but if he did it in worship of the demons or in honour of idols, let him do penance for three years.[106]

This is a new form of penance: not only is it tariffed according to the offence, but it can be performed more than once in a lifetime. Although it might at first glance seem only to provide negative and punitive enforcement of Christianity, penance in this form offered something else: in cognitive terms, it performed the function of bringing God to mind.

Traditional penance in the Western Church had been a weighty under-taking, performed by those who had committed major sins (*peccata capitalia*). In the sixth century, Bishop Cæsarius of Arles classed these as sacrilege, murder, false testimony, theft, persistent drunkenness, rapine, fornication, and abortion (though he sometimes also included others such as anger, pride, and envy).[107] The penitent confessed the sins in private, but the penance itself was a matter of public record. Initially, as in the classic exposition by St Basil of Cæsarea in the fourth century, they were made to stand outside the church in the part of the service where communion was given, gradually moving inside – perhaps over a period of years, depending on the seriousness of the sin and length of penance – to stand or kneel at the back of the church, and finally be re-admitted to communion.[108] In southern Gaul in the early sixth century, penitents were made to cut their hair, dress in a sombre garment, fast several days a week and stand at the back of the church.[109] But even when re-admitted, they never entirely lost the status of penitent, as they were disqualified from military service or marital relations once the formal part of the penance had been completed. Penance was such a major event that it could only be performed once in a lifetime.

Penance in its traditional form had underlined the identity and reality of the Christian community. It made transparent the contrition of the penitent, who was in effect demanding its prayers on his or her behalf. But the personal and social difficulties it created were so immense that by the sixth century, penance was mostly left until the deathbed. Bishops countenanced deathbed penance and sinners threw themselves on the mercy of God; Cæsarius of Arles allowed young men to do penance on a second occasion and others to fast and give alms instead.[110] But these were tinkerings at the edges of an old system, not a new one. While it has been suggested that Columbanus connected with existing tendencies in Merovingian Francia and earlier attempts to reform the clergy and the moral life of the laity,[111] the penitential techniques that he brought with him represented something entirely different in cognitive terms. They reinforced 'nonreflective' belief in the Christian God and also had the potential to bring Him to the attention of any non-Christians in the vicinity – including the 'idolaters' on the eastern borders of Austrasia.[112]

The crucial transformation of penance took place in sixth-century Ireland, where Christianity was still establishing itself. The early Irish Church had taken its penitential ideas from the continent via Britain. The brief texts of conciliar proceedings from the early British Church can only give an impression of the way in which penitence was administered to the laity there. There are many gaps and silences in these documents: there is no indication of the official public part of the procedures – whether penitents stood at the back of the church and whether they were enrolled amongst the penitents and their penances ended by formal laying-on of hands. Nevertheless, we can see that the British Churches considered the major sins to be drunkenness, fornication, bestiality, murder, plotting to poison someone, incest, theft and sodomy. They prescribed penances of fasting, austerity and, for the worst sins, exile. They have been influenced to some extent by local legal customs; but the basic outlines of the administration of penance in Britain resembles, as we might expect, that of the Church in Gaul. The text known as the *First Synod of St Patrick* (or the *Bishops' Synod*) reveals that Ireland seems to have taken up a similar pattern, although once again with local adaptations. This was not the work of Patrick himself but probably dates from the early sixth century. Some of the offences penalized correspond to Caesarius' 'capital' sins. The penitent had to stand outside the church during mass; and the penance might include fasting. While penance seems to have been routinely administered by a priest rather than a bishop and while there were importations from Irish legal custom, such as the testimony of witnesses to the completion of the penance, it appears to have followed the same basic pattern as penance in Gaul.[113]

The change in penance in Ireland came about as Christianity began to spread in the sixth century. Major monastic communities were established in the period 525–75 and these, like the Irish Church in general, appear to have had a degree of contact with Britain. In British monasteries, the influence of Cassian and Basil was apparent. Knowledge of Cassian's version of Evagrius of Pontus' teaching relayed in the *Institutes* and *Conferences* led to controversies over the degree of austerity practised in different communities, but also meant knowledge of the practice of confession to a more spiritually advanced member of the community as well as a focus on the mental processes of the monk. Evagrius had taught that there were eight evil 'thoughts' and prescribed *diakrisis*, a constant examination of thoughts to determine whether they were good or evil. Basil, in Rufinus' Latin version of his monastic teachings, also focused on the monk's interior disposition, referring to wiser physicians of the soul who might diagnose its state. The impact of these ideas is evident in the *Preface on Penance* ascribed to the sixth-century British monk and cleric Gildas.[114] In this, monks are supervised by the abbot: he decides on their spiritual condition as well as imposing penances on them for any faults committed. The wide range of offences implies repeatable penance and Gildas begins, tentatively, to extend the monastic practice of penance outside the monastery. Non-monastic clergy who have committed sexual sins are to perform the same penance as their monastic equivalent and deplore their guilt and ask pardon of God in the same way as the monk.

Gildas was a correspondent of the British monk and cleric UUinniau, a significant figure on both sides of the Irish Sea and better known as St Finnian of Clonard (who has also been identified with St Finnian of Movilla). Finnian, who was both monk and bishop, composed what is in effect the first of a new genre of penitential handbooks, although it also takes in a number of organisational aspects of the Irish Church. But its core content was a new style of penance. It developed Gildas' tentative attempt to extend monastic-style penance to clergy: they were not merely to confess to sins such as stealing their neighbours' livestock, but to scrutinize their innermost thoughts for signs of the 'great and capital sins'. Finnian set out not just to punish obvious derelictions but also to foster compunction and a genuine change of heart. The penances imposed on clerics include fasting and exile and are repeatable. But Finnian innovated further, moving beyond the interior disposition of the cleric to the interior disposition of the ordinary Christian as well. The sixth clause of the *Penitential* required even a layman who intended serious harm to others to confess his evil thought and to do penance:

> If anyone has decided on a scandalous deed and plotted in his heart to strike or kill his neighbour, if (the offender) is a cleric, he shall do penance for half a year with an allowance of bread and water and for a whole year abstain from wine and meat and thus he will be reconciled to the altar; but if he is a layman, he shall do penance for a period of seven days; since he is a man of this world, his guilt is lighter in this world and his reward is less in the life to come.[115]

Finnian makes a highly significant declaration at the outset of his work:

> If *anyone* has sinned by thought in his heart and immediately repents, he shall beat his breast and seek pardon from God and make satisfaction and (so) be whole.

But if he frequently entertains (evil) thoughts and hesitates to act on them, whether he has mastered them or been mastered by them, he shall seek help from God by prayer and fasting day and night until the evil thought departs and he is whole.[116]

Here Finnian is not only addressing 'anyone' – monk, cleric *and* layperson – but also expressing the idea that an all-knowing Christian God can see into an individual's heart. The *Penitential* does not tell the individual to confess his sinful thought or thoughts to God; instead, it tells him to strike his breast and ask for pardon. The implication is that God is aware of the thought and is equally aware of genuine contrition. God already knows what the individual has thought.

These are extremely important statements in the context of a converting populace. At the time Finnian was writing, probably in the 540s (or possibly a decade or so later), Christianity was expanding. But although, according to Thomas Charles-Edwards, it was probably clear that paganism was a 'lost cause' by the 530s, this does not imply that it had disappeared altogether from Ireland by this date and his estimate may even be a little premature.[117] The last High King of Ireland to follow non-Christian inauguration rituals died in 565.

While the assumption that God can see into an individual's heart and mind is fundamental to Christian theology, this is not a 'natural' idea. Christians understand that He has full access to what cognitive studies of belief term 'strategic information': that is, what is important to people and what they do in secret; or information that has consequences for social interactions.[118] This has meant that Christian missionaries encounter peoples who believe in the existence of a very powerful creator god; yet he has no regular cult. This is because he is not intuited as having any interest in or interaction with humanity. In the context of conversion to Christianity, this can create a problem. The Genesis account of creation on the one hand provides a Christian parallel to non-Christian intuitions of a mighty deity who has created the earth and the universe. On the other, if converts identify the Christian God as their creator god, their initial representation of the latter might be as a deity remote, otiose and with no relevance to everyday life. Converts from polytheistic religions may need to be convinced that God is able to see what they do in secret or into their innermost thoughts. If this does not happen, they are liable to create syncretistic forms of belief, acknowledging the Christian deity as supreme, but also continuing with the cult of the gods, spirits or ancestors who will be of more help to them in everyday situations. Some early Old Irish texts refer to the Christian God as 'God to the gods', or *ardri*, an expression related to 'High King'.[119] This contains a vital clue to the initial understanding of the new deity as a sort of over-god. A crucial step for missionaries in moving converts past this stage is to convince them that the all-powerful Christian creator God has access to 'strategic information': what is important to people, what they know and what they do, especially what they do in secret.[120] Finnian's penitential sets out to establish this fundamental belief.

Perhaps of even more lasting significance is Finnian's extension of the monastic idea of iterative penance to the laity. Penances for sins such as fornication are tariffed according to the seriousness of the offence. The layman who has 'converted from his evil-doing unto the Lord' and has been guilty of fornication and bloodshed is to perform a penance lasting three years. He has to go unarmed except for a staff and cannot live with his wife. The man who has intercourse with a neighbour's wife or daughter has to accept a penance lasting a year, as does a man who has intercourse with his own female slave; or repudiates a barren wife; or a wife who leaves her husband for another man. The number of times penance is entered on depends on the number of times a person confesses to one of the sins listed, not on the principle that penance may only be embarked on once in a lifetime. Iteration of penance is extremely important in cognitive terms, as it contributes to the creation of 'nonreflective' belief in God. A pattern of repeated confession and iteration of penance demands that people repeatedly ask themselves what God will think of their behaviour: over time the habit of mental reference to the Christian God will become automatic. 'Nonreflective' belief in turn strengthens 'reflective' belief – of which Christian doctrine and theology are prime examples. Finnian's innovations turned the penitential process for the laity into a way of bringing the Christian God to mind.

On the continent, sixth-century bishops viewed penance in traditional terms, failing to recognize the potential of its repetition for strengthening belief. As we have already seen, Cæsarius of Arles had allowed young men to perform penance on a second occasion and there is also a little evidence that repetition may have been permitted in North Africa, but these represent minor alterations in details of the older system rather than a new beginning.[121] Examination of conscience was a process separate from performance of penance.[122] The one place where iteration of penance might have been a reality is in Spain – at least according to the bishops assembled at the Third Council of Toledo in 589. But they displayed only unremitting hostility to new developments and a desire to maintain traditional patterns and prerogatives:

> Whereas we understand that in certain churches of the Spains men do penance for their sins, not according to canon, but in most offensive wise (*foedissime*) in such sort that so often as it pleases them to sin, so often they demand of the priest to be reconciled; and accordingly for the suppression of so execrable a presumption, it is commanded by the holy council that penances be given in accordance with the plan of the ancient canons, that is that first (the priest) shall require him who repents of this deed, having been suspended from communion, to make among the other penitents frequent recurrence to the imposition of hands; and that when the period of satisfaction is fulfilled to the approval of the priest's judgement, he restore him to communion. But as regards those who relapse into their former sins whether within the time of penance or after reconciliation, let them be condemned according to the severity of the earlier canons.
>
> Whosoever, whether in health or sickness demands Penance from a bishop or a priest … if the person be a man whether whole or sick, he do first shave him and so accord him Penance; but if it is a woman she is not to receive Penance unless she have first changed her attire: for oftentimes by the careless according to Penance to the lay-people they fall back again into their deplorable offences after the reception of Penance.[123]

Unfortunately we have no way of knowing which Spanish churches had administered iterative penance, although it is tempting to think that it might have been the churches of the Bretons or Britons referred to in the *Parrochiale Suevum*.[124] The contacts between British/Breton monasticism and Ireland that provided the context for Finnian's pioneering *Penitential* could also have allowed the dissemination of his ideas to this outpost in Iberia.

The principal vector for the spread of the new style of penance was the Columbanian group of monasteries in Burgundy. Columbanus composed a *Penitential*, which owes a great deal to Finnian. This is a composite – 'a file of documents rather than a single text' – with sections devoted to monks, clerics and laity.[125] Columbanus is heavily dependent on Finnian not just for concept but also for detail. But he nowhere repeats its first two clauses which imply God's access to 'strategic information', although he takes his cue, near the beginning of the 'monastic' section, from the clauses in Finnian which distinguish between sins of thought and deed. It is also noticeable that while Columbanus prefaces his 'clerical' section with the idea of spiritual doctors curing souls he makes no further references to thoughts and the clerical penances which follow apply to deeds.

Columbanus is not focused on the problems of the earlier stage of Christianization that had galvanized Finnian into action. Instead, his *Penitential* deals with residual rural traditions amongst a Christian population rather than the menace of more widespread paganism or elite syncretistic practice. While it assigns penances to laypeople who have 'eaten and drunk beside temples' either out of greed or 'in worship of demons or veneration of idols', this, as we have seen, relates to continuation of traditional practices at traditional sites. But the Columbanian *Penitential* also creates a wider set of situations in which consideration of God's views about the behaviour of individuals was set in motion, extending the range of sins for which the laity would have to do penance: these now include bestiality; smothering a child; repeated theft; perjury; shedding blood in a brawl; and lusting after a neighbour's wife.[126] This extension of offences requiring expiation by penance not only increased the number of times Christians were presented with the opportunity to think about God, but may also have helped spread knowledge about Christianity amongst any real pagans on the eastern frontiers of Francia with whom they came into contact. The usefulness of the new practice of penance is shown by its diffusion through the Columbanian monasteries in eastern Francia and the composition of penitential handbooks in the regions of northern Francia, the Rhineland and southern Germany in the eighth century.[127] There is uncertainty as to whether, in Italy, use of the new type of penitential handbook spread outwards from Columbanus' Italian foundation of Bobbio, or whether it was introduced in Carolingian times. (The *Life of St Barbatus of Benevento* uses vocabulary reminiscent of that of Columbanian penance: but although its narrative is set in the seventh century, it was written in the ninth or even the early tenth, so it cannot be used to resolve the question.)[128] The latter was certainly the case in Spain, where the conservative attitudes expressed at Toledo seemed to persist.[129]

Historians have attempted for some time to explain the spread and popularity of the new style of penance and its handbooks: the recent trend in discussion has been to emphasize continuities rather than changes.[130] A cognitive perspective, however, enables us to trace the reasons behind the appearance of the new style penance and its engagement with thought – not just monastic, or clerical, but also the thought of the ordinary layperson. From this standpoint, it is easy to see why penitentials proved so popular and were composed and used in many parts of Western Europe, before Carolingian churchmen began to worry about their lack of control over them.[131] It is also easy to see the source of Finnian's concern with thought: on the one hand in a monastic background steeped in knowledge of Cassian and Basil and on the other in the realities of a society where Christianity was still in the process of replacing paganism. Perhaps more surprising for those familiar with Gregory of Tours only as author of the *Ten Books of Histories* or even with his other works of hagiography (which, as noted above, are often read by historians in a political context) is his acute sense of the way in which God could be brought to mind. Gregory reveals his concern with the mind at the outset of *Glory of the Martyrs*, when he declares that he is following the advice of the Apostle Paul by writing and proclaiming what edifies – or, alternatively, builds – the church of God

> and what enriches barren minds to recognition of perfect faith by means of holy teaching.[132]

When Gregory concludes the same work by equating martyrdom with the conscious, 'reflective' resisting of vice by the ordinary believer and advises his audience to

> manfully and firmly place the sign of salvation on your forehead or your chest . . .[133]

he is advocating what we might see as a way of underpinning 'reflective' belief by 'nonreflective', virtually automatic, practices.

It is also significant that when Gregory deals with paganism in *Glory of the Martyrs* or *Glory of the Confessors* he locates it in the past – as well as illustrating its powerlessness in the face of Christianity. In *Glory of the Martyrs*, he borrows from the Spanish poet Prudentius, who died in the early fifth century, the story of a Roman priest who cannot perform an augury before the emperor because of the presence of a Christian soldier.[134] In *Glory of the Confessors*, he describes how a wagon containing a representation of the goddess Berecynthia was drawn around the fields and vineyards to ensure their productivity: but when Bishop Simplicius of Autun – who probably lived in the fourth century – made the sign of the cross, the statue toppled and the oxen drawing the wagon could not move. Four hundred men out of the crowd following the wagon sacrificed to the deity to see if she or the oxen would move, but when nothing happened, they converted to Christianity.[135] Gregory may have been aware of the ritual of earlier Germanic fertility cults, but Berecynthia was an eastern goddess, a circumstance that underlines the general and schematic nature of his representation.[136]

In the second chapter of *Glory of the Confessors*, Gregory tackles the issue of *ex-votos* – the condemned practice of 'fulfilling vows' at sacred trees or lakes – head-on. He narrates the Christianization of a sacred lake, possibly the lake of Saint-Andéol, by a bishop of Javols, in south-western France. The period in which the events are set is never precisely indicated, but Gregory refers to a mountain and a church bearing the name of St Hilary of Poitiers, who died in 367/8. Gregory claimed that:

> at a fixed time a crowd of rustics went there, and, as if offering libations to the lake, threw [into it] linen cloths and garments that served men as clothing. Some [threw] pelts of wool, many [threw] models of cheese and wax and bread as well as various [other] objects, each according to his own means … They came with their wagons: they brought food and drink, sacrificed animals and feasted for three days. But before they were due to leave on the fourth day, a violent storm approached them with thunder and lightning. Much later a cleric from that city [of Javols] became bishop and went to the place. He preached to the crowds that they should cease this behaviour lest they be consumed by the wrath of heaven. But their coarse rusticity rejected his preaching. Then, with the inspiration of the Divinity, this bishop of God built a church in honour of the blessed Hilary of Poitiers at a distance from the banks of the lake. He placed relics of Hilary in the church and said to the people, 'Do not, my sons, do not sin before God. For there is no religion in a lake. Do not stain your hearts with these empty rituals, but rather acknowledge God and direct your devotion to his friends. Respect St Hilary, a bishop of God whose relics are located here. For he can serve as your intercessor for the mercy of the Lord.' The men were stung in their hearts and converted. They left the lake and brought everything

they usually threw into it to the holy church. So they were free from the mistake (*ab errore*) that had bound them. Next the storm was banned from the place. After the relics of the blessed confessor were placed there, the storm never again threatened this festival of God.[137]

Van Dam suggests that these events may have taken place in the sixth century, but its time-frame is vague.[138] The nature of the votive deposits mentioned here in combination with the sacrifice of animals suggests that we are dealing with offerings made in connection with harvests and fertility rather than with the issues of healing and curing suggested by the Synod of Auxerre. It is noticeable that Gregory never mentions the representations of limbs condemned by the synod. But his general oppositional schema is clear: non-Christian vs. Christian belief, the church and relics vs. lake and offerings. The practice of offering *ex-votos* is Christianized and taken inside a church.[139] He tells another highly pointed tale, the narrative of the way in which his great-grandfather, also Bishop Gregorius, allegedly discovered the burial-place of a Christian martyr, Benignus, at Dijon. His ancestor, he says,

> always thought that some pagan had been buried there. For the countryfolk fulfilled their vows there and quickly received what they sought.[140]

It was gradually revealed to Bishop Gregorius that this place was the tomb of a Christian martyr. Gregory is once more suggesting that the tombs of the saints are the true locus of the sort of power that people – here once again characterized as rustics – intuitively felt to be located in lakes, stones and trees.

The language of 'paganism' and demons used in the sermons of Martin and Cæsarius and also by ecclesiastical councils, in an attempt to impress on their audiences the seriousness of their divided loyalties is not employed by Gregory. He writes of 'error' and '*rusticitas*' – although as we have seen from the Lombard laws and from Gregory's own loud professions of shock about the habits of Spanish 'Arians', resorting to traditional places of power was a habit extending beyond the peasantry. But actual paganism was something of the past amongst the Franks, even though they had relatively recently made the transition to Christianity. It is misleading to write in terms of 'pagan survivals' as it is extremely doubtful that any overt worship of actual pagan deities survived in Francia or in Gallaecia, whatever picture Martin of Braga's classicizing terminology may suggest. It is the case however, that there were practices involving natural features (which may also have involved intuitions about lesser supernatural beings, such as the 'Lamiae', 'Dianas' and 'Nymphs' associated with woods and springs by Martin).[141] In the past, as well as 'pagan survivals', other labels, have been attached to these practices: 'superstition'; 'not-Christian'[142] culture, or 'popular belief'. But Gregory recognized them as being based in what we could call non-Christian 'nonreflective' belief and deliberately worked to promote a Christian alternative. This was presented as involving God and its location was now – preferably – a church; but it still involved *ex votos*, stone (or dust from stone) liquids and sometimes even trees associated with saints.[143] From a cognitive perspective Cæsarius, Martin, the bishops assembled at ecclesiastical councils, along with Finnian and the promoters of the new type of penance, were all working toward the same goal: to replace non-Christian 'nonreflective' belief by Christian 'nonreflective' belief, making Christian 'reflective' belief and doctrine more plausible.

Rest In Peace

There has been a considerable amount of discussion in recent years about the funerary rituals of the Germanic peoples. Edward James has summarized the development of Germanic cemeteries across what he calls 'Barbaricum' – that is, the areas occupied by these peoples before they came into sustained contact with the Roman Empire – up to the fourth century as one where cremation was the predominant practice, apart from in southern Scandinavia. From around 400 CE, right across 'Barbaricum', we see a series of very rich furnished inhumations. This is the prelude to a general change from cremation to inhumation and

> heralds the emergence of what became the characteristic cemetery form for barbarians of the Migration Period and beyond: the *Reihengräberfelder* or 'row-grave' cemeteries.[1]

These cemeteries have been the subject of much functionalist and constructivist interpretation. In the 1990s, for example, Guy Halsall, surveying evidence from the Frankish kingdom of Austrasia, argued that in the sixth century we find large cemeteries where the grave-goods appear to have reflected principally age and gender, whereas in the smaller cemeteries characteristic of the seventh century, assemblages reflected rank and wealth.[2] More recently, Halsall has also argued that the so-called *foederati* burials of north-western Gaul in the fourth century, previously interpreted as Germanic, contained items of Roman manufacture; that they were high status burials of people of varying ethnicities; and that their appearance reflects the adoption of Germanic or Frankish customs by locals in a time of social stress.[3] This argument leads us into the other principal focus of funerary study in recent years: ethnicity. The so-called 'cultural-historical' approach that describes a buckle brooch as 'Visigothic' or 'Frankish' has been completely rejected by some historians, who remind us that an object cannot itself possess ethnicity.[4] Others would contest the comprehensive denial of links between objects and population groups.[5] None of these discussions take account of beliefs about or understandings of death and the afterlife. The beliefs and intuitions in these respects of the person – or persons – in the graves and the people who placed them there are seldom if ever discussed – though there are many illustrations in academic books of what the writer or writers thought funeral rituals consisted of. These depictions involve either a cremation (with the deceased frequently placed on what looks like a rather inadequate pyre) or an inhumation in which the departed is carried to the grave on a bier, with the mourners standing around in various attitudes of mourning.[6] In reality, the funerary practices of the Germanic peoples involved complex and protracted rituals that, considered as a totality, could go on for years.

Archaeological evidence of the continuation of burial with grave goods amongst the Germanic peoples after they accepted Christianity indicates that Christian funerary ritual failed to address their anxieties about the souls of the dead, as did their re-opening and re-utilization of graves. The impact of pestilence may have compounded the problem. Another major source of anxiety appears to have been the nature of the Christian afterlife. Unlike the non-Christian one, it was highly differentiated and one's fate in it depended on one's conduct one earth. Worryingly for the Christianized Germanic peoples, many sections of the Church appeared to suggest that it had no place for non-Christian ancestors, whom they would have expected to meet in the next life. This final chapter looks at these questions and discusses some of the means – theological, eschatological and liturgical – developed by the Church to allay such anxieties and to help Christians accept that they would, in the company of their ancestral dead, rest in peace.

Intuitions about the dead

In his study of religion and cognition, *Religion Explained*, Pascal Boyer notes that:

> The souls of the dead or their 'shadows' or ' presence' are the most widespread kind of supernatural agent the world over.[7]

Although we know a person is dead, we cannot or do not immediately cut off all our mental interaction with them. We go on thinking about them and mentally revisiting the picture we had of them while they were alive, or pondering our former relations with them as living persons. In this sense those who have just died are very close to us and their presence can be felt very vividly, or even 'seen'. Anthropologists have observed that while it is quite common for peoples they have studied to have vague notions about death or 'the dead' in general, they often cherish much more detailed representations of the recently deceased, revolving around the transitional period between death and some further state. Consciousness of the polluting nature of the corpse focuses attention on the period of decay as a transitional or liminal period; and is also a common feeling that the presence of the recently dead is dangerous rather than reassuring.[8]

Early Catholic funerary ritual and the beliefs behind it

The oldest versions of Christian funerary ritual ignored such feelings and beliefs: Christianity regarded death as instantaneous and leading to a separation between living and dead – and also between the body and the soul of the dead – until the general resurrection of the body and the Last Judgment at the end of time.

Christian funerals in the early centuries are rituals of separation, in which the living bid farewell to the deceased until the end of time and the Last Judgment. Early Catholic funerary ritual was intended to suggest the repose of the soul, the resurrection of the body, and an optimistic anticipation of a good outcome for the individual at the Last Judgment. The earliest surviving complete rite for the dying and dead from the Western Church – dating from the fourth or fifth century – reveals that it involved the administration of the Eucharist to the dying person (even to penitents); prayers and psalms immediately after death; the washing of the body and its conveyance to the church accompanied by psalms and antiphons; a church service which included lessons from the book of Job, psalms, prayers and responses; and finally inhumation, again accompanied by a psalm and an antiphon.

In contrast to other belief-systems, the Christian afterlife, which the single soul enters after death, is highly conceptualized. In its very earliest period the idea of the afterlife was hardly articulated, as Christians believed the imminence of the *parousia*, the Second Coming of Christ on earth. As time wore on, ideas about the afterlife became more detailed. There was more focus on the Last Judgment; while in the meantime in Heaven, God and the heavenly hierarchy were joined by the souls of the martyrs. It gradually became understood that not only the martyrs, but also those considered saints would be instantly admitted to, or have some sort of foretaste of, Heaven on their deaths. The souls of the irredeemably bad would go straight to Hell.[9] These were provisional judgments, to be confirmed only at the end of time, when the general resurrection of the body would take place and God would judge the living and the dead.[10] For the ordinary believer, however, who had been neither particularly good nor particularly bad, the fate of the soul after death was a rather different one. It was parked somewhere in the afterlife in *refrigeria* ('places of refreshment'), *receptacula* ('receptacles') or, less impersonally, the bosom of Abraham, there to await the Last Judgment.

As well as condemning ritual lamentations, which they associated with non-Christian beliefs, many early Christian writers sought to present the funeral as an occasion of joy and triumph over death.[11] Where joy was concerned, as Geoffrey Rowell has observed, the Church eventually lost the battle.[12] St Augustine of Hippo himself described his failure to overcome his own despair and sorrow during his mother's funeral.[13] Despite their suggestion of hope for the individual at the Last Judgment, the earliest Catholic funerary rites served to emphasize the separation of the living from the dead until the end of time. St Augustine made strenuous attempts to deny any possibility of communication between the living and the dead – though even he was forced to concede that prayers for the deceased were of consolation to the living.[14] Thus while the Church would develop the idea of limited communication with the 'very special dead' in the form of the saints, it ignored popular intuitions about the lingering presence of the recently dead as far as possible – though in fourth-century Roman cemeteries where the Christian dead lay buried near their pagan contemporaries, relatives frequently commemorated them with ritual banquets near their tombs and sometime even 'fed' them through tubes built into the graves.[15]

Some elements of Christian epigraphy may have evolved to express opposition to popular intuitions of the presence of the dead. From the fourth century onwards, beginning in Rome itself, we see the appearance of inscriptions on tombs expressing the idea that the deceased is resting there peacefully: *requiescit in pace* (s/he rests in peace); *recessit in pace* (s/he retreated in peace); *dormit in pace* (s/he sleeps in peace) and other variants on the theme of sleep and rest. The formulae of the epitaphs appear to be designed to establish the idea that the Christian body reposed in peace in the grave, while the soul tranquilly awaited the Last Judgment in the next world in secluded *refrigeria*. As one commentator has observed:

> The contrast between the image of the Christian dead lying peacefully in their tomb, and the images of the Roman dead as either dust, or a semi-living spirit, is great. It is not unreasonable to conclude that such a contrast was intentional, and that it was very much a part of why the new Christian memorial formulae were adopted.[16]

From threatening revenant to beneficent ancestor

A basic divergence between Christianity and Germanic paganism lay in different understandings of the relationship between body and soul – or souls. In common with many other cultures, Germanic pagans thought in terms of more than one soul.

They intuited the existence of a free soul, representing the personality on one hand, and on the other, one or more body souls, which endow the body with life and consciousness. We can find lingering traces of belief in soul dualism surviving in a number of European folk tales and motifs, such as the story preserved in the *History of the Lombards* of Paul the Deacon about Gunthram, a Christian King of the Franks.[17] This tells how, when the king was out hunting, he lay down to sleep. While he was asleep, his companion saw a small reptile come out of his mouth. It attempted to cross a stream, so the man laid down his sword, which it used as a bridge, before disappearing into a hole in a hill on the other side. After a while, the reptile came back and went into Gunthram's mouth. When he awoke, the king related a wonderful dream in which he had crossed an iron bridge and gone under a mountain where he had discovered a great mass of gold. His companion told him what he had seen and the place was dug up to reveal 'countless treasures' – out of which, Paul assures his readers, the king had a solid gold canopy made which he placed over the tomb of St Marcel at Châlon.[18]

There can be considerable variants in the beliefs underlying such stories, but certain fundamental patterns are discernible. Generally, the free soul is considered to be active during unconsciousness while the body souls are active when the individual is awake. It is never entirely clear where in the body the free soul resides during wakeful consciousness.[19] But when an individual is asleep or unconscious, the free soul may roam far and wide, visiting the living and – in certain cases – the dead. The belief in the potential mobility of the soul lies at the heart of belief in shamanism: and while the terms shaman and shamanism are often applied in the strict sense to a type of Siberian or South American religious specialist, the widespread belief in the mobile soul led to the emergence of specialists of this type in many cultures. In the Germanic religions, the cult of Woden is believed to have had shamanistic aspects, reflected in the role of Woden as god of the dead as well as of battle.

Christian theology, on the other hand, derived its teachings on the soul from Greek philosophy. Originally, the Archaic Greeks had intuited a number of souls. But by the end of the fifth century BCE, the *psyche*, associated with the breath, combined with the free soul and would go on to absorb other body soul concepts to produce the idea of a single, unitary soul. This would be incorporated in Christian teaching, where some traces of multiple soul belief survived: for early Christian theologians such as Origen, working partly in the intellectual tradition of Platonism, the single soul was made up of a number of areas or parts – including, for example, the *psyche* and also the *nous*; these ideas would be transmitted to, and play an important part in, early monastic thought.[20] However, these were only traces: it was a single, unitary soul that gave life to the body. The Christian version of the relationship between body and soul is set out in the extraordinary short treatise *On Lazarus* by the fourth-century Iberian bishop, Potamius of Lisbon.[21] Potamius was one of the earliest supporters of the Illyrican bishops Ursacius and Valens, who had advanced Homoian Trinitarian theology as a way of capturing non-Christian intuitions of divinity for Christianity. Potamius soon abandoned Homoianism, but nevertheless should be given credit for his sustained attempts to address popular beliefs. *On Lazarus* deals with the raising of the dead Lazarus by Christ. It makes it clear that there is one single soul, the 'charioteer' who has kept the elements making up the body together. This Christian version of the relationship between body and soul is followed by an account of Christ's raising of the dead man, a statement of His power over death (and also of the beneficent nature of this Christian resurrection). But it remains an isolated work amongst Christian homilies, until in the seventh century the *Dialogues* attributed to Gregory the Great tackled the same subject, explaining how the body is moved and operated by the (single) soul:

> In considering the movements of the body, it is from the lowest activity that we infer the soul's presence in the body … Imagine a house under construction and visualize the lifting of immense weights and large columns suspended from mighty cranes. Tell me who is doing this work? Is it the visible body that pulls those massive materials with its hand, or is it the invisible soul that activates the body?[22]

At the core of *On Lazarus* lies an extraordinary description of the decomposition of the dead Lazarus' body. The text makes it clear that death and decomposition begin at the moment when Lazarus' soul departs. With dual or multiple souls, however, death is a much more complex and far from instantaneous process. The body soul or souls will exit the body to disappear, perhaps into a tree or a bird. The free soul, also released from the body, lingers near it in the world of the living, in a liminal state between life and death. In cultures where dual or multiple soul belief exists, funerary rituals are rituals of transition, designed to ensure that the free soul, still in the world of the living after death (the departure of the body soul/s), makes a safe and permanent transit to the world of the dead.[23] If this is not done, it may still linger in the land of the living; or it may re-enter the body to become a deadly revenant, terrorising its family or community. The aim of funerals is to transform a potential ghost or malignant revenant into a beneficent ancestor, conducting it safely to the world of the dead. Before this stage, it is still a potentially malevolent or unwelcome ghost and may try to take the living into its shadow existence or at least pilfer subsistence from them – hence the common custom of making food offerings to the dead. As the anthropologist Robert Hertz pointed out in the early years of the twentieth century, the liminal period in which the soul or spirit has not finally reached the afterlife is generally believed to have corresponded to the period it took for the flesh to decay.[24] In order to ensure the safe transition of the soul to the village, land or world of the ancestors, funerary ritual needs to ensure that polluting and dangerous decaying flesh is dealt with. Thus peoples all over the world have ritually practised cremation, excarnation or mummification. Although these appear at first sight to be to be radically different procedures, they all ensure that the body is reduced to stable elements and that the soul cannot re-enter it. The alternative procedure is elaborate burial ritual, often with grave-goods and funerary feasting, to usher the soul safely into the land of the ancestors. Families without the means to do this can perform whatever little ritual they can afford – and perhaps also ensure that their relative is buried in the vicinity of the dead whose souls had already made the successful transition.[25]

Funerary rituals of the Germanic peoples

Archaeological evidence indicates that before coming into contact with Christianity, the Germanic peoples either cremated their dead or buried them with grave goods. In fact, cremation urns might also contain certain types of grave goods as well as the ashes of the dead. The Sîntana de Mureş-Černjachov culture of southern Russia and the Balkans, which has been associated with the Goths before they moved westwards, created cemeteries where we find a mixture of cremations, burials with grave goods and unfurnished burials; there are also occasional cenotaphs. Inhumation predominates in those in modern Romania (and some Romanian cemeteries contain only inhuma-tions); further east the picture appears to be more mixed. A wide variety of grave goods accompanied both cremations and inhumations. It also seems that inhumation gradually took over from cremation. The peoples of the Wielbark and Lubosyzce cultures, who are thought to be forerunners of the Burgundians,[26] practised both inhumation and cremation: the remains of hearths and posts have been found at some cemeteries.[27] In the areas of Pannonia where the Lombards settled, we see rich 'ducal' graves and also large inhumation cemeteries such as Hegykö, Szentendre and Tamási, where organization seems partly to have been based on age and gender, along the lines suggested by Halsall's study of Frankish cemeteries.[28] James has recently highlighted the emergence of inhumation as the predominant rite, as the Germanic peoples moved out of 'Barbaricum'. He focuses on the actual change in ritual itself: his discussion is functionalist in approach, emphasizing the social reasons which led 'barbarian' chiefs to copy Roman funerary customs and also to acquire precious Roman artefacts, some of which would, eventually, be buried with them. There is no consideration of the intuitions underlying these practices.[29]

The change from cremation to furnished inhumation is sometimes presented as an indication of a substantive change or difference in religious terms. Heather, for example, has characterized the appearance of both cremation and furnished inhumation in cemeteries of the Sîntana de Mureş-Černjachov culture as indicating use by two groups of people 'with quite different beliefs about the afterlife, and how to prepare an individual for it'.[30] This is at variance with the findings of anthropologists who see the same basic understandings of the purpose of funerary ritual underlying both rites.[31] We should seek the reasons for the change from one to the other in economic and/or geographical factors: cremation is a very expensive undertaking in terms of both labour and materials.[32]

As the Germanic peoples settled on the frontiers of empire or inside it, they were often buried in furnished graves in the *Reihengräberfelder* that James characterizes as typical of the late Migration Period – more typical of the era in which they came into contact with the Roman Empire than of their previous existence in 'Barbaricum'. The deposition of objects in graves and the custom of burying people dressed and with jewellery and/or weapons continued after Goths, Franks, Burgundians and Lombards settled beside Catholic populations – or in the case of the Franks became Catholic. (It is difficult to say much about the Sueves.) Recently, archaeologists and historians have been preoccupied with debates about whether it is possible to read ethnicity into weapons, jewellery and other objects found in graves.[33] The now common trope that the Visigoths in south-western Gaul are archaeologically invisible originates in this essentially functionalist and constructivist view of burial, a view that also dominates discussions of the changes in the types and numbers of objects found. While useful cautionary observations regarding the deficiencies of older excavations and their publication have emerged from them, these discussions take no account of beliefs about or understandings of death and the afterlife. The fact that such practices continued testifies to the continuing power of intuitions about the dead. Cemeteries in which there are some inhumations with vessels, weapons, jewellery and other objects and others with none can indicate either the different economic and social status of the persons buried there, or a gradual conversion to Christian norms of burial. In a cemetery used over a long period, such as that of Collegno (Turin), taphonomic evidence, taken in conjunction with the presence or absence of grave-goods, can provide some clues. Amongst the Lombard burials at this site, archaeologists believe they can chart a chronological progression: from the earliest graves with post-holes at the corners and evidence of wooden internal constructions along with certain types of grave-goods, c. 570 to c. 640; to stone-edged graves with other types of objects; and finally, in the eighth century, to burial in narrow earth graves and with no objects, in conformity with Christian norms. But there are many instances in which poorer Goths, Lombards, Burgundians or Franks were buried with no goods beside their better-off contemporaries. In the Burgundian cemetery of Monnet-la-Ville, only 48 out of a total of 202 graves contained any sort of object. The excavators suggest that use of this cemetery declined after the mid-500s, so the period of major use lasted only about a century; and it is very likely some of the burials where no objects were recovered dated from the same period as some of those with jewellery, buckles, and so on. If two fifth, sixth, and even seventh-century burials are roughly contemporary, even if one grave contains objects and the other does not, we cannot rule out the possibility that the families of both deceased shared the same ideas about the dead. The understanding of death as a liminal period and the necessity of ritual to assist the soul safely into the other world remains the same whether a fuller or an abridged version of funerary ritual is performed. The continued presence of structures over, or in, graves and of objects buried with the dead, characteristic of the entire spectrum of Germanic peoples into the seventh century, indicates the continuing power of such intuitions and practices.

Another custom – observed frequently amongst the Franks and Visigoths – which relates to intuitions about the dead is the post-depositional opening and re-use of graves. This used to be treated as evidence of 'grave-robbing', but recent work indicates the possibility of a range of motives behind the re-opening of interments.[34] Evidence of grave opening and re-use can be seen in large Visigothic cemeteries as at Duraton and Herrera de Pisuerga in central Spain, where photographs reveal complete or largely complete skeletons along with what are clearly the disarticulated bones of a number of other individuals.[35] Unfortunately, these older excavations did not meet modern standards and it is difficult to establish a reliable chronology of the interments.[36] Rather more recent work, such as the excavations at Alcalà de Henares, suggests that this custom was practised in the sixth century: excavators of this site in the 1970s commented on 'abundant' re-use, with large quantities of bones accompanying the more recent burials. Here, rather than placing the new interments on top of what looks like a random heap of disarticulated bones, the majority of cases seem to have involved inserting the latter at the foot of the grave.[37] A similar configuration has been remarked

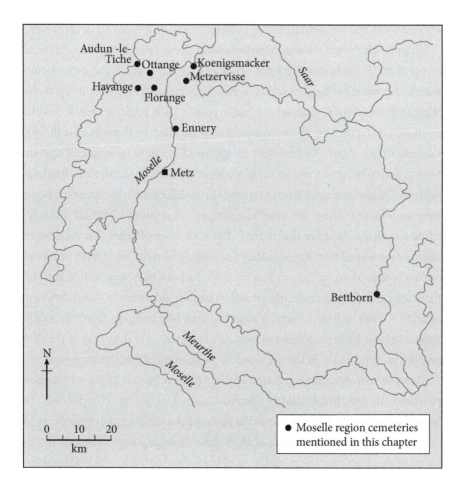

at Almodóvar del Pinar, in burials thought to date from the second half of the sixth century.[38] In Francia, the Merovingian cemetery of Audun-le-Tiche (Moselle) contains examples of post-depositional openings of tombs and re-arrangement of bodies.[39] Alain Simmer has remarked on the frequency of re-use in the Moselle region in the seventh century in general, not just at Audun, but also (for example) at Hayange and Ottange. At Ottange, almost all the tombs were re-used, while re-use occurred in over a third of those at Audun.[40] Not all cemeteries saw such extensive re-utilizations: the rescue excavation of Metzervisse has revealed a much lower proportion (four out of fifty-nine tombs), but its interments have been dated from the seventh to the ninth century, so here we may be seeing the custom go out of fashion in this area.[41] In a different region of Francia, the Merovingian graves of Lagny-sur-Marne seem to contain a high number of re-utilizations, though the excavators at the moment date this cemetery to the fifth and sixth centuries.[42]

Simmer characterizes the motives behind these re-utilizations as 'difficult to penetrate'.[43] He is puzzled by the lack of care with which the older bones, which only went back a generation or two, were treated. However, it is possible that the graves were re-opened not just to receive their latest occupant, but also to check on the process of decomposition of the flesh of those buried there at an earlier date. After the flesh had disappeared, it could be assumed that the person was to be numbered securely amongst the ancestors: once this had been achieved, many may have thought it made little difference what order the bones were re-interred. There are parallel examples of modern Christian funerary ritual where the dead are disinterred after a number of years and their bones anxiously scanned to make sure they are clean: any remains of flesh or discolouring is seen as an indication that their life had not been a good one and that their soul may be experiencing an unfavourable judgment in the (Christian) afterlife.[44] Thus in some cases, Visigothic and Merovingian funerary rituals appear to have been prolonged to include the checking of the decay of the flesh and the incorporation of the deceased in the community of the ancestors.

One piece of conciliar legislation appears to be related in some way to these practices. In 585, the Frankish Church Council of Mâcon complained that 'many' were opening tombs 'while the limbs of the dead were not yet decayed' and 'superimposing' the bodies of their dead or taking over 'religious places' for their dead without the permission of the owner of the tombs.[45] The former statement may reflect a lack of understanding of the process of checking on decay – while the latter may indicate that in some instances other people's tombs (and ancestors?) were being appropriated. The Council decreed that in the latter cases, the 'superimposed' bodies could be ejected. The recently excavated Merovingian Burgundian cemetery of Alésia ('Champs de l'Église', Alise-Sainte-Reine, Côte-d'Or), where the inhumations date from the sixth and seventh centuries, is about 170 km north of Mâcon, and contains graves which reflect practices comparable to those in other Visigothic or Frankish cemeteries, with superimposed bodies or disconnected bones in burials. Not all the disconnected bones were found in graves: some had been placed in wooden boxes or wrapped in cloth, before being inserted in separate ossuaries resembling graves: the excavators suggest some (but not all) of these were created when some new burials displaced older ones. The state of the disconnected bones indicates that these dismemberments and removals were made within a few years of the original interments.

The afterlife and the ancestors

Not only does Christian teaching depart from widespread beliefs and intuitions about the soul and its relationship to the body, but there is also a marked contrast between the Christian version of the afterlife and those of many other belief-systems. Christianity is a religion of salvation, or as Max Weber defined it, an other-worldly religion, its highly differentiated afterlife predicated on the conduct of the individual while alive, with the good being rewarded and the bad punished. By contrast, religions that concentrate on the here-and-now ('this-worldly' religions) tend to view life after death as a version – perhaps a fainter, distorted or less enjoyable version – of the known world. Though we sometimes see elements of afterlife differentiation developing, this is commonly on the basis of status rather than moral conduct. Thus Scandinavian mythology as preserved and developed in literary sources visualized an underworld realm of the dead in which warriors were received into Valhalla.[46] But this is a later development and to a certain extent a literary one, influenced by Christianity. Germanic pagans in the earlier period are likely to have regarded the afterlife as a version of the life they knew.[47] And, in common with other cultures, they would have regarded it as the home of the souls of their parents, grandparents and ancestors, with whom they would be united when they themselves died.

A story which encapsulates these differences is the narrative in which Radbod, the pagan duke of Frisia in the late seventh and early eighth centuries was on the point of becoming a Christian – indeed had one foot in the baptismal pool. When tactlessly told by the churchman Wulfram of Sens that he would not meet any of his ancestors in Heaven (because as pagans they were damned to Hell), he promptly took his foot out again, declaring that he would rather spend eternity in Hell with his ancestors, than in Heaven with a few paupers.[48] We cannot take the story entirely at face value: Radbod had originally reacted against his father's welcoming of Christianity, believing that it was an instrument of Merovingian hegemony and the story comes from a Christian source. Nevertheless, the tale neatly sums up some of the most significant differences between pagan and Christian afterlives. The latter is differentiated into what the Church believed were attractive and unattractive sections: Heaven for the good, Hell for the bad. Not only was this differentiation a notion foreign to Radbod – who noted the suspiciously 'small number' of people in the Christian Heaven – but his ancestors were not present, rendering it instantly unappealing. The *Dialogues* attributed to Pope Gregory the Great pronounced that there was no room in the Christian Heaven for the pagan ancestor: 'saintly men on earth do not pray for deceased infidels and godless people.'[49] They taught that the soul of the good Christian would instead enjoy the society of the souls of his or her fellow Christians and the saints. Radbod was less than impressed by the idea of such company – in his view he was being offered the society of 'paupers', as opposed to the heroic ancestral dead.

Aspects of funerary ritual amongst the Germanic peoples suggest that they thought certain locations were particularly auspicious for the safe transit of the soul into the community of the ancestors. In Anglo-Saxon England, during the 'Conversion Period', a conspicuous feature of funerary practice is the re-use of Bronze Age barrows, Roman ruins, even Roman roads or ancient features in the landscape – as burial sites. Some authorities calculate that there such positioning occurs in perhaps as many as 25 per cent of cemeteries (though this figure may be on the high side).[50] Burial beside older structures is often seen in functionalist terms as an attempt to underpin the contemporary social and political order: but it also involved a choice of location that strongly invoked the past.[51] In Spain, the occupants of some of the most famous Visigothic-era cemeteries – for example Duraton, Alcalà de Henares, Herrera de Pisuerga – were buried not just beside Roman roads but near the remains of Roman villas and towns.[52] The seventh-century Frankish 'row-grave' cemetery of Bettborn (Moselle) is situated on a hill among Roman substructures and at a point where roads cross; that of Audun-le-Tiche (seventh century), around a *fanum* used between the first and fourth centuries CE; that of Florange alongside a Roman road; that of Koenigsmacker (second half of sixth–seventh century) on Gallo-Roman structures on a terrace twelve or so metres above the Moselle.[53] There are many similar examples where the groups who settled chose to bury their dead beside ruins and substructures left by older societies, probably partly because of a belief that this would facilitate the transition of the spirit to the other world. They also interred their dead beside those of earlier groups of inhabitants. At Collegno in northern Italy, a family group of 'Ostrogothic' burials, including that of a warrior with cranial deformation and also a leg syndrome caused by long periods in the saddle, was situated beside two Bronze Age cremations: the presence of these was probably indicated by mounds which have long since disappeared. A Lombard cemetery would, in due course, take its place close beside them.[54] At Briord (Ain), one of a number of Burgundian cemeteries, Les Plantées, took over a graveyard dating from the first century CE and a basilica church of later date. The lack of evidence for Suevic cemeteries has led scholars to fall back on contextualisation by comparison with Merovingian Francia; but the putatively Sueve burials of Eido da Renda (Beiral do Lima) are in a small Roman necropolis (with Roman structures nearby).[55] Locations from which spirits had already made the transition to the other world were highly appropriate for their own rituals.

The major differences between these beliefs and rituals on one hand and those of Christianity on the other begs the question of the position of clerics, Homoian or, in the case of the Franks, Catholic, with regard to them. We have no direct evidence, but the *Lives* of Martin of Tours and Columba of Iona, from other early medieval environments, throw some light on the question. In the first, composed soon after his death in the 390s, Martin comes across a crowd of peasants, bearing a body on a bier, and mistakes the procession for a fertility ritual. Thinking they are carrying the image of a 'demon', that is, a fertility divinity, he stops the cortège, which is miraculously rooted to the spot. Once the saint realises that he has interrupted a funerary procession rather than sacrifices to heathen gods, he releases them, taking no further interest in proceedings. The funerary procession is not a Christian one, but such rituals, performed by peasants, are evidently of no concern to him.[56] Another perspective is offered by Adomnán's *Life of Columba*, written approximately a century after his death in 597, which depicts the saint deliberately leaving a house where one of his monks lay dying:

> The holy man came to visit him in his last hour, standing for a time beside his bed and blessing him. But he soon left the monk, for he wished not to see the man die.[57]

The later Irish text known as the *Monastery of Tallaght* reveals that in Ireland priests were not allowed to come into contact with a dying man.[58] The justification it gives is Biblical, citing Leviticus 21.10-12, which instructs that the sons of Aaron – that is, priests – should not defile themselves by contact with the dead.[59] This creates – once again – a distancing effect between clerics and the moment of death. Given that the cemeteries of the Germanic peoples testify to rituals centring on the idea of the dead body as dangerous and polluting, Gothic clergy may have, like Columba, blessed the sick but avoided the moment of death and the place where the dead body lay.

Christianity and its anxieties

While there is no co-ordinated approach to these phenomena and there may be wide regional and chronological variations within Francia and Visigothic Spain, it does appear that customs of funerary rituals of transition and burial in locations believed to be propitious survived for a considerable time after Franks and Visigoths had technically accepted Christianity, whether of the Catholic or Homoian variety. We have much less evidence in the case of Ostrogothic Italy, a kingdom of relatively short duration. Some of this consists of finds made a long time ago for which we have no proper context; while some would seem to indicate the differing ethnic backgrounds of people classed as

'Goths'.[60] Some scholars suggest – at least in the case of the Goths in cities – a degree of assimilation to Roman burial customs.[61] This may be the case, though in the light of the short-lived nature of the Ostrogothic kingdom and the paucity of evidence, we should perhaps suspend judgment: the complexities are evident in the record from Ravenna. There, the funerary area of the Via Darsena, in the region of the *Campus Coriandri*, the site of 'Arian' extramural churches in the time of Theoderic and not far from his own mausoleum, was rich in finds, but was unsystematically excavated in the nineteenth century.[62] However, one of the most intriguing pieces of evidence comes not from the archaeological record, but from a written source, the *Variae* of Theoderic's Roman administrator, Cassiodorus. This is an instruction by Theoderic to one of his *saiones* for the removal of precious metal from graves with no owner (*ubi dominus non habetur*).[63] It goes on to state that remains should be protected by buildings and graves adorned by columns or marble (*aedificia tegant cineres, columnae vel marmora ornent sepulchra*). This instruction does not represent a legalization of tomb-robbing. In an attempt to create a distinction between this type of removal – portrayed as being for the good of the living and of the state – and acts of grave-robbing or tomb violation, the directions stipulate that the remains of the deceased (literally their 'ashes') should not be disturbed, (*quia nolumus lucra quaeri, quae per funesta possunt scelera reperiri*). But it does imply that Theoderic's view of funerary ritual at this point was more in tune with standard Christian beliefs and norms than with more traditional rites, in keeping with his desire for *Romanitas*. Had other Ostrogoths come to share these beliefs? This question is at the moment un-answerable because of the scarcity and problematic nature of the evidence and may well remain so. The drift towards Catholicism suggested in the written sources would imply that some Goths were buried according to Catholic rites – which is what archaeologists suggest was occurring in urban areas. Thus there may have been an acculturation of Goths in the cities that led to their acceptance of Christian teaching on death and burial.

Was this also the case in Burgundy? Christian funerary epigraphy from the south and west in particular would indicate that some of the incomers had accepted Christian norms of burial in the late fifth and early sixth centuries. At the same time, evidence from one Burgundian cemetery suggests a marked degree of nervousness about the safe transit of the soul of the deceased to the afterlife amongst some of the first individuals to be buried with an epitaph carved in stone. At Briord (Ain), the cemetery of En Pontonnier contains the epitaphs of two men and three women with Germanic names: Manneleubus and Baldaridus who died in 487 and 488 respectively; Rudehilde (d. 491), Arenberga (d. 501), and Vilioberga (d. 501). According to the inscriptions, both men died at the age of sixty. This means they had been born in the time of the 'First Burgundian Kingdom' and had lived through the catastrophe of defeat by Aëtius' Hunnic allies, the settlement of the Burgundians in Sapaudia and its subsequent expansion into this region. According to the epitaphs, Manneleubus had freed six slaves and Arenberga one: her epitaph states explicitly that she did this 'for the redemption of her soul' (*pro redemtione animae suae*).[64] The most startling fact about the inscriptions is that we know that two (and quite possibly three) were placed *inside* the tomb.

A functionalist interpretation of similarly positioned inscriptions – based on the construction of inhumation rituals primarily as reflectors of social status or aspirations – maintains that they were intended for the benefit of a temporary audience, the mourners who attended the funeral.[65] But the context of the En Pontonnier inscriptions suggests that there is more than social status involved. These people – tellingly, two males long past warrior age and three females – look like first generation converts. Scholars favour the opinion that they, and indeed this cemetery as a whole, should be regarded as Catholic. Their epitaphs demonstrate that Manneleubus and Arenberga had assimilated the Christian teaching that the fate of the soul after death is dependent not on rites of transition but on the merit of the individual's life on earth. The freeing of slaves, therefore was commemorated as the conscious performance of a good deed in the hope of being adjudged worthy of Heaven. But it was accompanied by a reminder to the dead themselves that they should 'rest in peace', by means of an inscription placed in the grave with them. The inscription was invested with an apotropaic function in circumstances where the intuition of the unquiet grave had not been entirely banished.

Anxiety about the effectiveness of Christian funerary ritual amongst those professing Christianity manifested itself in a different way in Lombard Italy. There, funerary ritual continued for some time in traditional mode. Archaeologists have suggested that in many respects early Lombard inhumations recall Lombard burials in Pannonia, in which the dead might be deposited in hollowed-out tree-trunks and with two posts at each end supporting a 'house of the dead' above ground.[66] At cemeteries as diverse as Romans d' Isonzo (Gorizia) and Collegno (Turin), the earliest tombs are deep, with similar post-holes at the corners.[67] The Pannonian burials are indicative of elaborate mortuary rituals: the 'houses of the dead' could have held the body during a protracted wake or for desiccation before inhumation. Some of the deceased at Collegno appear to have been buried in man-made approximations of tree-trunks with the 'houses' above them. There are clear indications that these rituals were carried out by Christians: four graves of this type at Collegno, all from the earliest phase of inhumations (c. 570–c. 640–50), contain gold-foil crosses indicating Christian affiliation.[68] Gold-foil crosses have been found in around 340 Lombard interments of the late sixth and seventh centuries, sewn on to a garment on the breast or to a cloth placed over the face.[69] The four graves with crosses are located close to the burial of a decapitated horse, presumed to have belonged to the inhabitant of a neighbouring grave, now destroyed: a warrior assumed to be related to the four Christian deceased, but who had his horse buried beside him in a non-Christian rite. This sequence of burials would suggest on one hand a rapid conversion to Christianity amongst what looks like a family group, but on the other a reluctance to abandon the traditional rites by which the soul was conducted into the afterlife.

The eighth-century Lombard writer Paul the Deacon attributes another funerary custom to the Lombards:

> if any one were killed in any place either in war or in any other way, his relatives fixed a pole (*pertica*) within their burial ground upon the top of which they placed a dove made of wood that was turned in that direction where their beloved had expired so that it might be known in what place he who had died was sleeping.[70]

One such post appears to have been placed at the corner of an empty grave at Collegno. Post-holes interpreted as those of *perticae* are have been found near actual inhumations in Celimarro (Calabria).[71] The two most famous Lombard cemeteries in Italy – '*ad perticas*' or '*in pertica*' – at Pavia and Cividale have been partly or entirely built over, so cannot help us resolve the question of whether Paul's explanation of these posts is correct.[72] The bird-figures placed on top of them are thought by some scholars to represent the soul of the deceased, as birds and souls are frequently associated as such amongst the Germanic peoples.[73] If this is the case the pole and bird may represent the body soul and free soul (or perhaps the pole represented a tree into which the body soul might pass, if the grave was occupied). Though some of its members may have called themselves Christians, the community that buried its dead at Collegno still subscribed to these ideas and practices, perhaps up to the 640s.

The impact of pestilence

The necropolis of Santo Stefano *in Pertica* outside the Roman walls of Cividale contained several tombs constructed in a way that suggests a fear of the dead.[74] Among the forty-three graves excavated here was a group of fifteen burials, interpreted as a family group of seven 'rich' burials and eight 'poor' burials. These inhumations are different from other Lombard burials, even those in the same cemetery. The 'rich' interments are those of six young people or children and an aged warrior: the age and sex of the others is often difficult to establish. The former group was buried with goods including gold foil crosses, indicating that they identified themselves as Christians. Three (or so the excavator thought) were buried prone; all were protected by up to five slabs of stone laid at regular intervals in the earth above them. While this method of interment might at first look like a means of frustrating would-be grave robbers, the 'poor' inhumations, though much more shallow, are also protected by a single layer of stone – albeit broken and irregular, not like the solid slabs over the 'rich' burials.[75] It seems much more likely that these measures were designed to prevent the inhabitants of the graves from becoming revenants. The fact that two of the gold foil crosses are – unusually – stamped with the same design adds to the impression that we are dealing with deaths occurring close together. Were the 'rich' burials those of victims of the plague of c. 589–90 – and were they buried in this way because their community shared the intuition that they would return from the dead to carry others off?[76] Whatever the answer, it seems that that Christian funerary ritual was considered especially inadequate in these cases: another 'rich' burial of a young person in the same cemetery, with a gold foil cross similar to one found with this group – and therefore likely to date from around the same time – was placed in the soil, with no protective stone layers or surround.[77]

The 'poor' burials from this section of the Santo Stefano necropolis were interpreted by their excavator as those of servants or dependents of the warrior and young people in the 'rich' burials nearby. But their meagre grave goods – knives, beads, a comb, a buckle – could alternatively indicate a date in the latter part of the seventh century. Burial near the 'rich' group and also under stones may be an indication of attempts to isolate and neutralize potential revenants in this part of the cemetery in another, later outbreak of pestilence. Between 541 and c. 750 the Justinianic Pandemic affected many regions of Europe.[78] In the sixth century Gregory of Tours describes its appearance in Clermont-Ferrand; in Marseilles in the 580s and Rome in 590. Paul the Deacon describes an outbreak in Italy in the sixth century; the pestilence in Rome in 590; and another outbreak in Rome and Pavia in 680.[79] It devastated Ireland and England in the 660s. Although we cannot trace its movements in detail – in its typical 'saltatory' mode it appeared and disappeared without warning – it could have had the effect of slowing down the complete acceptance of Christian teaching about the dead or norms of burial, as communities feared that those first to die were liable to return to kill them as well.[80] Michael Kulikowski has noted the way in which in the pandemic even changed burial habits in the Spanish cities, former centres of Roman rule and Catholic Christianity, where, after the arrival of pestilence, there was an increase in multiple burials: several burials in a larger grave or more commonly the consecutive burial of several occupants in one, single tomb.[81] It appears that in Spain, from the late sixth century onwards, Christians from a Roman background began re-opening graves, in order to check that the dead were being reduced to stable bone and were not liable to turn into malevolent revenants. In the Eure-et-Loire region of Francia, the re-use of megalithic burial grounds appears to coincide with the period of the Justinianic Pandemic, suggesting that plague victims may have been buried at these sites: at a later date such structures would have leper-houses or asylums placed beside them, perhaps because of the associations with disease they had acquired in this period.[82] Plague must have encouraged the supposition that intuitions, rather than Christian doctrine, held the key to dealing with mortality. In northern Italy, where Lombard families and groups settled and in the seventh and eighth centuries took over older churches on their lands, using them for funerary purposes – a process seen by archaeologists as one of putting down roots and becoming Catholic – there are numerous signs of the re-use of graves and the tidying-away of the bones of the previous occupants, possibly in response to outbreaks of plague, as well as cases of interment with grave-goods.[83]

Modes of reassurance

Despite the gulf that initially existed between Christian teaching and non-Christian intuitions regarding death and the afterlife, the seventh and eighth centuries saw the narrowing of the gap between the two. The major changes came with the early development of what we would recognize as Purgatory and also with attempts at the retrospective Christianization of ancestors. There were also initiatives in some parts of what had been Burgundy to convince the laity that God would intervene at their death to help their souls to reach the Christian afterlife – and indeed that He was privy to their 'strategic' information and would intervene to help them in general. By the eighth century, we can even see the first development of a Christian liturgy for the dying to help their souls through the dangerous period when it left the body and usher it into the Christian afterlife.

Although reactions to plague are likely to have worked initially against the acceptance of Christian ideas of death and the afterlife, the repeated outbreaks of pestilence may in the end have contributed to their acceptance. The seventh century saw an important change in the Christian conception of the afterlife, with the emergence of early versions of what would develop over the centuries into the fully-fledged doctrine of Purgatory. In the older version of the afterlife, there were many sinners who, if their sins were not gross, were nevertheless condemned to wait out eternity in *refrigeria*, places of refreshment, until their souls were purified in the purgative fire preceding the Last Judgment. In traditional thinking there was no possibility of the living communicating with them. But as new forms of iterative penance developed, the question of what happened if a penance remained incomplete on an individual's death arose – particularly in an era when pandemic must have made this a frequent possibility. Hagiographic literature originating in the Columbanian group of monasteries in Neustria and Italy in the 640s has the souls of pious monks and nuns reaching the gates of Heaven – only to be sent back to expiate their sins on earth, through sickness and suffering. A new development in thinking about this problem came with the Irish monk Fursey's description of a visit to the afterlife in which he claimed he had heard that it was possible for penance to be continued there. After leaving Ireland, he worked in England for several years, before moving to Neustria and founding the monastery of Lagny. His vision was set down in writing on the continent after his death in the 650s, but it was known in England, where Bede reproduces a version of it in his *Ecclesiastical History*.[84] Bede's work also offers other versions of the afterlife, where the souls of those who had sinned – but not so greatly that they were instantly condemned to Hell – were purged of their sins in a variety of scenarios. Even deathbed penitents were incorporated in this vision. In the eighth century, an English abbess notified St Boniface about the vision experience of a monk of Wenlock, who had seen in the afterlife fiery pits that were not Hell: some of the souls there would be saved at the Last Judgment (while others crossed a bridge across a river of fire, before arriving in Paradise).[85] At the same time the Church suggested that the offering of prayers or masses for souls in these proto-Purgatories might ease their suffering or reduce the length of their stay there, thus laying the foundations for a medieval economy of salvation in which Christians could pay priests and monks to pray for the souls of their deceased relations. This offered the living a means of communication – albeit vicarious – with their family dead, combined with the reassurance that their souls had passed safely into the next world, from whence they could not return.

The exclusion of the pagan ancestor from Heaven was exemplified not only in the story of Radbod and in the *Dialogues* attributed to Gregory the Great, but would also be demonstrated by the Roman synod of 745. This council condemned two bishops working in Germany, Aldebert and Clement, who was described as an Irishman, at the instigation of the missionary St Boniface. Of Clement, the Synod noted that:

> Contrary to the teaching of the Fathers, he affirms that Christ descended into hell to deliver all those, believers and unbelievers, servants of Christ as well as worshippers of idols, who were confined there.[86]

Clement painted a reassuring picture for his Germanic audience, who would understand that they would be re-united with their ancestors after death in what amounts to a familiar, undifferentiated and encouragingly crowded version of the afterlife. There are indications from elsewhere that other clerics were willing to take a rather more merciful view in order to reassure their flocks that Christianity would not cut them off forever from their forbears – while at the same time emphasizing that a good life on earth was necessary for a good outcome in the afterlife. The anonymous *Life of Pope Gregory* by a monk of Whitby, composed in the early eighth century, contains a number of tales designed to instruct recent Anglo-Saxon converts. One relates how Pope Gregory was so moved by the thought of a just act performed by the Emperor Trajan that he wept copious tears – tears by which the soul of the pagan Trajan was retrospectively baptized. The implication of this story was that a long-dead pagan – though also by implication one who had given some evidence of just or moral behaviour – would be able to join his descendants in the Christian otherworld. A similar idea is expressed in a much later English poem in which St Erkenwald (Eorcenwald, bishop of London, 675–93) baptizes by tears a dead British pagan judge whose judgments had been just. Clement's version of the afterlife may have been an unacceptable one but he was evidently not the only priest or monk willing to provide comfort to the anxious who feared eternal separation from the ancestral dead.[87]

Powerful individuals and groups might also – perhaps encouraged by clerics who shared the more merciful view – take the matter of the ancestors into their own hands, Christianizing them retrospectively. Rodelinda, wife of the Lombard ruler Perctarit (672–88) had a church dedicated to the Virgin built at the site of the *perticas* burial ground outside the walls of Pavia, probably in the 670s.[88] Whether she had been encouraged by a sympathetic bishop, or whether this was a unilateral initiative on her part is not clear. Whichever was the case, she was both declaring her own Christianity and devotion to the Virgin and also her identification with the Lombard dead. In the 730s a traditional inauguration ceremony was performed there when Hildeprand was 'raised up by the Lombards' to be king.[89] Evidently, the ancestral dead still mattered – though they had now been re-framed in a Christian context. The same tactic of re-framing the ancestors is also apparent in some Lombard epigraphy, evident in the famous epitaph commissioned by Aldo in the church of S. Giovanni in Conca, Milan.[90] It proclaims his loyalty to family memory, while also advertising his role in the restructuring of the church, his wife's burial there and his own intention to be buried there. The process of retrospective Christianization of the ancestors through the construction of new Christian funerary chapels or churches in older graveyards is evident elsewhere: Bailey K. Young has argued that in eastern Merovingian Francia, the construction of chapels in wood or stone on burial grounds was more common than one might at first imagine.[91] Béatrice Privati's publication of the excavation at Sézegnin, near Geneva, points to the existence of a wooden building interpreted as a chapel.[92] Thus it seems to have been the case that the hard-line approach to the ancestral dead might sometimes be softened in theory; and it could effectively be mitigated in practice, by the creation of churches in ancestral cemeteries.

Some of the most intriguing items found graves of this era are the 'Daniel' plate-buckles (or plaque-buckles) discovered in Switzerland and in the Jura, the Savoie and Burgundy regions of France. Although generally referred to, for convenience, as Burgundian, they date from the sixth and seventh centuries – that is, the period when, after 534, the former Burgundian kingdom had been annexed and formed part of Merovingian Francia.[93] They are remarkable in many ways. Like the Lombard gold foil crosses, they are grave goods indicative of Christianity; but whereas the foil crosses were manufactured purely for funerary use, buckles constituted an item of clothing or adornment for the living, though they are commonly found in grave goods (and plate-buckles are commoner in male than female Frankish graves).[94] We cannot be certain whether these buckles were ever worn – or whether, as their unusual decoration and inscriptions might suggest – they were crafted with a funerary use in mind.

These rectangular bronze belt-fittings bore central depictions, generally of the Biblical scene of Daniel in the lions' den, though one is of Christ's entry into Jerusalem and another depicts two praying figures. The central scene is surrounded by inscriptions; some buckles also have lettering on the back. The inscriptions often give the name of the craftsman who made them, together with that of a recipient: in one case, the latter is a cleric, in another (perhaps) a deacon. As such buckles are not items of clerical apparel, it has been suggested that it was made for the cleric, who presented it to the person in whose grave it was found. In some cases, the lettering is enigmatic, but in the form of a

Daniel and Habakkuk on plate-buckle from Châlon-sur-Saône

palindrome, indicating magical or apotropaic significance.[95] Some buckles have a hidden compartment, interpreted as a container for relics: analysis of one revealed traces of imported cotton fibre, another indication of their function as portable reliquaries.[96]

Together with this reliquary function, the prevalence of the depiction of Daniel on these objects has attracted much attention. They have been characterized as prophylactic or apotropaic in nature, produced with the aim of protecting the wearer in a funerary context, through their inscription, the relic (where present) and their imagery. In the legend of the Vulgate *Book of Daniel* (or the apocryphal *Bel and the Dragon*), God not only miraculously protects Daniel in the lions' den, but also sends an angel to transport the prophet Habakkuk to him, to bring him food.[97] One of the buckles includes a representation of Habakkuk as well as of Daniel and the lions. In a funerary context, reference to this narrative indicates that God would shield the soul from harm, nourish it and bring it to a good outcome. The buckles are Christianized grave goods, which simultaneously acknowledge intuitions of death as a liminal process and the existence of fears about the soul, while at the same assuring wearer than when the soul leaves the body, it will be shielded and cared for by God Himself, just as Daniel was. One commentator observes that Daniel's name and example 'figure in the litany of *Commendatio animae*, no doubt particularly familiar to Merovingian Christians.'[98] But there is no evidence to indicate that the litany existed or was widely known at this stage. Instead, the presence of the buckles in graves seems a positive indication that it was not. They were produced under the direction of clerics or monasteries, both groups that are known to include metalworkers at this period, then distributed to named individuals – or manufactured for a named cleric.[99] It appears that monasteries and clerics in Burgundy were setting out to address one of the most profound gaps between Christian doctrine and popular intuitions – the areas of death and the transit of the soul to the afterlife.

The regional nature of the distribution of the buckles is also of significance. They are largely found in the eastern parts of the former Burgundian kingdom, especially north of Lake Geneva, and not in the same area as the epitaphs of an earlier date discussed above (p. 150). They were discovered mainly in the areas of earliest Burgundian settlement and the sources hint that there might have been a stronger Homoian presence there during the reign of Gundobad. One buckle in particular even suggests that the Church was now ready to confront the problem not only of intuitions about death but also those about God. The 'Landelinus' buckle, though crudely executed in technical terms nevertheless conveys a wide range of meanings. While it depicts a mounted figure reminiscent of non-Christian iconography, it also references a number of Biblical texts and the ambiguity is probably intentional. At its centre is a fierce warrior Christ mounted on a stallion, with the Chi-Ro symbol to one side of him and the Beast of the Apocalypse on the other. The inscription refers to a 'numen' and living 'a thousand years'; and the figure is plausibly interpreted as that of Revelation 19.11-15:

> And I saw heaven opened and behold a white horse; and he that sat upon him was called Faithful and True, and in righteousness, he doth judge and make war.
>
> His eyes were as a flame of fire and on his head were many crowns …
>
> … And out of his mouth goeth a sharp sword that with it he should smite the nations.

In addition to its millenarian aspect, the buckle also expresses a view of the Christian God. Not only does the intense stare of the eyes match the description of the apocalyptic text: it also reflects the all-seeing nature of Christ, just as the extra-large ears reflect his all-hearing ability. The triumphant Christ of the Apocalypse is also a God who sees and hears everything, who has access to 'strategic' knowledge about what the owner of the buckle thinks and does. At the same time the object itself declares an apotropaic quality – the inscription read 'Landelinus made [this] *numen*' or sacred power: 'he who possesses it, may he live a thousand years in the Lord.'[100]

'Landelinus' buckle

This focus on the intervention of God reminds us that that the 'Arian' – Homoian – Christian view of God had originally been designed to capture intuitions of a creator god, remote from the world, who did not intervene in human affairs. We have no way of telling exactly how far beyond this stage Homoianism in Burgundy advanced: the discussions between the Catholic Bishop Avitus of Vienne and Gundobad's *sacerdotes* (see Chapters 3 and 4 above) suggest that some of the latter thought in terms almost of three separate Gods. What Burgundian warriors thought in terms of must remain conjecture, but it is quite possible that their understanding of the Christian God was still a largely intuitive one and that this basic understanding persisted in this region into the Frankish period.[101]

We have no way of knowing exactly when Christian funerary liturgy began to focus on the transition of the soul into the afterlife: but a ritual accompaniment to death itself – as opposed to a rite for the person who had already died – appears in the Gellone Sacramentary, which, according to Deshusses, was copied in the 790s for Bishop Hildoard of Cambrai.[102] This is regarded as 'a new moment in the death ritual'.[103] The prayer *Proficiscere anima* is recited by those gathered around the deathbed. It connects them with the entire community of the blessed both in Heaven and on earth and exhorts the soul of the dying person to go forth from the body in the name of the Father, Son and heavenly host. The prayer is followed by a prose litany: 'Free, Lord the soul of your servant' – urging God to intervene as he had intervened to deliver Noah, Enoch and Elijah, Moses, Job, Daniel, Jonah, David and finally Peter and Paul.[104] The Sacramentary, which originated in late eighth-century Francia also contains a series of ante-mortem rituals 'On the migration of the soul'.[105]

By the late eighth century, the Church in Francia had at last evolved a liminal stage missing from its earlier death rituals: it had created a ritual of transition for the soul, surrounding the dying person with the prayers of the living and the imploring the intervention of Heaven. All these actions focused on the elements that had been the cause of such anxiety to the Germanic peoples not just as they entered the world of Christianity but for centuries after – the exit of the soul from the body and its safe transition to a life beyond the grave.

***

To end a book with a chapter on death and at the point where the Frankish Church produced a deathbed liturgy addressing the most basic intuitions and fears about the dead might look like an attempt to suggest some sort of closure or resolution. This is not the intention. The aim has been to open up further areas for discussion and to signal possibilities for future research. Where death and funerary ritual are concerned, for example, many discussions are still conducted in functionalist terms; or focus on arguments about the ethnicity or non-ethnicity of objects; or proclaim the 'archaeological invisibility' of peoples. One of the most frustrating aspects of current approaches, even if there has recently been a heartening move away from the labelling of any post-depositional disturbance or manipulation of bodies as 'grave-robbing', is the widespread lack of attention to the reasons behind the opening and reuse of graves. This area demands further thought. Another desiderandum is the further consideration of the impact of the Justinianic Plague. Its sporadic but devastating appearance may initially have served to reinforce traditional intuitions about the dead – thus providing the impetus for the Church to formulate a version of the Christian afterlife and Christian rites for the dying which coped better with people's fears. We need to know more about the presence of pandemic and its relationship to traditional burial practices and as scientists are currently developing new ways of testing remains for signs of the aDNA of pestilence, we may be able to estimate its role more clearly in the history of beliefs about the dead and funerary ritual.

This book has been about history but has also attempted to indicate that for historians of religion, a cognitive approach is extremely useful when data is scarce, opening up new frameworks for the comparative study of divinities and for our understanding of peoples' first encounters with Christianity. It could easily be extended to other groups on the fringes of the Roman Empire – Gepids, Marcomanni, Rugians and Herules, as well as to the aggressively 'Arian' Vandals in North Africa and to the later Thuringii, Alamanni and Saxons. The struggles of many rulers to escape the limitations of this 'entry-level' Christianity throw further light on the connection between Catholicism and the emergence of royal authority – as has already been done to some extent for Anglo-Saxon England – but we might look further at the relationship between Homoianism or syncretism and military rituals. A cognitive approach can create new ways of looking at belief and practice in areas where Catholic Christianity was the official religion. Instead of thinking in terms of a conflict between Christianity and 'pagan' survivals, or 'superstition', it suggests it is more productive to think in terms of 'nonreflective' beliefs that were not Christian and of attempts to replace them by Christian 'nonreflective' beliefs supporting Christian 'reflective' belief. This in turn suggests a way ahead in terms of early medieval religion, based not on broad-brush studies, but on micro-histories of individual areas, examining the manner in which Christian pastoral structures – dioceses, parishes, monasteries – and more familiar elements of 'reflective' belief, encouraged by masses, sermons, saints' lives and homilies, were supported by 'nonreflective' elements such as tomb-cults, the presence of relics and the use of iterative penance. Other significant elements to be brought into this picture would be the presence or absence of non-Christian sites of power – stones, water, trees – and their Christianization (or lack of it). The funerary liturgy in use in the area and any changes in burial rites could also be factored in. We also need to consider what other aspects of Christian practice might be considered as creating 'nonreflective' belief: could a cognitive approach be used, for example, in the area of food taboos and ideas of ritual pollution which we find in some areas of the early medieval Church? There are many areas to be explored through the use of the cognitive science of religion, which not only gives us many things to think with (and will undoubtedly go on to give us more) but also many things to think about …

Notes

Chapter 1

1 P. Heather, *The Goths* (Oxford, 1996), 128.

2 G. Halsall, *Barbarian Migrations and the Roman West 376–568* (Cambridge, 2007), 211.

3 K. Escher, *Les Burgondes, I^e–VIe Siècle apr. J.-C.* (Paris, 2006), 24–32; 61–6.

4 P. de Vingo, *From Tribe to Province to State* BAR International Series 2117 (Oxford, 2010), 59.

5 For a recent overview, see E. James, *Europe's Barbarians AD 200–600* (London, 2009).

6 James, *Europe's Barbarians*, 128.

7 Halsall, *Barbarian Migrations*, 35–45.

8 Heather, *Goths*, 166–78, at 178.

9 C. Mercier and M. Mercier-Rolland, *Le Cimitière Burgonde de Monnet-la-Ville* (Paris, 1974), 34; H. Gaillard de Sémainville, 'À propos de l'implantation des Burgondes: réflexions, hypothèses et perspectives', in *Burgondes Alamans Francs Romains dans l'est de la France, le sud-ouest de l' Allemagne et la Suisse* (Besançon, 2003), 17–39. G. Baggieri, 'Approccio antropologico sul cavaliere guerriero longobardo della necropoli di San Mauro a Cividale', in E. A. Arslan and M. Buora (eds), *L' Oro degli Avari. Popolo delle Steppe in Europa* (Milan, 2000), 206–9, discusses a 'mysterious' and similar dental formation in a warrior, who may be an Avar, buried with his horse in a Lombard cemetery at Cividale.

10 For the latter, see Heather, *Goths*; P. Heather and J. Matthews, *The Goths in the Fourth Century* (Liverpool, 1991); P. Heather (ed.), *The Visigoths – From the Migration Period to the Seventh Century. An Ethnographic Perspective* (Woodbridge, 1999); E. James, *The Franks* (Oxford, 1991); I. N. Wood, *The Merovingian Kingdoms, 450–751* (London and New York, 1994); S. J. Barnish, and F. Marazzi (eds), *The Ostrogoths From the Migration Period to the Sixth Century* (Woodbridge, 2007); N. Christie, *The Lombards. The Ancient Longobards* (Oxford, 1995); G. Ausenda, P. Delogu, and C. Wickham (eds), *The Langobards Before the Frankish Conquest: An Ethnographic Perspective* (Woodbridge, 2009); K. Escher, *Burgondes*.

11	See R. Collins, 'King Leovigild and the conversion of the Visigoths' in *idem*, *Law, Culture and Regionalism in Early Medieval Spain* (Aldershot, 1992), II, 1–12; and E. A. Thompson, 'The conversion of the Spanish Suevi to Catholicism', in E. James (ed.), *Visigothic Spain: New Approaches* (Oxford, 1980), 77–92.

12	R. Fletcher, *The Conversion of Europe 371–1386 AD* (London, 1997); P. R. L. Brown, *The Rise of Western Christendom: Triumph and Diversity, 200–1000 AD* (Oxford, 1996 and 2003).

13	K. Dowden, *European Paganism: the Realities of Cult from Antiquity to the Middle Ages* (London, 1999); C. M. Cusack, *The Rise of Christianity in Northern Europe 300–1000* (London, 1998).

14	V. I. J. Flint, *The Rise of Magic in Early Medieval Europe* (Oxford, 1991). For reactions, see A. Murray, 'Missionaries and magic in dark-age Europe', *Past and Present* 136 (1992), 186–205; and R. Kieckhefer, 'The specific rationality of medieval magic', *AHR* 99 (1994), 813–34. In a recent study of relics, *Holy Bones, Holy Dust. How Relics Shaped the History of Medieval Europe* (New Haven, CT and London, 2011), 50–1, Charles Freeman follows Flint.

15	J. C. Russell, *The Germanization of Early Medieval Christianity: A Sociohistorical Approach to Religious Transformation* (Oxford, 1994). See the critical review by H. Rosenberg, *Journal of Early Christian Studies* 5 (1997), 127–8.

16	M. Dunn, *The Christianization of the Anglo-Saxons c. 597–c.700* (London, 2009).

17	For a robust response to critics of the cognitive approach, see E. Cohen, J. A. Lanman, H. Whitehouse and R. N. McCauley, 'Common criticisms of the Cognitive Science of Religion – answered', *Council of Societies for the Study of Religion Bulletin* 37 (4) (2008), 112–5.

18	See R. North, *Heathen Gods in Old English Literature* (Cambridge, 1997); P. A. Shaw, *Pagan Goddesses in the Early Germanic World. Eostre, Hreda and the Cult of Matrons* (London, 2011).

19	P. Boyer, *The Naturalness of Religious Ideas* (Berkeley, Los Angeles and London, 1994), 296. See also S. Atran, *In Gods We Trust: the Evolutionary Landscape of Religion* (Oxford and New York, 2002), 10.

20	E. T. Lawson, 'The wedding of psychology, ethnography, and history: methodological bigamy or tripartite free love?' in H. Whitehouse and L. Martin (eds), *Theorizing Religions Past: Archaeology, History and Cognition* (Walnut Creek, CA, Lanham, New York, Toronto and Oxford, 2004), 1–6, at 4.

21	Boyer, *Naturalness*, 141–54.

22	Boyer, *Religion Explained. The Human Instincts That Fashion Gods Spirits and Ancestors* (London, 2002), 262–302.

23   H. Whitehouse, 'Theorizing religions past', in Whitehouse and Martin (eds), *Theorizing Religions Past*, 215–32, at 223.

24   J. L. Barrett, *Why Would Anyone Believe in God?* (Lanham, MD, Boulder, New York, Toronto and Plymouth, 2004), 31–44; *idem, Cognitive Science, Religion and Theology* (West Conshohocken, PA, 2011), 100–2.

25   K. Schäferdiek, 'Die Anfänge des Christentums bei den Goten und der sogenannte Gotische Arianismus', *ZKG* 112 (2001), 295–310; *idem*, 'Germanic and Celtic Christianities', in A. Casiday and F. W. Norris (eds), *The Cambridge History of Christianity*, vol. 2, *Constantine to c. 600* (Cambridge, 2007), 52–69. The decisive German contribution to our understanding of Homoianism continues with U. Heil's study of the Homoian Church in Burgundy: *Avitus von Vienne und die homöische Kirche der Burgunder* (Berlin and Boston, 2011).

26   See M. Dunn, 'Intuiting gods: creed and cognition in the fourth century', *Historical Reflections/Reflexions Historiques* 38 (2012), 1–23.

27   R. Horton, 'African conversion', *Africa* 41 (1971), 85–108; *idem*, 'On the rationality of conversion', *Africa* 45 (1975), 219–35; 373–99.

28   Barrett, *Why Would Anyone Believe*, 9.

29   Barrett, *Why Would Anyone Believe*, 12.

30   Boyer, *Religion Explained*, 260.

31   Boyer, *Religion Explained*, 241.

Chapter 2

1   For an overview of earlier general interpretations of Germanic and Celtic religions and deities, see H. R. Ellis Davidson, *The Lost Beliefs of Northern Europe* (London, 1993), 144–59, 'The Interpreters'. Some of Dumézil's ideas still form part of current discussions: see M. Arnold, *Thor. Myth to Marvel* (London, 2011), 45–7, who uses Dumézil's theories of the common Indo-European origins of gods. At 35, he also discusses some of Lévi-Strauss' ideas.

2   R. Fletcher, *The Conversion of Europe From Paganism to Christianity 371–1386 AD* (London, 1997), 4.

3   H. R. Ellis Davidson, *The Road to Hel: A Study of the Conception of the Dead in Old Norse Literature* (Cambridge, 1943); *Gods and Myths of Northern Europe* (Harmondsworth, 1964); *Myths and Symbols in Pagan Europe: Early Scandinavian and Celtic Religions* (Manchester, 1988); *Lost Beliefs*; B. Branston, *The Lost Gods of England* (2nd edn, London, 1974); R. North, *Heathen Gods in Old English Literature* (Cambridge, 1997). The approach embodied in the

last work meant that it was no longer possible to say, as David Wilson did, in *Anglo-Saxon Paganism* (London and New York, 1992), 3, that information from the thirteenth-century work of Snorri Sturlusson, is 'projected-back to pagan Anglo-Saxon England, as though the differences in time and space were irrelevant, and pagan beliefs remained static and uniform.'

4   See Dunn, *Christianization of the Anglo-Saxons*, Ch. 4 for earlier approaches.

5   A. R. Birley, *Tacitus: Agricola and Germany* (Oxford, 1999), xxx.

6   Heather, *Goths*, 9.

7   A. Bracciotti, *Origo Gentis Langobardorum. Introduzione, testo critico, commento*, Biblioteca di Culture Romanobarbarica 2 (Rome, 1998), 7–9.

8   *Germania* 40: Birley, *Agricola and Germany* 58 and 126–7.

9   *Germania* 43: *ibid.* 59, 130.

10   *Germania* 9: *ibid.* 42.

11   For Tacitus, weekdays and the identification of Germanic gods, see R. Simek, *Götter und Kulte der Germanen* (Munich, 2004), 57–63.

12   *Origo* 1, Bracciotti (ed.), 105–7. See also the version of the tale in Paul the Deacon *HL* I, 8. English translation in E. Peters (ed.) and W. D. Foulke (trans.), Paul the Deacon, *History of the Lombards* (Philadelphia, PN, 1974), 16–17; and Appendix, 316–7, for the *Origo*.

13   *DLH* II 28: trans. L. Thorpe, *History of the Franks* (Harmondsworth, 1974), 141–2.

14   *DLH* IV, 25; V, 38; IV, 1; V, 21: *History of the Franks*, 219, 301, 197, 288.

15   North, *Heathen Gods*, 26–43; Dunn, *Christianization of the Anglo-Saxons*, 61.

16   See North, *Heathen Gods*, 1–25.

17   Martin of Braga, *De Correctione Rusticorum*, 18, in C. W. Barlow (ed.), *Martini Episcopi Bracarensis Opera Omnia* (New Haven, CT, 1950), 202. See also the partial English translation in J. N. Hillgarth, *The Conversion of Western Europe, 350–750* (Englewood Cliffs, NJ, 1969), 55–63, at 62; Canon 15 of the Council of Narbonne, 589, in C. de Clercq (ed.), *Concilia Galliae a. 511–a. 695, Corpus Christianorum, Series Latina* 148A (Turnhout, 1963), 257. A. Ambrosia de Pina, 'S. Martinho de Dume e la sobrevivencia de la mitologia suevica', *Bracara Augusta* 9–10 (1958), 58–66, assumes that the Sueves were familiar with later Scandinavian deities such as Sif and also with the concept of Valhalla.

18   Cæsar, *De bello gallico*, VI, 17: trans. H. J. Edwards, *The Gallic War, Julius Cæsar* (Cambridge, MA, 1917), 104. For Tacitus' borrowing from earlier authors, see North, *Heathen Gods*, 78–9.

19   T. Derks, *Gods, Temples and Ritual Practices. The Transformation of Religious Ideas and Values in Roman Gaul* (Amsterdam, 1998), 81–94; and also

J. Webster, '"Interpretatio": Roman word power and the Celtic gods', *Britannia* 26 (1995), 153–61.

20   On Nzame and another powerful African creator, Mebeghe, see Boyer, *Religion Explained*, 160.

21   C. H. Talbot (ed.), *The Anglo-Saxon Missionaries in Germany* (London and New York, 1954), 76.

22   Tacitus, *Annales*, XIII, 5: trans. M. Grant, *Tacitus. The Annals of Imperial Rome* (London, 1996), 311–12.

23   See M. Kingsley, *Travels in West Africa. Congo Français, Corisco and Cameroons* (London, 1897), 508 for observations on last-ditch appeals to the mightiest god in an African context.

24   Derks, *Gods, Temples and Ritual Practices*, 91.

25   Webster, '"Interpretatio"', 157, observes that 'It is, for example, more likely that the high proportion of name-pairings involving the Roman war god Mars (36 from the total of 65) reflects the concerns of soldier dedicants, rather than the often-cited warlike nature of the Celtic gods.' See also *eadem*, 'Necessary comparisons: a post-colonial approach to religious syncretism in the Roman Empire', *World Archaeology* 28 (1997), 324–38; and also her 'Creolizing the Roman provinces', *American Journal of Archaeology* 105 (2001), 209–25.

26   Derks, *Gods, Temples and Ritual Practices*, 9: 'a transformation of the indigenous universes resulting from integration in the Roman Empire ... visible in a change of names'. Derks is looking at the association of Roman and native names, but the assumption is generally valid. See also Derks, 'The perception of the Roman pantheon by a native elite: the example of votive inscriptions from Lower Germany', in N. Roymans and F. Theuws (eds), *Images of the Past* (Amsterdam, 1991), 235–65.

27   Translated in Dowden, *European Paganism*, 276.

28   *Ibid.*

29   See North, *Heathen Gods*, 1–25.

30   *Germania* 39: Birley, *Agricola and Germany*, 56.

31   North, *Heathen Gods*, 230.

32   Jordanes, *Getica* v, 41 and v, 40.

33   Heather, *Goths*, 10.

34   E. A. Thompson, *The Huns* (Oxford, 1996), 97.

35   A. H. Merrills, *History and Geography in Late Antiquity* (Cambridge, 2005), 100–69, 'Jordanes'.

36   *Ibid.*, esp. 138.

37   *Aeneid* III, 1–69.

38   Merrills, *History and Geography*, 61–2.

39   P. Heather and J. Matthews, *Goths in the Fourth Century*, 154; E. A.
      Thompson, *The Visigoths in the Time of Ulfila* (Oxford, 1966), 57; North,
      Heathen Gods, 139–41; P. Pieper, 'Autopsie und Experimenta zur
      Runeninschrift auf dem Goldreif von Pietroasa', in W. Heizmann and A. van
      Nahl (eds), *Runica-Germanica-Mediaevalia, Ergänzungsbände zum Reallexikon
      der Germanischen Altertumskunde* (Berlin and New York, 2003), 595–646;
      A. Schwarcz, 'Cult and religion among the Tervingi and Visigoths and
      their conversion to Christianity', in P. Heather (ed.), *The Visigoths – From
      the Migration Period to the Seventh Century. An Ethnographic Perspective*
      (Woodbridge, 1999), 447–59.

40   North, *Heathen Gods*, 138.

41   M. Kingsley, *West African Studies* (3rd edn, London, 1964), 406. She also
      observes, at 131, that Nzambi was frequently 'confused' by Africans with the
      Virgin Mary when the Portuguese introduced Catholicism to parts of West
      Africa.

42   Freyja was famously insulted by Hjalti Skeggjason, one of the supporters of
      conversion of Iceland to Christianity, who was outlawed at the Allthing for his
      blasphemy: K. von See, 'Der Spottvers des Hjalti Skeggjason', *Zeitschrift für
      deutsches Altertum* 97 (1968), 155–8.

43   Boyer, *Religion Explained*, 159–60.

44   Kingsley, *West African Studies*, 408.

45   North, *Heathen Gods*, 136.

46   *De S. Barbato Episcopo Beneventano in Italia*, AASS, Feb. III, 139–42 at 139:
      *His vero diebus quamuis sacri baptismatis unda Longobardi abluerentur,
      tamen priscum gentilitatis ritum tenentes, siue bestiali mente degebant, bestiæ
      simulachro, quæ vulgo Vipera nominatur, flectebant colla, quæ debite suo
      debebant flectere Creatori.*

47   See W. Pohl, 'Deliberate ambiguity: the Lombards and Christianity', in G.
      Armstrong and I. Wood (eds), *Converting Peoples and Christianizing Individuals*,
      International Medieval Research 7 (Turnhout, 2000), 47–58, esp. 51; J-M.
      Martin, 'À propos de la vita de Barbatus, évêque de Bénévent', *Mélanges de l'
      École française de Rome, Moyen Âge, Temps Modernes* 86 (1) (1974), 137–64.
      The association with Woden seems least likely, as in the Old English Nine Herbs
      Charm, Woden 'smites' a snake which bit a man: see North, *Heathen Gods*, 85–7.

48   In the seventeenth century an archdeacon writing under the pseudonym
      'Marius de Vipera' produced a *Chronologia Episcoporum et Archiepiscoporum
      Metropolitanae Ecclesiae Beneventanae* (Naples, 1636).

49 J–M. Martin, 'La Longobardia meridionale', in S. Gasparri (ed.), *Il Regno dei Longobardi in Italia* (Spoleto, 2004), 327–65 and also P. Peduto, 'Insediamenti longobardi del ducato di Benevento (sec. VI–VIII)', 367–442 in the same volume.

50 For the shrine of the Archangel Michael at Monte Gargano, see C. Carletti and G. Otranto (eds), *Culto e Insediamenti Micaelici nell' Italia Meridionale fra Tarda Antichità e Medioevo* (Bari, 1994).

51 *Vita Barbati De S. Barbato Episcopo Beneventano In Italia*, *AASS*, Feb. III, 140: *qui scrutatur renes et corda.*

52 Derks, *Gods, Temple and Ritual Practices*, 119–30; P. A. Shaw, *Pagan Goddesses in the Early Germanic World. Eostre, Hreda and the Cult of Matrons* (London, 2011), 37–48.

53 *Ibid.*, 45.

54 *Ibid.*, 47.

55 Bede, *De Temporum Ratione* c. 15: trans. F. Wallis, *Bede: The Reckoning of Time* (Liverpool, 1999), 53.

56 *Ibid.*, 53–4.

57 Shaw, *Pagan Goddesses*, 73–97 for a full discussion of Bede's text and the debates over the existence of this goddess and possible interpretations of her name.

58 Barrett, *Why Would Anyone Believe*, 89.

59 K. L. Jolly, *Popular Religion in Late Anglo-Saxon England* (Chapel Hill, NC, 1996), 134.

60 A. Hall, *Elves in Anglo-Saxon England. Matters of Belief, Health, Gender and Identity* (Woodbridge, 2007).

61 W. Boudriot, *Die Altgermanische Religion* (Bonn, 1928), 51; *Corrector* 103, translation in J. McNeill and H. Gamer, *Medieval Handbooks of Penance* (New York, 1938), 335.

62 Boudriot, *Altgermanische Religion* 51, *Corrector* 152, McNeill and Gamer *Medieval Handbooks*, 339; Boudriot *Altgermanische Religion* 52, *Corrector* 150, McNeill and Gamer, *Medieval Handbooks*, 338.

63 Martin of Braga, *De Correctione Rusticorum*, C. W. Barlow (ed.) *Martini Episcopi Bracarensis Opera Omnia*, Papers and Monographs of the American Academy in Rome, XII (New Haven, CT, 1950), 159–203. Translated (largely but not completely) as *On the Castigation of Rustics* in J. N. Hillgarth, *The Conversion of Western Europe* (Englewood Cliffs, NJ, 1969), 55–63.

64 See A. Róna-Tás, *Hungarians and Europe in the Early Middle Ages* (Budapest and New York, 1999), 151. Thompson, *The Huns*, does not deal with Hunnic religion.

65   Tacitus, *Germania*, ch. 40: trans. Birley, *Agricola and Germany*, 58.

66   Sozomen, *Ecclesiastical History* 6, 37, 13, translated in P. Schaff and H. Wace (eds), *Socrates, Sozomenus: Church Histories, Nicene and Post-Nicene Fathers* (2nd Series, vol. 2. 1890, reprinted Peabody, MA, 1999), 374.

67   Thompson, *Visigoths*, 61 and n. 1.

68   H. Wolfram, trans. T. Dunlap, *History of the Goths* (Berkeley, 1987), 108.

69   *GC* 76; trans. R. Van Dam, *Gregory of Tours. Glory of the Confessors* (Liverpool, 1988), 80.

70   North, *Heathen Gods*, 26–43.

71   Tacitus, *Germania*, ch. 39: trans. Birley, *Agricola and Germany*, 57.

72   *Ibid.*

73   See H. Whitehouse, 'Rites of terror: emotion, metaphor and memory in Melanesian initiation cults', *Journal of the Royal Anthropological Institute* 2 (4) (1996), 703–15; *idem, Arguments and Icons: Divergent Modes of Religiosity* (Oxford, 2000), 7–9; Whitehouse and Martin (eds) *Theorizing Religions Past*, 11.

74   Boyer, *Religion Explained*, 279–82.

75   Wolfram, *Goths*, 108.

76   *Vita Barbati De S. Barbato Episcopo Beneventano In Italia, AASS*, Feb. III, 140: *Quin etiam non longe a Beneuenti mœnibus ... deuotissime sacrilegam colebant arborem, in qua suspenso corio, cuncti qui aderant terga vertentes arbori, celerius equitabant, calcaribus cruentantes equos; vt vnus alterum posset præire: atque in eodem cursu retrouersis manibus in corium iaculabantur. Sicque particulam modicam ex eo comedendam superstitiose accipiebant. Et quia stulta illic persoluebant vota, ab actione nomen loco illi, sicut hactenus dicitur, Votum imposuerunt.*

77   Martin, 'À propos de la vita', 149–50.

78   Martin proposes an alternative reading, missing the point of the spears being thrown backwards.

79   K. Fischer Drew, *The Lombard Laws* (Philadephia, 1973), 53–4: Rothair's Laws, 7.

80   Boyer, *Religion Explained*, 270.

81   *Germania*, ch. 39, trans. Birley, *Agricola and Germany*, 58.

82   North, *Heathen Gods*, 47.

83   North, *Heathen Gods*, 26–48, also making a connection to the wagon tour of the last Merovingian.

84   Wolfram, *Goths*, 108.

85   Wolfram, *Goths*, 108.

86 Dunn, *Christianization of the Anglo-Saxons*, 79–83.

87 *VP* 6, 2, English trans. E. James, *Life of the Fathers* (Liverpool, 1985), 53–4.

88 Boyer, *Naturalness*, 141–54.

89 For a translation of the relevant parts of Childebert's ordinance decreeing the removal of both, see B. Filotas, *Pagan Survivals, Superstitions and Popular Cultures in Early Medieval Pastoral Literature* (Toronto, 2005), 86; Filotas, 64 and 86 also notes the difference between simulacra and idols. J. M. Wallace-Hadrill, *The Frankish Church* (Oxford, 1983), 32, dates the ordnance to 533 or soon after, as it seems to be contingent on Canon 20 of the Council of Orléans of that year, while Filotas gives the traditional date of 554.

90 *Registrum* VIII, 4: D. Norberg (ed.), *S. Gregorii Magni Registrum Epistularum* vol. II, Corpus Christianorum, Series Latina 140a (Turnhout, 1982), 521.

91 D. M. Deliyannis (trans.), *Agnellus of Ravenna. The Book of Pontiffs of the Church of Ravenna* (Washington, DC, 2004), 165–6. The entry is for the episcopate of Aurelian, a Catholic bishop in the time of Theoderic.

92 C. M. Cusack, *The Sacred Tree: Ancient and Medieval Manifestations* (Newcastle upon Tyne, 2011), ix.

93 See Dowden, *European Paganism*, 62–5.

94 Dowden, *European Paganism*, 70.

95 Dowden, *European Paganism*, 74.

96 Dowden, *European Paganism*, 39–57.

97 *Life of St Boniface*, ch. 6: Talbot, *Anglo-Saxon Missionaries in Germany*, 45.

98 Dowden, *European Paganism*, 65.

99 *Ibid.*

100 Boyer, *Naturalness*, 147.

Chapter 3

1 The label Homoian is coming into more frequent use: for example, U. Heil, *Avitus von Vienne und die homöische Kirche der Burgunder* (Berlin and Boston, 2011).

2 Translation in R. Williams, *Arius* (2nd edn, London, 2001), 278.

3 R. P. C. Hanson, The *Search for the Christian Doctrine of God* (Edinburgh, 1988), 217–35.

4 Translation in Hanson, *Search*, 163.

5 For the Greek philosophical roots of *ousia,* and its use in early creeds, see C. Stead, *Divine Substance* (Oxford, 1977). Hanson, *Search*, 181–90, points out

that in the early stages of the development of Trinitarian doctrine, the technical terms *hypostasis* and *ousia* were generally assumed in the West to mean more or less the same thing, rather than having the distinct meanings of 'person' and 'substance' which would be attached to them slightly later.

6   Translation in Hanson, *Search*, 363–4.

7   Hanson, *Search*, 348–71; W. A. Löhr, 'A sense of tradition: the Homoiousian church party', in M. R. Barnes and D. H. Williams (eds), *Arianism After Arius: Essays on the Development of Fourth Century Trinitarian Conflicts*. Edinburgh, 1993, 81–100; *idem, Die Entstehung der homöischen und homöousianischen Kirchenparteien – Studien zur Synodalgeschichte des 4 Jahrhunderts* (Bonn, 1986), 44–102, 142–8.

8   Sozomen, *Ecclesiastical History* IV, 17, 2, in P. Schaff and H. Wace, *Socrates, Sozomenus: Church Histories, Nicene and Post-Nicene Fathers* (2nd Series, vol. 2. 1890, reprinted Peabody, MA, 1999), 312, gives a figure of about 400 bishops present; the *Sacred History of Sulpitius Severus* 41, translated in P. Schaff and H. Wace, *Sulpitius Severus, Vincent of Lerins, John Cassian, Nicene and Post-Nicene Fathers* (2nd Series, vol. 11. 1894, reprinted Peabody, MA, 1994), 116–7 asserts that eighty of these were 'Arians'. However, Maximinus, the Homoian who debated with St. Augustine in the 420s, thought that there had been 330 signatories to the Creed of Rimini: see 'Debate with Maximinus', 2, in R. J. Teske (ed.), *The Works of St Augustine. A Translation for the 21st Century, I/18: Arianism and Other Heresies* (New York, 1995), 188.

9   Hanson, *Search*, 364; for the letter of instruction sent by Constantius, see the translation in L. R. Wickham, *Hilary of Poitiers. Conflicts of Conscience and Law in the Fourth-century Church* (Liverpool, 1997), 81.

10   Hanson, *Search*, 380 for a translation of the final section.

11   D. H. Williams, *Ambrose of Milan and the End of the Nicene-Arian Conflicts* (Oxford, 1995), 32. See H. C. Brennecke, *Studien zur Geschichte der Homöer* (Tübingen, 1988), 5–56; Hanson, *Search*, 271–86; Löhr, 'Sense of Tradition', 83–7; and Williams, *Ambrose*, 22–37 for the events and creeds of Rimini-Seleucia-Nike-Constantinople.

12   R. Williams, *Arius*, 101–3.

13   M. Wiles, 'Attitudes to Arius in the Arian Controversy', in Barnes and Williams (eds), *Arianism After Arius*, 31–43; *idem, Archetypal Heresy. Arianism Through the Centuries* (Oxford, 1996), 6; R. Lyman, 'A topography of heresy: mapping the rhetorical creation of Arianism', in *Arianism After Arius*, 45–62; R. P. Vaggione, 'Of monks and lounge lizards: 'Arians', polemics and asceticism

in the Roman East', in *Arianism After Arius*, 181–214; L. Ayres, *Nicaea and Its Legacy. An Approach to Fourth-Century Trinitarian Theology* (Oxford, 2004), 107; D. H. Williams, 'Another exception to later fourth-century "Arian" typologies: the case of Germinius of Sirmium', *Journal of Early Christian Studies* 4 (1996), 335–57. See also R. C. Gregg and D. E. Groh, *Early Arianism: A View of Salvation* (London, 1981); R. Williams, *Arius*.

14   S. Parvis, *Marcellus of Ancyra and the Lost Years of the Arian Controversy 325–345* (Oxford, 2005), 135, hypothesizes that they might possibly have met Arius when he was exiled to Sirmium (modern Sremska Mitrovica, Serbia) after his condemnation at the Council of Nicaea in 325. However, both Ursacius and Valens must have been young at this date (and we cannot, in any case, be absolutely certain that they were natives of the cities they ruled as bishops). Ayres, *Nicaea*, 124 thinks that their meeting is an 'intriguing' possibility. The *Letter of the Western Bishops* to Constantius of 343 (see Hanson, *Search*, 305–6) refers to *imperitis atque improbis duobus adolescentibus Ursacio et Valente*, a description suggesting their youth, though this may have been relative, as the minimum canonical age for consecration as a bishop is thirty. The *Letter* also suggests that they were authors of a tract or tracts, but nothing has survived.

15   T. A. Kopecek, *A History of Neo-Arianism* (Cambridge, MA, 1979), 85.

16   Hanson, *Search*, 246–62. At the same time, they apologized to Athanasius of Alexandria for any allegations they had made about him. This apology had nothing to do with theological issues: it related to their membership of the official 'Mareotic commission' of 335, which had resulted in his deposition and banishment at the Council of Tyre. This commission had investigated Athanasius' conduct and not his doctrine.

17   Wickham, *Hilary of Poitiers*, xx: see also Hanson, *Search*, 591 and Parvis, *Marcellus*, 125, for examples. For 'court bishops', see E. D. Hunt, 'Did Constantius II have "court bishops"?', *Studia Patristica* 19 (1989), 86–90.

18   Hanson, *Search*, 363–5; trans. F. Williams, *The Panarion of Epiphanius of Salamis*, vol. II (Leiden, New York and Köln, 1994), 455–6.

19   As suggested by Hanson, *Search*, 313.

20   See M. Dunn, 'Intuiting gods: creed and cognition in the fourth century', *Historical Reflections/Reflexions Historiques* 38 (2012), 1–23.

21   E. A. Thompson, *The Visigoths in the Time of Ulfila* (Oxford, 1966), xiii and 81; Heather and Matthews *Goths in the Fourth Century*, 133–4.

22   Thompson, *Visigoths*, 97.

23   Theodoret, *Ecclesiastical History* 4, 33, in P. Schaff and H.Wace (eds), *Theodoret,*

Jerome, Gennadius, Rufinus, Nicene and Post-Nicene Fathers (2nd series, vol. 3, 1892, reprinted Peabody, MA, 1994), 131; Sozomen, *Ecclesiastical History*, 6, 37 translated in Schaff and Wace (eds), *Socrates, Sozomenus*, 373.

24 Heather and Matthews, *Goths in the Fourth Century*, 140.

25 Williams, *Ambrose*, 204–23, discusses the possibility that Auxentius' *Epistula de vita et obitu Ulfilae* was composed shortly after his death in 383, but also suggests an alternative context, that of a 'Homoian revival' in Milan after 384. This might account for its presentation of Ulfila's anti-*ousian* views in such intemperate language. See also Heather and Matthews, *Goths in the Fourth Century*, 133–53.

26 Translation, Heather and Matthews, *Goths in the Fourth Century*, 148–9.

27 *Ibid.*

28 Translation, Hanson, *Search*, 563–4.

29 See Hanson, *Search*, 557–97, for developments in Homoian theology.

30 Wiles, *Archetypal Heresy*, 44.

31 Heather, *Goths*, 58–65.

32 Heather and Matthew, *Goths in the Fourth Century*, 20; see also Heather, *Goths*, 59–60 and Thompson, *Visigoths*, 1–24.

33 For Germinius, see Williams, 'Another exception' and the references given there; for Palladius, Secundianus and the Council of Aquileia, M. Meslin, *Les Ariens d' Occident 335–430* (Paris, 1967), 59–99.

34 Hanson's discussion of 'Homoian people' at *Search*, 579–97, includes a number of eastern bishops whose theology is not unequivocally Homoian; see also W. A. Löhr, 'Western Christianities', in A. Casiday and F. W. Norris (eds), *Cambridge History of Christianity* vol. 2, *Constantine to c. 600* (Cambridge, 2007), 9–51 at 12. For Potamius of Lisbon's adoption and subsequent abandonment of Homoianism, see A. Montes Moreira, 'Le retour de Potamius de Lisbonne à l' orthodoxie nicéenne', *Didaskalia* 5 (1975), 330–54. Although Athanasius would claim that Auxentius of Milan, a Cappadocian appointee of Constantius II, was anathematized along with the Illyricans at the first session of the Council of Rimini, the surviving documents do not confirm this. See Williams, *Ambrose*, 76–83; N. B. McLynn, *Ambrose of Milan. Church and Court in a Christian Capital* (Berkeley, Los Angeles and London, 1994), 22–31; and Hanson, 466–7 and 596–7. See also Meslin, *Les Ariens*, 59–99 and J. Zeiller, *Les Origines Chrétiennes dans les provinces danubiennes de l'Empire Romain* (Paris, 1918), 417–64.

35 Homoianism developed supporters outside the region – and of course, was subscribed to by hundreds of bishops as the imperial creed in 359–60. See

Hanson's discussion of 'Homoian people' at *Search*, 579–97 and Löhr, *Die
Entstehung*, 58–62, 127–41. Hanson includes eastern figures such as Akakius,
bishop of Caesarea who subscribed to the Creed of Constantinople but who
expressed different views beforehand and Eudoxius who might have been
Eunomian ('neo-Arian') rather than Homoian. As he indicates at 344–6, one
name associated with the 'Blasphemy of Sirmium' was the centenarian Ossius
of Cordoba, whose endorsement of the document was possibly extracted
under pressure for political reasons; and who was followed by his Iberian
colleague Potamius of Lisbon. The 'Blasphemy' would also be endorsed by
Liberius, Bishop of Rome: see Löhr, 'Western Christianities', 12. Auxentius, a
Cappadocian appointed by Constantius II as Bishop of Milan in 355, is counted
as Homoian: but although Athanasius would claim he was anathematized along
with the Illyricans at the first session of the Council of Rimini, the surviving
documents do not support him. Auxentius was a popular bishop, attacked by
pro-Nicenes for maintaining a principled adherence to the Creed of Rimini
which he had signed: his main adversary was Hilary of Poitiers and the size
and importance of the diocese of Milan would have made him a natural target.
See Williams, *Ambrose*, 76–83; McLynn, *Ambrose of Milan*, 22–31; and Hanson,
Search 466–7 and 596–7. See also Meslin, *Les Ariens*, 59–99 and Zeiller,
Origines Chrétiennes, 417–64.

36   Translation, Hanson, *Search*, 344–5.

37   Translation, Hanson, *Search*, 380.

38   Hanson, *Search*, 570.

39   Hanson, *Search*, 564.

40   See Williams, *Ambrose*, 21–2, n. 40; M. Simonetti, *La Crisi Ariana nel IV Secolo*
     (Rome, 1975), 229–30.

41   E. A.Thompson, 'Constantine, Constantius and the Lower Danube frontier',
     Hermes 84 (1956), 372–81.

42   E. A. Thompson, *The Historical Work of Ammianus Marcellinus* (Cambridge,
     1947), 47ff.

43   Dunn, 'Intuiting gods', 14–16.

44   Socrates, *Ecclesiastical History* IV, 33, in Schaff and Wace (eds), *Socrates,
     Sozomenus*, 115.

45   Heather and Matthews, *Goths in the Fourth Century*, 20–1; P. Heather,
     'The crossing of the Danube and the Gothic conversion', *Greek, Roman and
     Byzantine Studies* 27 (1986), 289–318, argues that 376 represents the date of
     a formal conversion agreement. However, much of the information he cites
     suggests that some Tervingi were already Christians: ' … before the reign of

Valens, the Goths and the Tervingi had long been exposed to Christianity'
(293).

46   Heather, *Goths*, 61.

47   Heather and Matthews, *Goths in the Fourth Century*, 135.

48   Heather and Matthews, *Goths in the Fourth Century*,155.

49   Schäferdiek, 'Germanic and Celtic Christianities', 53.

50   R. C. Blockley (ed.), *The Fragmentary Classicising Historians of the Later Roman
      Empire* II (Liverpool, 1983), 74–7.

51   Brennecke, *Studien*, 87–157; T. D. Barnes, *Athanasius and Constantius. Theology
      and Politics in the Constantinian Empire* (Cambridge, MA and London, 1993),
      149–54; Hanson *Search*, 676–737; Ayres, *Nicaea*, 173–86 and 187–242.

52   For the Council and Creed of Constantinople, see Hanson, *Search,* 812–23, and
      877; Ayres, *Nicaea*, 253–9.

53   See N. B. McLynn, 'From Palladius to Maximinus: passing the Arian torch',
      Journal of Early Christian Studies 4 (4) (1996), 477–93.

54   Heather and Matthews, *Goths in the Fourth Century*, 140–1.

55   J. Stevenson (ed.), *Creeds, Councils and Controversies: Documents Illustrating
      the History of the Church AD 337–461* (London, 1983), 148.

56   McLynn, 'From Palladius to Maximinus', 484.

57   D. M. Gwynn, 'Archaeology and the "Arian Controversy"', in D. M. Gwynn and
      S. Bangert (eds), *Religious Diversity in Late Antiquity* (Leiden, 2010), 229–63.

58   Sozomen, *Ecclesiastical* History, VII, 17 in Schaff and Wace, *Socrates,
      Sozomenus*, 387–8; J. H. W. G. Liebeschuetz, *Barbarians and Bishops. Army,
      Church and State in the Age of Arcadius and Chrysostom* (Oxford, 1990), 152–3.

59   Heather, *Goths*, 137.

60   Heather, *Goths*, 138.

61   Heather, *Goths*, 131–51.

62   Heather, *Goths*, 115–16.

63   Heather, *Goths*, 152.

64   Heather, *Goths*, 152–4.

65   Halsall, *Barbarian Migrations*, 227–33.

66   Hydatius, 98: *Rechila rex Suevorum Emerita gentilis moritur mense Augusto, sui
      mox filius suus Catholicus Rechiarius succedit in regnum, nonnullis quidem sibi
      de gente sua emulis, sed latenter*: R. W. Burgess (ed. and trans.), *The Chronicle of
      Hydatius and the Consularia Constantinopolitana* (Oxford, 1993), 98–9.

67   Burgess, *Chronicle of Hydatius*, 118–9. One of Rechiar's kin also converted
      to Christianity, opting for Homoianism as an expression of fidelity when he
      became a member of the Vandal ruler's *Gefolge*: L. A. Garcia Moreno, 'La

Iglesia y el Cristianismo en la Galecia de época sueva', in *Espacio y tiempo en la percepción de la Antigüedad Tardía, Antigüedad Cristiana* XXIII (Murcia, 2006), 39–55, at 44 n. 29.

68 Schäferdiek,'Germanic and Celtic Christianities', 55.

69 *DLH* II 28: Thorpe, *History of the Franks,* 140–1; Schäferdiek, 'Germanic and Celtic Christianities', 55, notes Gundioc's descent from what he calls 'Visigothic' nobility.

70 De Vingo, *From Tribe to Province to State,* 51.

71 B. Dumézil, *Les Racines Chrétiennes de l' Europe* (Paris, 2005), 202.

72 A. T. Fear (ed. and trans.), Orosius, *Seven Books of History Against the Pagans.* (Liverpool, 2010), notes at 380 that Orosius, who claims in Bk. VII chap. 33 that the Burgundians who had entered the Empire 'had recently all become Catholics', was probably trying to excuse the Emperor Honorius for allowing this part of the Empire to slip out of control.

73 Socrates, *HE* VII 30: Schaff and Wace (eds), *Socrates, Sozomenus,* 169–70.

74 *Ibid.*

75 Escher, *Burgondes,* 26–7.

76 Acts 2.41.

77 Suggested by Dumézil, *Racines Chrétiennes*, 200.

78 Escher, *Burgondes,* 65.

79 Escher, *Burgondes,* 68; Gaillard de Sémainville, 'À propos de l'implantation', 19, suggests that the 'relatively important proportion of oriental elements' among the Burgundians may have been a result of the dissolution of Attila's confederation after his defeat in 451. De Vingo, *Tribe to Province to State,* 104; Mercier and Mercier-Rolland, *Le Cimitière Burgonde de Monnet-la-Ville,* 34. For a new perspective on skull deformations, see S. Hakenbeck, '"Hunnic" modified skulls: physical appearance, identity and the transformative nature of migrations' in D. Sayer and H. Williams (eds) *Mortuary Practices and Social Identities in the Middle Ages* (Exeter, 2009), 64–80.

80 Dumézil, *Racines Chrétiennes,* 525 n. 36 draws attention to the *Consularia Italica* § 583, *MGH AA*, IX, 305: *Gundiochus rex Burgundionum cum gente et omni praesidio annuente sibi Theoderico ac Gothis intra Galliam ad habitandum ingressus societate et amicitiae Gothorum functus.*

81 G. W. S. Friedrichsen, *The Gothic Version of the Gospels* (London, 1926), 187.

82 R. W. Mathisen, 'Barbarian bishops and the churches "in barbaricis gentibus" during Late Antiquity', *Speculum*, 72 (1997), 664–97 at 679.

83 'Debate with Maximinus' in Teske (ed.), *Works of St Augustine, Arianism and Other Heresies*, 175–336.

84   McLynn, 'From Palladius to Maximinus'.

85   See Mathisen, 'Barbarian bishops'.

86   Burgess, *Chronicle of Hydatius*, 118–19, translates *natione Galata effectus apostata* as 'a Greek apostate'.

87   Letter 23: trans. D. Shanzer and I. Wood, *Avitus of Vienne, Letters and Selected Prose* (Liverpool, 2002), 229.

88   *DHL* II, 33: Thorpe, *History of the Franks*, 147–8.

89   Deliyannis, *Agnellus of Ravenna, Book of Pontiffs*, 199.

90   J-O. Tjäder, *Die nichtliterarischen lateinschen Papyri Italiens aus der Zeit 445–700* vol. II Papyri 29–59 (Stockholm, 1982), 147.

91   Heather, *Goths*, 245, appears to suggest that the *spodeis* are part of a writing-office rather than ascetics.

92   Heather, *Goths*, 213.

93   Heather, *Goths*, 210 claims Palencia as an Arian see, but this does not seem to be the case: see García Moreno, 'La Iglesia y el Cristianismo en la Galecia', at 40.

94   M. Cecchelli and G. Bertelli, 'Edifici di culto Ariano in Italia', *Actes du XIe Congrès Internationale d' Archéologie Chrétienne* vol. I, Collection de l'École française de Rome 123 (Rome, 1986), 233–47.

95   H. Woodruff, 'The iconography and decoration of the mosaics of La Daurade', *The Art Bulletin* 13 (1931), 80–104. Woodruff favoured a date of fifth–sixth century for the mosaics and thought there was strong Ravennate influence on them.

96   De Clercq (ed.), *Concilia Galliae a. 511–a. 695*, Conc. Aurelianense 511, Canon 10, 7–8.

97   Letter 7, Shanzer and Wood, *Avitus of Vienne*, 295–302.

98   See Williams, 'Another exception' and also M. Simonetti, 'Osservazioni sull' "Altercatio Heracliani cum Germinio"', *Vigiliae Christianae* 21 (1967), 39–58.

99   Heather and Matthews, *Goths in the Fourth Century*, 148–9.

100 *Ibid.*, 144.

101 Jerome, Letter 106, *Ad Sunniam et Fretelam* in J. Labourt (ed.), *Saint Jérôme, Lettres* vol. 6 (Paris, 1955), 104–44.

102 Friedrichsen, *Gothic Version of the Gospels*, 15–68.

103 Friedrichsen, *Gothic Version of the Gospels* 187–93.

104 Matthew – 22 leaves (76 missing, 75 per cent lost); John – 45 leaves (29 missing, 40 per cent lost); Luke – 70 leaves (36 missing, 35 per cent lost); Mark: – 50 leaves + 1 Speyer leaf (7 missing, 8 per cent lost).

105 Wiljarith is also known as the scribe who copied Books One to Six of Orosius' work *Against the Pagans*. See J-O. Tjäder, 'Der Codex argenteus in Uppsala

und der Buchmeister Viliaric in Ravenna', in U. E. Hagberg (ed.), *Studia Gotica* (Stockholm, 1972), 144–64.

106 For more on glosses and translation, see Heather and Matthews, *Goths in the Fourth Century*, 155–73.

107 M. J. Hunter, 'The Gothic Bible', in G. W. H. Lampe (ed.), *The Cambridge History of the Bible* vol. 2, *The West From the Fathers to the Reformation* (Cambridge, 1969), 338–62 at 346.

108 *Ibid.*, 360.

109 Heather and Matthews, *Goths in the Fourth Century*, 171.

110 Friedrichsen, *Gothic Version of the Gospels*, 240–5.

111 W. H. Bennett, *The Gothic Commentary on the Gospel of John* (New York, 1960), 69. Bennett, 9, suggests that the linguistic features of the commentary are essentially the same as those of the *Codex Argenteus*, implying that they are roughly contemporary.

112 *Ibid.*, 66.

113 R. Gryson (ed.), *Scripta Arriana Latina, Corpus Christianorum Series Latina* 87 (Turnhout, 1982), xviii–xx; 1–145. *Contra Paganos* can be found at 118–41.

114 Heather and Matthews, *Goths in the Fourth Century*, 144.

115 Salvian, *On The Present Judgment*, Book 5, ch. 2: trans. E. M. Sanford, *Salvian, On the Government of God* (New York, 1930), 133–42.

116 Letter 29, Shanzer and Wood, *Avitus of Vienne*, 227.

117 Heil, *Avitus von Vienne*, 132–9, notes the novelty of this text in discussions of the divinity of the Holy Spirit.

118 *DLH* V, 43 and VI, 40: Thorpe, *History of the Franks*, 307–10 and 371–4.

119 *MGH Epistolae* vol. III, *Epistolae Wisigoticae*, ep. 9, 671–75. The translation used is from the *Epistolae* website: http://epistolae.ccnmtl.columbia.edu/letter/44.html [accessed July 13, 2013]. For the Visigothic context of the letter, see Y. Hen, *Roman Barbarians* (Basingstoke and New York, 2007), 55–6.

120 *Ibid.*

121 Heather and Matthews, *Goths in the Fourth Century*, 103–31.

122 Gryson (ed.), *Scripta Arriana Latina*, 47–92.

123 Meslin, *Les Ariens*, 406.

124 A. Urbano, 'Donation, dedication, and Damnatio Memoriae: the Catholic reconciliation of Ravenna and the church of Sant' Apollinare Nuovo', *Journal of Early Christian Studies* 13 (2005), 71–110.

125 R. Mathisen, 'Ricimer's church in Rome: how an Arian barbarian prospered in a Nicene world', in A. Cain and N. Lenski (eds), *The Power of Religion in*

Late Antiquity (Farnham and Burlington, VT, 2009), 307–26; M. C. Cartocci, 'Alcune precisazioni sulla intitolazione a S. Agata della "Ecclesia Gothorum" alla Suburra', in *Teoderico Il Grande e i Goti D' Italia* (Spoleto, 1993), 611–20.

126 Letter to Chlodosuintha, wife of the Lombard ruler Alboin: partial translation in Hillgarth, *Conversion*, 78–9.

127 *Ibid.*

128 Paul the Deacon, *The Lives of the Fathers of Merida* in A. T. Fear (trans.) *Lives of the Visigothic Fathers* (Liverpool, 1997), 45–105, quotation at 84.

129 *DLH* VI, 18: Thorpe, *History of the Franks*, 349.

130 Zaragoza II, 592, Canon 2: J. Vives (ed.), *Concilios Visigóticos e Hispano-Romanos.* (Barcelona-Madrid, 1963), 154–5.

131 For his letters to the emperor, see Shanzer and Wood, *Avitus of Vienne*, 141–53. B. H. Rosenwein, 'Perennial prayer at Agaune', in S. Farmer and B. H. Rosenwein (eds), *Monks and Nuns, Saints and Outcasts. Religion in Medieval Society* (Ithaca, NY, 2000), 37–56 emphasizes the local dimension of the enterprise. R. Snee, 'Gregory Nazianzen's Anastasia church: Arianism, the Goths, and hagiography', *Dumbarton Oaks Papers* 52 (1998), 157–86, at 183 highlights anti-'Arian' activity by the Akoimetoi.

132 See, for example, Gregory of Tours *DLH* IV, 26 on the Visigothic princess Brunichildis, who became a Catholic on her marriage: Thorpe, *History of the Franks*, 221–2. For the letter of Vigilius: Barlow, *Martini Episcopi Bracarensis Opera*, 290–3; J. O. Bragança, 'A carta do Papa Vigílio ao Arcebispo Profuturo de Braga', *Bracara Augusta* 21 (1967), 65–91.

133 E. A. Thompson, *The Goths in Spain* (Oxford, 1969), 33.

134 Canon 29: de Clercq (ed.), *Concilia Galliae a. 511–a. 695*, 31.

135 Shanzer and Wood, *Avitus of Vienne*, 223.

136 Heil, *Avitus von Vienne*, 47–57.

137 J. Moorhead, *Theoderic in Italy* (Oxford, 1992), 95–6.

Chapter 4

1 For example, J. Moorhead, *Theoderic in Italy* (Oxford, 1992), 95.

2 R. Horton, 'African conversion', *Africa* 41 (1971), 85–108; *idem*, 'On the rationality of conversion', *Africa* 45 (1975), 219–35 and 373–99.

3 Halsall, *Barbarian Migrations*, 282.

4 Moorhead, *Theoderic in Italy*, 13.

5 Jordanes, *Getica*, 271.

6   J. Shepard, 'Manners maketh Romans? Young barbarians at the emperor's court', in E. Jeffreys (ed.), *Byzantine Style, Religion and Civilization In Honour of Sir Steven Runciman* (Cambridge, 2001), 135–58.

7   Moorhead, *Theoderic in Italy*, 11–31.

8   Moorhead, *Theoderic in Italy*, 52.

9   *Ibid.*, 63–4.

10 J. Marenbon, *Boethius* (Oxford, 2003), 66–95.

11 *Variae* IV, 34: *MGH AA* 12, Lib. IIII, 34, 129.

12 Moorhead, *Theoderic in Italy*, 91–2; 114–39; 259–60.

13 Moorhead, *Theoderic in Italy*, 60.

14 Deliyannis, *Agnellus of Ravenna, Book of Pontiffs*, 161, 165, 171, 177, 183.

15 See C. La Rocca, 'Una prudente maschera "Antiqua". La politica edilizia di Teoderico', in *Teoderico Il Grande e i Goti D' Italia* (Spoleto, 1993), 451–516; B. Ward-Perkins, 'Where is the archaeology and the iconography of Germanic Arianism?', in D. M. Gwynn and S. Bangert (eds), *Religious Diversity in Late Antiquity* (Leiden, 2010), 265–89; D. M. Deliyannis, *Ravenna in Late Antiquity* (Cambridge, 2010), 139–200; and M. Verhoeven, *The Early Christian Monuments of Ravenna: Transformations and Memory* (Turnhout, 2011), 115–35 and especially 137–58.

16 *DLH* II, 33: Thorpe, *History of the Franks*, 147–8.

17 *(Gunde)badus rex clementiss(imus) emolumento proprio spatio mult(ip)licat(o)*. See K. Escher, *Genèse et Évolution du Deuxième Royaume Burgonde: les Témoins Archéologiques*, BAR International Series 1402 vol. II (Oxford, 2005), CD-ROM 2: Fichier Lapidaire, L. 081.

18 Letter 21, Shanzer and Wood, *Avitus of Vienne*, 201–3.

19 Heil, *Avitus von Vienne*, 47–57.

20 Heather, *Goths*, 239.

21 Heather, *Goths*, 239.

22 M. Aimone, 'Romani e Ostrogoti fra integrazione e separazione. Il contributo dell' archeologia a un dibattito storiografico', *Reti Medievali Rivista*, 13, 1 (2012), 31–96, at 39.

23 For an overview of the debates see Halsall, *Barbarian Migrations*, 443–5.

24 Heather, *Goths*, 238–9.

25 See Aimone, n. 22 above.

26 Heather, *Goths*, 238.

27 Heather, *Goths*, 236.

28 Tjäder, *Die nichtliterarischen lateinschen Papyri*, vol. 2, 100–1.

29 P. Heather, 'Merely an ideology? – Gothic identity in Ostrogothic Italy', in S. J.

Barnish and F. Marazzi (eds), *The Ostrogoths From the Migration Period to the Sixth Century* (Woodbridge, 2007), 31–60, 46.

30   R. Davis (ed. and trans.), *The Book of Pontiffs (Liber Pontficalis)* (Liverpool, 2000), xii–xiv; S. J. Barnish, 'The *Anonymus Valesianus* II as a source for the last years of Theoderic', *Latomus* 42 (1983), 572–96.

31   *Contra hereticos*: Gryson, *Scripta Arriana* Latina, 142–5.

32   M. Cecchelli and G. Bertelli, 'Edifici di culto Ariano in Italia', *Actes du XIe Congrès Internationale d' Archéologie Chrétienne* vol. I, Collection de l'École française de Rome 123 (Rome, 1986), 233–47.

33   Translation in Deliyannis, *Agnellus of Ravenna, Book of Pontiffs*, 198–9.

34   Heather, *Goths*, 261–4.

35   *DLH* II, 34: trans. Thorpe, *History of the Franks, 148–9.*

36   Heil, *Avitus von Vienne*, 132–9, notes the novelty of some of the discussions of the divinity of the Holy Spirit.

37   Fragments 15, 16, 22, 23, 24, 25 and 27: translation in Shanzer and Wood, *Avitus of Vienne*, 173–80.

38   Fragments 13 and 14: translation in Shanzer and Wood, *Avitus of Vienne*, 172–3.

39   Fragments 18 and 19: translation in Shanzer and Wood, *Avitus of Vienne*, 174–5.

40   Heil, *Avitus von Vienne*, 129. Cf. Hanson, *Search*, 570 for a similar theology.

41   Shanzer and Wood, *Avitus of Vienne*, 231.

42   Heil, *Avitus von Vienne*, 80–4.

43   Canon 33: de Clercq, *Concilia Galliae a. 511–a. 695*, 33.

44   See Hag. 2.13.

45   For a recent discussion of these issues, see de Vingo, *From Tribe to Province to State*, 147–57.

46   See Letters 70 and 75, Shanzer and Wood, *Avitus of Vienne*, 306–8.

47   Halsall, *Barbarian Migrations*, 200–2.

48   Shanzer and Wood, *Avitus of Vienne*, 143.

49   Escher, *Burgondes*, 134, points to the lack of clear information.

50   Marius of Avenches quoted by Escher, *Burgondes*, 264, accuses the Burgundians of atrocities in churches during the siege of Milan.

51   Halsall, *Barbarian Migrations*, 301.

52   Barlow, *Martini Opera*, 251–2. In 591, Pope Gregory the Great had to concede to Bishop Leander of Seville that single immersion could be used in Catholic Spain.

53   A. Ferreiro, 'The missionary labor of St Martin of Braga in 6th century

Galicia, *Studia Monastica* 23 (1981), 11–26; A. Ferreiro, 'Braga and Tours: some observations on Gregory's *De virtutibus Sancti Martini*', *Journal of Early Christian Studies* 3 (2) (1995), 195–210 and the wealth of references given there, especially in note 3. M. J. Violante Branco, 'St Martin of Braga, the Sueves and Gallaecia', in A. Ferreiro (ed.), *The Visigoths, Studies in Culture and Society* (Leiden, 1999), 63–97, stresses Martin's 'peculiar and close relationship to Gaul' (83). G. Martinez Diez, 'La coleccíon canonica de la iglesia sueva: los Capitulos Martini', *Bracara Augusta* 21 (1967), 224–43, however, had previously pointed out the lack of canons of Gallic councils in the collection attached to the legislative work of the First and Second Councils of Braga.

54 Barlow, *Martini Opera*, 80–115.

55 Barlow, *Martini Opera*, 116–44.

56 For discussion of the *Parrochiale*, see P. David, *Études Historiques sur la Galice et le Portugal du VIᵉ au XIIᵉ Siècle* (Lisbon and Paris, 1947), 19–44; P. C. Díaz, 'El Parrochiale Suevum: organización ecclesiástica, poder político y poblamiento en la Gallaecia Tardoantigua' in J. Alvar (ed.), *Homenaje a José Mª Blázquez* vol. VI (Madrid, 1998), 35–47; S. Castellanos and I. Martín Viso, 'The local articulation of central power in the north of the Iberian Peninsula (500–1000)', *Early Medieval Europe* 13 (2005), 1–42, at 5–8.

57 John of Biclaro, *Chronicle*, in K. B. Wolf, *Conquerors and Chroniclers of Early Medieval Spain* (2nd edn, Liverpool, 1999), 61.

58 Friedrichsen, *Gothic Version of the Gospels*, 187.

59 Heather, *Goths*, 213.

60 C. Munier (ed.), *Concilia Galliae a. 314– a. 506*, 189–228, at 192.

61 G. I. Halfond, 'Vouillé, Orléans (511) and the origins of the Frankish conciliar tradition', in R. W. Mathisen and D. Shanzer (eds), *The Battle of Vouillé 507 CE Where France Began* (Boston and Berlin, 2012), 151–65 at 151.

62 R. Collins, *Visigothic Spain* (Oxford, 2004), 25.

63 Collins, *Visigothic Spain*, 46.

64 Collins, *Visigothic Spain*, 56.

65 J. D. Dodds, *Architecture and Ideology in Early Medieval Spain* (Philadelphia, 1993), 15–16.

66 R. Collins, *Early Medieval Spain* (2nd edn, New York, 1995), 48–9.

67 See Isidore of Seville, *History of the Kings of the Goths*, in K. B. Wolf, *Conquerors and Chroniclers of Early Medieval Spain* (2nd edn, Liverpool, 1999), 81.

68 *Lives of the Fathers of Merida*, in A. T. Fear (trans.), *Lives of the Visigothic Fathers* (Liverpool, 1997), 45–105.

69   Trans. Wolf, *Conquerors and Chroniclers*, 60–1

70   J. Orlandis, 'El Arrianismo Visigodo tardio', *Cuadernos de Historia de España* 65 (1981), 5–20.

71   *DLH* VI, 18: trans. Thorpe, *History of the Franks*, 349.

72   This builds on arguments advanced by R. Collins. 'King Leovigild and the conversion of the Visigoths' in *idem*, *Law, Culture and Regionalism in Early Medieval Spain* (Aldershot, 1992), II, 1–12.

73   One of his two sons, Hermenegild had rebelled against him in the 580s: while this revolt is presented by Gregory of Tours and in the *Dialogues* attributed to Gregory the Great as having a religious character, with Hermenegild cast in the role of Catholic champion and martyr, this is not how Iberian chroniclers saw it. See discussion in R. Collins, 'King Leovigild and the conversion'; *idem*, *Visigothic Spain*, 50–69.

74   Collins, *Early Medieval Spain*, 53–5.

75   *DHL*, VI, 40; trans. Thorpe, *History of the Franks*, 371–4.

76   Heather, *Goths*, 209.

77   For Zaragoza II, see J. Vives, *Concilios Visigóticos e Hispano-Romanos* (Barcelona-Madrid, 1963), 154–5.

78   De Vingo, *From Tribe to Province to State*, 59.

79   I. N. Wood, *The Merovingian Kingdoms, 450–751* (London and New York, 1994), 49, describes the late elimination of rivals as 'surprising'. Wood, 'Gregory of Tours and Clovis', *Revue Belge de Philologie et d' Histoire* 63 (2) (1985), 249–72, describes Gregory's treatment of Clovis at 271 as 'remarkably unsatisfactory' in 'many ways', but at 255 suggests that it is still possible that his overall interpretation of the reign may stand.

80   *DLH* II, 42: trans. Thorpe, *History of the Franks*, 156–8.

81   See Dumézil, *Racines Chrétiennes*, 218.

82   *Ibid*; *Contra* Collins, *Early Medieval Europe, 300–1000* (3rd edn, Basingstoke, 2010), 110, who says Remigius' injunction to listen to advice given to him by bishops would make no sense if not addressed to a Christian.

83   Partial translation of the letter in Hillgarth, *Conversion*, 78–9.

84   *DLH* II, 28: trans. Thorpe, *History of the Franks*, 140–1.

85   Wood, 'Gregory of Tours and Clovis', 253–4.

86   S. Crawford, 'Children, death and the afterlife in Anglo-Saxon England', *Anglo-Saxon Studies in Archaeology and History* 6 (1993), 83–9; Dunn, *Christianization of the Anglo-Saxons*, 142–4.

87   *DLH* II, 30: trans. Thorpe, *History of the Franks*, 143. For the problems surrounding the date of this battle and whether it was the occasion of Clovis'

'conversion', see I. Wood, *The Merovingian Kingdoms 450-751* (Harlow, 1994), 45-6.

88   *DLH* II, 31: trans. Thorpe, *History of the Franks*, 143-5.

89   Y. Hen, 'Clovis, Gregory of Tours and pro-Merovingian propaganda', *Revue Belge de Philologie et d' Histoire* 71 (2) (1993), 271-6.

90   Wood, 'Gregory of Tours and Clovis', 255.

91   See Dunn, *Christianization of the Anglo-Saxons*, 141-4 and the references given there; *eadem*, 'Lombard religiosities reconsidered: "Arianism", syncretism and the transition to Catholic Christianity', in A. P. Roach and J. Simpson (eds), *Heresy and the Making of European Culture. Medieval and Modern Perspectives* (Farnham, 2013), 85-105, esp. 94-6.

92   Shanzer and Wood, *Avitus of Vienne*, 369: The Latin reads *aut sacerdotum hortatu aut quorumcumque sodalium* – so the ruler is encouraged not just by priests and friends but by associates.

93   *DLH* II, 40: Thorpe, *History of the Franks*, 155-6.

94   See Wood, *Merovingian Kingdoms*, 44-5.

95   These issues are discussed by Dumézil, *Racines Chrétiennes*, 213.

96   G. Halfond, 'Vouillé, Orleans (511) and the origins of the Frankish conciliar tradition', in Mathisen and Shanzer (eds), *Battle of Vouillé*, 151-65 at 162.

97   J. M. Wallace-Hadrill, *The Frankish Church* (Oxford, 1983), 27.

98   *Ibid.*, 25.

99   S. Dick, '"Langobardi per annos regem non habentes, sub ducibus fuerunt." Formen und Entwicklung der Herrschaftsorganisation bei den Langobarden. Eine Skizze', in Pohl and Erhart (eds), *Die Langobarden*, 335-44. For the Lombards in general, see N. Christie, *The Lombards. The Ancient Longobards* (Oxford, 1995); G. Ausenda, P. Delogu and C. Wickham (eds), *The Langobards Before the Frankish Conquest: An Ethnographic Perspective* (Woodbridge, 2009).

100 S. Fanning, 'Lombard Arianism reconsidered', *Speculum* 56 (1981), 241-58, at 246-9. See also Dumézil, *Racines Chrétiennes*, 337-49.

101 J. Zeiller, *Les Origines Chrétiennes Dans Les Provinces Danubiennes de l' Empire Romain* (Paris, 1918), 571-4, suggests that the Lombards were converted to Catholicism before they entered Italy through contact with the Marcomanni and in Catholic Noricum. See also T. S. Brown, 'Lombard religious policy in the late sixth and seventh centuries: the Roman dimension' in Ausenda, Delogu and Wickham (eds), *The Langobards*, 289-308.

102 *De Bello Gothico* 3.34.25-29: trans. H. B. Dewing, *Procopius, History of the Wars* vol. 4 (New York, 1924), 451.

103   R. A. Markus, *Gregory the Great and His World* (Cambridge, 1997), 99–107,
      emphasizes the anxieties about the Lombards expressed by Gregory before 600.

104   On Pelagius, see Fanning, 'Lombard Arianism', 242.

105   S. Gasparri, *I Duchi Longobardi* (Rome, 1978), 456, points out that the
      circumstances of Agilulf's accession and marriage with Theodelinda are
      unclear.

106   *HL* IV, 2: trans. Foulke, *History of the Lombards*, 166.

107   R. Valentini and G. Zuchetti (eds), *Codice Topografico della Città di Roma*,
      vol. II (Rome, 1942), 29–47.

108   IX, 66: D. Norberg (ed.) *S. Gregorii Magni Registrum Epistularum* vol. II,
      Corpus Christianorum, Series Latina 140a (Turnhout, 1982), 621–2.

109   XIV, 12: Norberg (ed.), *Registrum* vol. II, 1082–3.

110   C. Wickham, *Early Medieval Italy. Central Power and Local Society 400–1000*
      (London, 1981), 34.

111   *HL* IV, 22: trans. Foulke, *History of the Lombards*, 166–7.

112   Wickham, *Early Medieval Italy*, 34.

113   *Registrum* IX, 66.

114   C. Cipolla (ed.) *Codice Diplomatico del Monastero di San Colombano di Bobbio
      fino all' anno 1208*, Fonti per la storia d'Italia 52 (Rome, 1918), 100–3.

115   *HL* IV, 42: trans. Foulke, *History of the Lombards*, 193–4.

116   Cipolla (ed.), *Codice Diplomatico*, 104–15.

117   See Dunn, 'Lombard religiosities reconsidered'.

118   *Ibid.*

119   Translation in I. Wood, 'Jonas of Bobbio, the Abbots of Bobbio from the *Life
      of Columbanus*', in T. Head (ed.), *Medieval Hagiography* (New York, 2001),
      117–35, 127.

120   *HL* IV, 42: trans. Foulke, *History of the Lombards*, 194–5. For St. Eusebius, see D.
      A. Bullough, 'Urban change in early medieval Italy: the example of Pavia', *Papers
      of the British School at Rome* 34 (n.s. 21) (1966), 82–129, at 121–22.

121   *HL* IV, 42: trans. Foulke, *History of the Lombards*, 194.

122   See Fanning, 'Lombard Arianism', 252 n. 86, who points out that historians
      have only ever been able to identify Anastasius at Pavia and the unnamed
      individual at Spoleto in the *Dialogues* attributed to Gregory the Great, III, 29.

123   *HL* IV, 42, trans. Foulke, *History of the Lombards*, 195.

124   Wickham, *Early Medieval Italy*, 33.

125   See for example, P. T. R. Gray and M. W. Herren, 'Columbanus and the Three
      Chapters controversy – a new approach', *The Journal of Theological Studies* 45
      (1994), 160–71.

126 Cipolla (ed.) *Codice Diplomatico*, 91–6.

127 *HL* IV, 41: trans. Foulke, *History of the Lombards*, 190–1; Wickham, *Early Medieval Italy*, 35–6.

128 Wickham, *Early Medieval Italy*, 37.

129 L. Bethmann and G. Waitz (eds), *Carmen de synodo Ticinense, MGH SSrerLang* (Hannover, 1978), 189–91. See also W. Pohl, 'Heresy in Secundus and Paul the Deacon', in C. Chazelle and C. Cubitt (eds), *The Crisis of the Oikoumene. The Three Chapters and the Failed Quest for Unity in the Sixth–Century Mediterranean* (Turnhout, 2007), 243–64, at 260–1.

Chapter 5

1 For some interesting comparisons with what follows, see S. Rock, *Popular Religion in Russia. Double Belief and the Making of an Academic Myth* (Abingdon, 2007).

2 B. Filotas, *Pagan Survivals, Superstitions and Popular Cultures in Early Medieval Pastoral Literature* (Toronto, 2005), 45–6.

3 Boudriot, *Altgermanische Religion*, 4–6.

4 D. Harmening, *Superstitio: Überlieferungs- und theoriegeschichtliche Untersuchungen zur kirchlich-theologischen Aberglaubensliteratur des Mittelalters* (Berlin, 1979), 320–7.

5 Dowden, *European Paganism*,152.

6 A. I. Gurevich, *Medieval Popular Culture. Problems of Belief and Perception* (Cambridge, 1988), 37. See also W. Klingshirn, *Caesarius of Arles*, 283–4.

7 R. Künzel, 'Paganisme, syncrétisme, et culture religieuse au haut moyen âge. Réflexions de méthode', *Annales ESC* 4–5 (1992), 1055–69. This 'authentication' is to be carried out by reference to other written sources; by consideration of the location, purpose and audience of the text; by the appearance of vernacular terms in a Latin text; by departures from 'stereotypes'; by the appearance of elements given an 'incongruously Christian' interpretation; and by the appearance of a 'plausible' new element in a older description.

8 V. I. J. Flint, *The Rise of Magic in Early Medieval Europe* (Oxford, 1991), 43.

9 Y. Hen, *Culture and Religion in Merovingian Gaul A.D. 481–751* (Leiden, New York and Köln, 1995), 162–3.

10 Hen, *Culture and Religion*, 165.

11 *Ibid.*, 165–6.

12 *Ibid.*, 169–71. See also J-C. Schmitt, 'Les superstitions', in J. Le Goff (ed.), *Histoire de la France Religieuse*, vol. 1 (Paris, 1988), 425–53.

13 Hen has also pointed to the tendency for Carolingian texts to find 'pagan' survivals in the Merovingian past, where none may have actually existed: see 'Paganism and superstitions in the time of Gregory of Tours: *une question mal posée!*', in K. Mitchell and I. Wood (eds), *The World of Gregory of Tours* (Leiden, Boston and Köln, 2002), 229–40.

14 Boyer, *Religion Explained*, 272.

15 IV, 26: Norberg (ed.), *Registrum* vol. I, 244–6; IX, 205: Norberg (ed.), *Registrum* vol. II, 764; VIII, 19: *Registrum* II, 538; III, 59: *Registrum*, I, 207–8.

16 Canon XVI of Toledo III: J. Vives, *Concilios Visigoticos e Hispano-Romanos* (Barcelona and Madrid, 1963), 129–30.

17 For Auxerre, see de Clercq, *Concilia Galliae a. 511–a. 695*, 265–73; for its date, see R. Meens, 'Reforming the clergy: a context for the use of the Bobbio penitential', in Y. Hen and R. Meens (eds), *The Bobbio Missal – Liturgy and Religious Culture in Merovingian Gaul* (Cambridge, 2007), 154–67, at 160 n. 23. J. N. Hillgarth offers a translation of most of its canons in *The Conversion of Western Europe, 350–750* (Englewood Cliffs, NJ, 1969), 97–9.

18 See M. Meslin, *La Fête des Kalendes de Janvier dans L' Empire Romain*. Brussels, 1970; R. Arbesmann, 'The "cervuli" and "anniculae" in Cæsarius of Arles', *Traditio* 35 (1979), 89–119; C. Ginzburg, *Ecstasies* (London and Sydney, 1990), 182–204.

19 Barlow, *Martini Opera*, 140–1. These are presented as 'Oriental Canons', but though most repeat the rulings of earlier eastern councils, those dealing with these particular issues have no eastern precedents. Harmening, *Superstitio*, at 143, suggests that Cæsarian and oriental traditions came together in Martin.

20 *MGH Capitularia Merowingica* I, 2–3: J. M. Wallace-Hadrill. *The Frankish Church* (Oxford, 1983), 32. Wallace-Hadrill dates this to 533 or soon after, as it seems to be contingent on Canon 20 of the Council of Orléans of that year. Filotas, *Pagan Survivals*, 85–6 gives the traditional date of 554, which is questioned in the *MGH*.

21 Canon 16: de Clercq, *Concilia Galliae a. 511–a. 695*, 294.

22 Columbanus, *Penitential* 24, G. S. M. Walker (ed.), *Sancti Columbani Opera* (Dublin, 1970), 178–9.

23 See n. 19 above.

24 S. McKenna, *Paganism and Pagan Survivals in Spain up to the Fall of the Visigothic Kingdom* (Washington, DC, 1938), esp. 71–146; M. Meslin,

'Persistences paiennes en galice, vers la fin du VIᵉ siècle', in J. Bibauw (ed.), *Hommages à Marcel Renard* vol. II (Brussels, 1969), 512–24.

25 Dunn, *Christianization of the Anglo-Saxons*, 75.

26 See Vives, *Concilios* 398–9 and 498–9 for Canon XI of Toledo XII and Canon II of Toledo XVI.

27 Filotas, *Pagan Survivals*, 92–4.

28 Trans. K. Fischer Drew, *The Lombard Laws* (Philadelphia, 1973), 180.

29 *DLH* V, 43: trans. Thorpe, *History of the Franks*, 310. Gregory's further account of his own speech alludes to Abraham and the oak tree, Isaac and the ram, Jacob and the stone and Moses and the burning bush indicating an understanding of the 'altars of the Gentiles' as natural phenomena.

30 Meslin, *Kalendes*, 40ff.

31 Ginzburg, *Ecstasies*, 185–6.

32 Tours 567, Canon 23, in de Clercq, *Concilia Galliae a. 511–a. 695*, 191: *Sunt etiam qui in festivitate cathedrae domni Petri intrita mortuis offerunt et post missas redeuntes ad domus proprias ad gentilium revertuntur errores et post corpus Domini sacratus daemoni escas accipiunt.*

33 Ginzburg, *Ecstasies*, 185–6.

34 The sermons have been translated into English in three volumes by Sister M. M. Mueller: *Cæsarius of Arles: Sermons* (New York and Washington, DC, 1956, 1963, 1973). Sermons 51–3 (vol. 1) which raise many of these points are, as Hen points out, *Culture and Religion* at 165, only known from the eighth-century homiliary of Burchard of Würzburg. He raises the interesting question of whether they can be considered authentic.

35 Sermon 204: Mueller, *Cæsarius* vol. 3, 71–4. It is largely drawn from Maximus of Turin.

36 Cæsarius' views on the Kalends of January should be compared with the massive sermon *Contra paganos* preached on 1 January by Augustine of Hippo: see F. Dolbeau (ed.), *Vingt-six Sermons au Peuple d' Afrique* (Paris, 1996), 345–417.

37 Sermon 193: Mueller, *Cæsarius* vol. 3, 34.

38 See H. O. Old, *The Reading and Preaching of the Scriptures in the Worship of the Christian Church* vol. 3, *The Medieval Church* (Grand Rapids, MI and Cambridge, 1999), 80.

39 Barlow, *Martini Opera*, 164; A. Ferreiro, 'St Martin of Braga's policy towards heretics and pagan practices', *American Benedictine Review* 34 (1983), 372–95 suggests the possibility of an unknown common source.

40 Basing himself on Gen. 1.4: *et divisit deus inter lucem et tenebras*. See also Martin's *De Pascha* in Barlow, *Martini Opera*, 259–75.

41   Translation: Hillgarth, *Conversion*, 58.

42   *Ibid.*, 61.

43   Hillgarth misses out the condemnation of 'observing the foot', Barlow, *Martini Opera*, 198.

44   Barlow, *Martini Opera*, 140–1. See n. 19 above. Harmening, *Superstitio*, 143, suggests that Cæsarian and oriental traditions came together in Martin.

45   J. N. Hillgarth, 'Popular religion in Visigothic Spain', in E. James (ed.), *Visigothic Spain: New Approaches* (Oxford, 1980), 3–60 insists on the use of the term 'pagan' cults in relation to the beliefs condemned by Martin of Braga. He also suggests at 26 that in the seventh century Ildefonsus of Toledo wrote about the process of converting someone who came from paganism to Christianity. But the passage in question (*PL* 96, 118–19) seems to refer to someone who believes in God, but not necessarily as a god of the visible creation.

46   Hillgarth, *Conversion,* 61, my emphasis.

47   *Ibid.*

48   'shrines of the saints', Hillgarth, *Conversion,* 62; Barlow, *Martini Opera*, 202, *loca sanctorum.*

49   The translations used are those of Raymond Van Dam: *Glory of the Martyrs* (Liverpool, 1998) and *Glory of the Confessors* (Liverpool, 1998).

50   See for example I. Wood, 'Constructing cults in early medieval France: local saints and churches in Burgundy and the Auvergne 400–1000', in A. Thacker and R. Sharpe (eds), *Local Saints and Local Churches in the Early Medieval West* (Oxford, 2002), 155–87; D. Shanzer, 'So many saints – so little time: the *Libri Miraculorum* of Gregory of Tours,' *Journal of Medieval Latin* 13 (2003), 19–60; and Freeman, *Holy Bones, Holy Dust*, 56–7. For an earlier, functionalist approach that presents the cult of relics as 'therapy' and illness and healing as reflections of social exclusion and re-integration into the community, see R. Van Dam, *Leadership and Community in Late Antique Gaul* (Berkeley, Los Angeles and London, 1985), 256–76.

51   Hen, *Culture and Religion*, 86.

52   See the introduction to *GM*, 15.

53   *GM* introduction, 5; *GM* 1, Van Dam 20; *GM* 5, Van Dam 22.

54   *GC* introduction, 10–11.

55   *GM* introduction, 11–13.

56   G. de Nie, 'Cæsarius of Arles and Gregory of Tours: two sixth-century Gallic bishops and 'Christian magic', in D. Edel (ed.), *Cultural Identity and Cultural Integration. Ireland and Europe in the Early Middle Ages* (Dublin, 1995), 170–96.

57   Shanzer and Wood (eds), *Avitus of Vienne*, 154–6.

58   M. Conway, 'St. Radegund's reliquary at Poitiers', *The Antiquaries' Journal* 3 (1923), 1–12.

59   J. W. George, *Venantius Fortunatus, A Latin Poet in Merovingian Gaul* (Oxford, 1992), 30–1; 63.

60   *GM* 5, Van Dam 23–4.

61   *GM* 14, Van Dam 36.

62   *GM* 5, Van Dam 25.

63   *GM* 5, Van Dam 25.

64   *GM* 5, Van Dam 23.

65   *GM* 5, Van Dam 26–7.

66   J. Sørensen *A Cognitive Theory of Magic* (Lanham, MD, New York, Toronto and Plymouth, 2007), 70.

67   *Ibid.*, 69.

68   J. M. McCulloh, 'The cult of relics in the letters and "Dialogues" of Pope Gregory the Great', *Traditio* 32 (1976), 145–84 classes these as *brandea* (sing. *brandeum*). C. Leyser, '"Divine power flowed from this book": ascetic language and episcopal authority in Gregory of Tours' *Life of the Fathers*' in K. Mitchell and I. Wood (eds), *The World of Gregory of Tours* (Leiden, Boston and Köln, 2002), 281–94, looks at the theme of *virtus* in writing but also mentions at 287 the way in which 'miraculous power could rub off from the saint's body to objects through physical contact.'

69   *GM* 28, Van Dam 45–6.

70   *GM* 28, Van Dam 45–6.

71   GM 6, Van Dam 27.

72   *GC* 84, Van Dam 90.

73   *GM* 27, Van Dam 45–6.

74   GM 50, Van Dam 59–60.

75   *GC* 34, Van Dam 47–8.

76   *GM* 56, Van Dam 62–3.

77   M. Vieillard-Troiekouroff, *Les Monuments Religieux de la Gaule d' Après les Oeuvres de Grégoire de Tours* (Paris, 1976), 340–1.

78   *GM* 29, Van Dam 29.

79   See *GC* 17; *GC* 22; *GC* 35; *GC* 46; *GC* 79; *GC* 83.

80   *GC* 38, Van Dam 50.

81   *GC* 40, Van Dam 52.

82   *GC* 61, Van Dam 61.

83   *GC* 71, Van Dam 75–6.

84   *GC* 27, Van Dam 41–2.

85 *GC* 31, Van Dam 45.

86 *GC* 36, Van Dam 49.

87 *GC* 40, Van Dam 52–3.

88 See R. Van Dam, *Saints and Their Cults in Late Antique Gaul* (Princeton, 1993), 53.

89 *GM* 83, Van Dam 107–9; *GC* 20, Van Dam 34–5.

90 E.g. *GC* 55, 68, 97, 102, 103.

91 *GC* 43, Van Dam 55.

92 *GC* 22, Van Dam, 36–8. See *GC* 23; 26; 36; 52; 58; 60; 63, 65; 81; 82; 84; 87; 88; 89; 99; 100 for cures of chills and fevers.

93 Mutes: *GC*, 53; the blind: *GC* 26, 34, 53, 60, 82, 88, 92, 101; the possessed (*inergumini*) *GC* 32, 48, 58, 60, 92; contracted and twisted limbs or paralysis: *GC* 56, 57, 79, 93, 60, 88, 94, 101; toothache: *GC* 52, 93, 103.

94 *GC* 78, Van Dam 81–3; *GM* 50, Van Dam 76.

95 *GM* 90, Van Dam 114–15.

96 *GM* 27, Van Dam 47.

97 *GM* 1, Van Dam 20.

98 *GC* 70, Van Dam 74.

99 The classic discussion is P. Geary, 'Humiliation of saints', in S. Wilson (ed.), *Saints and Their Cults* (Cambridge, 1983), 123–40.

100 Sørensen, *Cognitive Theory of Magic*, 69–70.

101 Hen, *Culture and Religion*, 97–100. For local saints in two regions of Francia, see Wood, 'Constructing Cults'.

102 N. Veas Ruiz and J. C. Sanchez, 'El elemento acuático en las iglesia visigoda', in A. Gonzalez Blanco and J. M. Blázquez Martínez, *Cristianismo y Acculturación en Tiempos del Imperio Romano. Antigüedad Cristiana* VII (Murcia, 1990), 487–93.

103 Vives, *Concilios*, 195–6.

104 See G. Halfond, *The Archaeology of Frankish Church Councils AD 511–768* (Leiden, 2010), 196.

105 Canon 16, de Clercq, *Concilia Galliae a. 511–a. 695*, 29: *Sunt enim nonulli, qui cum paganis comedunt cibos; sed hos benigne placuit admonitione suaderi, ut ab erroribus pristinis revocentur. Quod si neglexerint et idolatriis vel immolantibus se miscuerint, paenitentiae tempus exsoluant.*

106 *Penitential* 24, Walker, *Columbani Opera*, 178–9.

107 H. G. J. Beck, *The Pastoral Care of Souls in the South-East of France During the Sixth Century* (Rome, 1950), 189.

108 The three letters 'On the Canons' addressed to Amphilochius of Iconium

translated in P. Schaff and H. Wace (eds), *Basil: Letters and Select Works*, *Nicene and Post-Nicene Fathers* (2nd series, vol. 8, 1895, reprinted Peabody, MA, 1999), 223–9, 236–40, 255–9.

109 Beck, *Pastoral Care*, 192–5, for conciliar legislation and performance of penance.

110 Beck, *Pastoral Care*, 216–7.

111 R. Meens, 'Remedies for sins', in T. F. X. Noble and J. M. H. Smith (eds), *Cambridge History of Christianity. Early Medieval Christianities c. 600–c. 1100* (Cambridge, 2008), 399–415 and 736–47, at 404.

112 For more on the origins of the new style of penance, see M. Dunn, 'Paradigms of penance', *Journal of Medieval Monastic Studies* 1 (2012), 17–39.

113 See *Synodus I S. Patricii*, 'First Synod of St Patrick', in L. Bieler (ed. and trans.), *The Irish Penitentials* (Dublin, 1963), 54–9.

114 See Dunn, 'Paradigms of penance', 23–7 and Gildas, *Praefatio Gildae de Poenitentia*, 'Preface of Gildas on Penance', Bieler, *Irish Penitentials*, 60–5.

115 *Paenitentialis Vinniani*, 'Penitential of Finnian', in Bieler, *Irish Penitentials*, 74–95, esp. 76–7.

116 Bieler, *Irish Penitentials*, 74–5. T. O' Loughlin, *Celtic Theology* (London, 2000), 57, places these passages in the monastic context of Cassian's emphasis on contrition and conversion of heart. This is elaborated at considerable length in the *Twentieth Conference* 'On repentance and reparation', where Abba Pinufius discusses the need to wipe from one's mind all recollection of major sins so as not to wallow in them; but at the same time the need to be constantly aware of and do penance for the little sins by which 'the righteous person falls seven times ... and gets up again'. See B. Ramsey, *John Cassian. The Conferences* (New York and Mahwah, NJ, 1997), 691–706.

117 T. M. Charles-Edwards, *Early Christian Ireland* (Cambridge, 2000), 240.

118 Boyer, *Religion Explained,* 171–91; Barrett, *Why Would Anyone Believe*, 89–90.

119 J. Carey, 'From David to Labraid: sacral kingship and the emergence of monotheism in Israel and Ireland', in K. Ritari and A. Bergholm (eds) *Approaches to Religion and Mythology in Celtic Studies* (Cambridge, 2008), 2–27. Carey offers the hypothesis that the idea of the 'one God *to the gods*' reflects attempts by Christian churchmen to 'assert the claims of the Christian God against those of the divinities whose worship he was superseding'. This is difficult to accept: Christian churchmen generally characterized pagan gods as 'demons' and their representations as things of wood, metal or stone – see the letter of Pope Boniface V in Bede *HE* II, 19, *Bede's Ecclesiastical History*, Colgrave and Mynors (eds), 168–71.

120 Boyer, *Religion Explained*, 181–3.

121 See O. D. Watkins, *A History of Penance*, vol. 2 (London, 1920), 566; there is also a little evidence for pious laypeople who spontaneously submitted minor faults to episcopal correction: Beck, *Pastoral Care*, 212–13.

122 See Beck, *Pastoral Care*, 206 for Cæsarius' views.

123 Watkins, *History of Penance*, vol. 2, 567. In Canons 11 and 12 of Toledo III, it is noticeable that the priest plays an important role in what otherwise seems to be a reassertion of traditional forms.

124 *Ad sedem Britonorum ecclesias que sunt intro Britones una cum monasterio Maximini et que in Asturiis sunt.* David, *Études Historiques sur la Galice et le Portugal*, 30–4, 56–60.

125 T. M. Charles-Edwards, 'The Penitential of Columbanus' in M. Lapidge (ed.), *Columbanus: Studies on the Latin Writings* (Woodbridge, 1997), 217–39 at 225.

126 Walker, *Sancti Columbani Opera*, 169–81.

127 Meens, 'Remedies for sins', 407; *idem*, Reforming the clergy: a context for the use of the Bobbio penitential', in Hen and Meens (eds), *The Bobbio Missal*, 154–67. For the 'minor Frankish penitentials' see the edition of R. Kottje, L. Körntgen, and U. Spengler-Reffgen (eds), *Pænitentialia Minora Franciae et Italiae Saeculi VIII–IX CCSL* 156 (Turnhout, 1994).

128 *De S. Barbato, AASS*, Feb. III, 139: *Cumque caritatem B. Barbati, illorumque perpenderet infirmitatem, concessit, vt sicut sanctissimus vir diuinis medicaminibus conabatur eos a peccatorum febribus, vt ex intimis squallida profluente sanie emundaret …*

129 Meens, 'Remedies for sins', 407.

130 Meens, 'Remedies for sins', 404–5.

131 Meens, 'Remedies for sins', 407–8.

132 *GM* Prologue, Van Dam 18, translates: *Ergo haec nos oportet sequi, scribere atque loqui, quae ecclesiam Dei aedificent et quae mentes inopes ad notitiam perfectae fidei instructione sancta faecundent* as '… it is proper for me to follow this advice [referring back to two citations from Paul] by writing and proclaiming what edifies the church of God and what enriches barren minds to recognition of perfect faith by means of holy teaching'. Or it might read: 'Therefore it behoves us to follow, to write and to speak those things which may build the church of God and which may make fruitful needy minds to acquaintance with perfect faith through holy teaching'.

133 *GM* 106, Van Dam 133.

134 *GM* 40, Van Dam 61–3.

135 *GC* 76, Van Dam, 80.

136 North, *Heathen Gods*, 22, accepts Gregory's testimony that she was worshipped in fourth-century Gaul.

137 *GC* 2, my translation, which differs slightly from Van Dam 18–19, who renders *Nulla est enim religio in stagnum* as 'For there is [to be] no religious piety to a lake'.

138 *Ibid.*

139 See Derks, *Gods, Temples and Ritual Practices*, 215–39 for a study of Roman pagan vows and offerings.

140 *GM* 50, Van Dam 74.

141 *Castigation of Rustics,* 8: Hillgarth *Conversion of Western Europe*, 57.

142 F. Lifshitz, *The Norman Conquest of Pious Neustria. Hagiographic Discourse and Saintly Relics 684–1090* (Toronto, 1995), 26.

143 See for example *GC*, Van Dam 20–1.

Chapter 6

1 E. James, *Europe's Barbarians AD 200–600* (Harlow, 2009), 131. See also H. Fehr, 'Germanische Einwanderung oder kulturelle Neuorientierung? Zu den Anfängen des Reihengräberhorizontes', *Zwischen Spätantike und Frühmittelalter: Archäologie des 4. bis 7. Jahrhunderts im Westen* (Berlin, 2008), 67–102.

2 G. Halsall, 'Social change around A.D. 600: an Austrasian perspective', in M. O.H. Carver (ed.), *The Age of Sutton Hoo* (Woodbridge, 1992), 265–78. See also Halsall's updated views in his *Cemeteries and Society in Merovingian Gaul. Selected Studies in Archaeology and History 1992–2009* (Leiden, 2010), 287–322.

3 G. Halsall, 'Archaeology and the late Roman frontier in northern Gaul: the so-called Föderatengräber reconsidered', in W. Pohl and H. Reimitz (eds), *Grenze und Differenz in Frühenmittelalter* (Vienna, 2000), 167–80; James, *Europe's Barbarians* 201–13; see also Halsall's *Cemeteries and Society*, 91–167.

4 See for example, G. Halsall, 'The origins of the Reihengräberzivilisation: forty years on', in J. Drinkwater and H. Elton (eds), *Fifth Century Gaul. A Crisis of Identity* (Cambridge, 1992b), 196–333; *idem, Early Medieval Cemeteries: An Introduction to Burial Archaeology in the Post-Roman West* (Skelmorlie, 1995); *idem,* 'Ethnicity and early medieval cemeteries', *Arqueología y Territorio Medieval* 18 (2011), 15–27; B. K. Young, 'Has anyone seen the barbarians? Remarks on the missing archaeology of the Visigoths in Gaul', in Mathisen and Shanzer (eds), *The Battle of Vouillé*, 183–201.

5   M. Kazanski and P. Périn, 'Identité ethnique en Gaule à l' époque des grandes migrations et des royaumes barbares: étude de cas archéologiques', *Antiquités Nationales* 39 (2008), 181–216; M. Kazanski and P. Périn, '" Foreign" objects in the Merovingian cemeteries of northern Gaul', in D. Quast (ed.), *Foreigners in Early Medieval Europe* (Mainz, 2009), 149–67; C. Giostra, 'Goths and Lombards in Italy: the potential of archaeology with respect to ethnocultural identification', *Postclassical Archaeologies* 1 (2011), 7–36.

6   See for example, de Vingo, *From Tribe to Province to State*, 218, 222, 223, 226 and 227 for burials; and for an example of an imagined cremation, the illustration in H. Williams, *Death and Memory in Early Medieval Britain* (Cambridge, 2006), 92.

7   Boyer, *Religion Explained*, 260.

8   Boyer, *Religion Explained*, 232–61, 'Why is religion about death?' For ideas of pollution and fear of the spirit of the dead (*mulo*) amongst modern Roma, as well as for their funerary rites of transition, see J. Okely, *The Traveller-Gypsies* (Cambridge, 1983), 215–30.

9   Tertullian, *Treatise on the Soul* (*De Anima*), in A. Robertson and J. Donaldson (eds), *Ante-Nicene Fathers* (vol. 3, 1885, reprinted Peabody, MA, 1999), 181–235, esp. 230–1, thought that only Christ himself could be in Heaven before the resurrection and Last Judgment, while the souls of martyrs would enjoy immediate admission to Paradise. The souls of the Christian dead would wait in Hades, located in the central part of the earth, until the general resurrection and Judgment. See, by contrast, Cyprian, *On the Mortality* (*De mortalitate*) in A. Robertson and J. Donaldson (eds), *Ante Nicene Fathers* (vol. 5, 1885, reprinted Peabody, MA, 1999), 469–75.

10   1 Pet. 4.5.

11   U. Volp, *Tod und Ritual in den christlichen Gemeinden der Antike* (Leiden-Boston, 2002), 176–185.

12   G. Rowell, *The Liturgy of Christian Burial* (London, 1977), 23.

13   *Confessions*, Book ix, ch. 12, in P. Schaff (ed.), *Nicene and Post-Nicene Fathers* (1st ser., vol. 1, 1886, reprinted Peabody, MA, 1999), 139–40.

14   For further discussion of these issues, see Dunn, *Christianization of the Anglo-Saxons*, Chapter 2.

15   M. J. Johnson, 'Pagan-Christian burial practices of the fourth century: shared tombs?', *Journal of Early Christian Studies* 5 (1997), 37–59.

16   M. A. Handley, *Death, Society and Culture: Inscriptions and Epitaphs in Gaul and Spain*, BAR International Series 1135 (Oxford, 2003), 9.

17   *HL* III, 34: Foulke, *History of the Lombards*, 147–8.

18   For this genre in European folk-tales, see J. N. Bremmer, *The Early Greek Concept of the Soul* (Princeton, NJ, 1987), 132–5.

19   *Ibid.*, 13–69. See H. Lixfeld, 'Die Guntramsage (AT 1645 A), *Fabula* 13 (1972), 67–107, for the tale of Gunthram.

20   Particularly in Evagrius of Pontus and John Cassian: see M. Dunn, *The Emergence of Monasticism* (Oxford, 2003), 21–4, 73–81.

21   M. Conti, *The Life and Works of Potamius of Lisbon*, Instrumenta Patristica XXXII (Turnhout, 1998), 58–74, 142–7.

22   *Dialogues*, IV. 5: trans. O. J. Zimmerman, *Saint Gregory the Great Dialogues* (Washington, DC, 1959), 196–8.

23   On funerary ritual as a rite of transition, see A. van Gennep, trans. M. B. Vizedom and G. L. Caffee, *The Rites of Passage* (London, 1960), 146–65.

24   R. Hertz, trans. R. and C. Needham, *Death and the Right Hand* (London, 1960), 44; van Gennep, *Rites*, 148: 'The chief rite of this period consists of either removing the flesh or waiting until it falls off by itself.'

25   P. Metcalf and R. Huntington, *Celebrations of Death. The Anthropology of Mortuary Ritual* (revised edn, Cambridge, 1991), 79–85.

26   Escher, *Les Burgondes*, 7–15.

27   See for example, S. Sadowski, 'The youngest phase of Wielbark Culture cemetery in Swaryczów, site 1', in B. Niezabitowska-Wiśniewska, M. Juściński, P. Łuczkiewicz and S. Sadowski (eds), *The Turbulent Epoch* (Lublin, 2008), 303–14.

28   I. Bona, *The Dawn of the Dark Ages* (Budapest, 1976), 33; I. Barbiera, 'Memory of a better death. Conventional and exceptional burial rites in central European cemeteries of the AD 6th and 7th centuries', in I. Barbiera, A. M. Choyke and J. A. Rasson (eds), *Materializing Memory*, BAR International Series 1977 (Oxford, 2009), 65–75. C. Giostra, 'Goths and Lombards in Italy: the potential of archaeology with respect to ethnocultural identification', criticizes the methodology used in I. Barbiera, *Changing Lands in Changing Memories. Migration and Identity During the Lombard Invasions* (Florence, 2005). See also I. Barbiera, 'Sixth-century cemeteries in Hungary and Italy: a comparative approach', in W. Pohl and P. Erhart (eds), *Die Langobarden – Herrschaft und Identität* (Vienna, 2005), 301–20.

29   James, *Europe's Barbarians*, 131.

30   Heather and Matthews, *Goths in the Fourth Century*, 63.

31   In the South Pannonian Lombard cemetery of Kajdacs, for example, there are late cremations dating from the period 536–68 amongst interments: I. Bóna and J. B. Horváth, *Langobardische Gräberfelder in West-Ungarn* (Budapest, 2009), 182.

32   Dunn, *Christianization of the Anglo-Saxons*, 88.

33   For example: James, *Europe's Barbarians*, 111–19; Halsall, *Barbarian Migrations*
     35–45 and 59–62; V. Bierbrauer, 'Archäologie der Langobarden in Italien:
     ethnische Interpretation und Stand der Forschung', in Pohl and Erhart (eds),
     Die Langobarden, 21–66; Giostra, 'Goths and Lombards in Italy'.

34   For the older approach, M. Todd, *The Early Germans* (Oxford, 1992), 82–3.
     For an early study of double burials, see H. Lüdemann, *Mehrfachbelegte*
     Gräber im Frühen Mittelalter (Würzburg, 1990). But now see C. Kümmel,
     Ur- und frühgeschichtlicher Grabraub. Archäologische Interpretation und
     kulturanthropologische Erklärung (Münster, New York, Munich and Berlin,
     2009) and M. C. van Haperen, 'Rest in pieces: an interpretive model of
     early medieval "grave robbery"', *Medieval and Modern Matters* 1 (2010),
     1–36; E. Aspöck, 'Past "disturbances" of graves as a source: taphonomy and
     interpretation of reopened early medieval inhumation graves at Brunn am
     Gebirge (Austria) and Winnall II (England)', *Oxford Journal of Archaeology* 30
     (2011), 299–324.

35   For example, A. Molinero Perez, 'La necropólis visigoda de Duraton.
     Excavaciones del plan nacional de 1942 y 1943', *Acta Arqueológica Hispanica*
     4 (1948), 1–198, Lámina XVII; J. Martinez Santa Ollala, *Excavaciones en la*
     necropólis visigoda de Herrera de Pisuerga (Madrid, 1933), Lámina XXIX.

36   See the comments of A. Jepure, 'Interpretationsprobleme der
     Westgothenarchäologie', in S. Brather (ed.), *Zwischen Spätantike und*
     Frühmittelalter: Archäologie des 4. bis 7. Jahrhunderts im Westen.
     Ergänzungsbände zum Reallexikon der germanischen Altertumskunde 57
     (Berlin and New York, 2008), 193–209. Jepure discusses double and multiple
     interments from the standpoint of the difficulty of establishing a chronology of
     the objects buried with the dead.

37   D. Fernández Galliano Ruiz, 'Excavaciones en la necropolis hispano-visigoda
     del Camino de los Afligidos (Alcalà de Henares)', *Noticiario Arqueloogico*
     Hispanico 4 (1976), 5–90, at 64. N. Roselló, 'Necropolis de Vistalegre (Aspe,
     Alicante)', *Arqeología Medieval Española* 11 (1987), 374–8, indicates instances
     of bones being placed at the foot of the new inhumation and others where the
     new body was simply laid on top of the old.

38   M. Almagro Gorbea, 'Hallazgos de epoca visigoda en Almodóvar del Pinar
     (Cuenca)', *Trabajos de prehistoria* 27 (1970), 311–26.

39   See A. Simmer, *Le Cimitière Mérovingien d' Audun-le-Tiche* (Paris, 1988), esp.
     139–53. A second phase of Audun's occupation began in the mid-seventh
     century: at this stage there was an increase in the number of ground-level
     sepulchres and surface markers. B. Effros, *Merovingian Mortuary Archaeology*

and the Making of the Middle Ages (Berkeley, Los Angeles and London, 2003), 204. See also F. Stein, 'Verhaltensweisen der Bestattungsgemeinschaft von Rency/Renzig bei Audun-le-Tiche in Lothringen', in D. Hägermann, W. Haubrichs, J. Jarnut, C. Giefern, (eds), *Akkulturation: Probleme einer germanisch-romanischen Kultursynthese in Spätantike und frühem Mittelalter* (Berlin and New York, 2004), 274–310; this is conceptualized in terms of an opposition between Roman Christian unfurnished burial and Frankish furnished burial.

40   A. Simmer, 'Le nord du département de la Moselle à l' époque mérovingienne', *Revue Archéologique de l' Est et du Centre-Est* 38 (1987), 333–96, 388.

41   R. Lansival, 'La nécropole mérovingienne de Metzervisse (Moselle)', *Revue Archéologique de l' Est* 56 (2007), 231–310.

42   See http://www.inrap.fr/archeologie-preventive/Ressources-multimedias/Audiovisuels/Reportages-videos/Reportages-2011/p-13082-lg0-Les-tombes-merovingiennes-de-Lagny-sur-Marne.htm [Accessed 13 July 2013].

43   Simmer, 'Le nord du département de la Moselle', 388.

44   See L. M. Danforth, *The Death Rituals of Rural Greece* (Princeton, 1982).

45   De Clercq, *Concilia Galliae a. 511–a. 695*, 246.

46   H. R. Ellis Davidson, *The Road to Hel. A Study of the Conception of the Dead in Old Norse Literature* (Cambridge, 1943), 65–120.

47   See Dunn, *Christianization of the Anglo-Saxons*, 8–9.

48   *Miracula S. Wulframni Episcopi Senonensis, AASS*, March III, 147.

49   *Dialogues*, IV, 46: trans. Zimmerman, *Gregory the Great Dialogues*, 257. See also Dunn, *Christianization of the Anglo-Saxons*, 173.

50   H. Williams, 'Monuments and the past in early Anglo-Saxon England', *World Archaeology* 31 (1998), 90–109.

51   Effros, *Merovingian Mortuary Archaeology*, 191–2 considers that 'cemeterial remains at sites in or over Roman ruins contained a disproportionate number of adult males'; though she adds that 'these statistics may not be entirely accurate'.

52   See the references at notes 35 and 37 above.

53   A. Laumon, 'La nécropole mérovingienne de Bettborn', *Annuaire de la Société d' Histoire et d' Archéologie de Lorraine*, 77 (1977), 51–71; Simmer, 'Le nord du département de la Moselle'.

54   L. Pejrani Baricco, 'Il Piemonte tra Ostrogoti e Longobardi', in G. P. Brogliolo and A. Chavarria Arnau (eds), *I Longobardi. Dalla caduta dell'Impero all' alba dell' Italia* (Milan, 2007), 255–65.

55   See J. J. Rigaud de Sousa, 'Novas considerações sobre a necropole do Beiral

(Ponte de Lima)', *Gallaecia* 5 (1979), 293–303; A. Viana, 'Necrópole Romano-Suevica (?) de Beiral', *Arquivo do Alto Minho* 10 (1961), 115–23.

56 Sulpicius Severus, *Vita Martini*, XII, in P. Schaff and H. Wace, *Nicene and Post-Nicene Fathers* (2nd series, vol. 11, Peabody, MA, 1894, repr. 1999), 9–10.

57 *Life* of St Columba, III, 6: trans. R. Sharpe, *Adomnán of Iona. Life of St Columba* (Harmondsworth, 1995), 210.

58 F. S. Paxton, *Christianizing Death. The Creation of a Ritual Process in Medieval Europe* (Ithaca and London, 1990), 84–5.

59 See the discussion in Paxton, *Christianizing Death*, 85–8.

60 For a summary of the difficulties of establishing an Ostrogothic archaeology of Italy, see now C. Giostra, 'Goths and Lombards in Italy' at 7; also de Vingo, *From Tribe to Province to State*, 197–206.

61 G. P. Brogiolo, E. Possenti, 'L' età gota in Italia settentrionale nella transizione tra tarda antichità e alto medioevo', in P. Delogu (ed.), *Le Invasioni Barbariche nel Meridione dell' Impero: Visigoti, Vandali, Ostrogoti* (Catanzaro, 2001), 257–95; E. Micheletto, 'Materiali di età gota in Piemonte: un aggiornamento', in R. Fiorillo and P. Peduto (eds), *Atti del III Congresso Nazionale di Archeologia Medievale* (Florence, 2003), 697–704.

62 See E. Cirelli, *Ravenna: Archeologia di una Città* (Borgo S. Lorenzo, 2008), 116; V. Manzelli, *Ravenna* (Rome, 2000), esp. 80–1; A. Augenti, E. Cirelli, N. Mancassola, V. Manzelli, 'Archeologia medievale a Ravenna: un progetto per la città et il territorio', in R. Fiorillo and P. Peduto (eds), *Atti del III Congresso Nazionale di Archeologia Medievale*, 271–6.

63 Cassiodorus, *Variorum Libri xii*, IV, 34: *MGH Auct. Ant.* 12, 129.

64 For these inscriptions see Escher, *Genèse et Évolution du Deuxième Royaume Burgonde*, Fichier Lapidaire, L. 053–7; H. Parriat and R. Perraud, 'Les inscriptions paléochrétiennes de Briord (Ain)', *La Physiophile* 79 (1973), 14–37; Gaillard de Sémainville, 'Implantation des Burgondes', 32–3.

65 Handley, *Death, Society and Culture*, 172. For an inscription inside a Christian Breton sarcophagus of the fifth or sixth centuries: W. Davies, J. Graham-Campbell, M. Handley, P. Kershaw, J. T. Koch, G. Le Duc and K. Lockyear, *The Inscriptions of Early Medieval Brittany* (Oakville, CT and Aberystwyth, 2000), 183–94. On inscriptions in this period in general, see A. Petrucci, *Writing the Dead. Death and Writing Strategies in the Western Tradition* (Stanford, 1998), 29–43.

66 L. Pejrani Baricco, *Presenze Longobarde. Collegno nell' Alto Medioevo* (Turin, 1004), 30–1 and 46, n. 28. See the discussion in Bóna and Horváth (eds),

Langobardische Gräberfelder, 182–4, with some examples from excavations at Szentendre-Pannnoniatelep at 93–136,

67   For Romans d' Isonzo, see the summary at www.archeologia.beniculturali.it/index.php?it/142/scavi/scaviarcheologici_4e048966cfa3a/5 [accessed 13 July 2013]; for Collegno, principally, Pejrani Baricco, *Presenze Longobarde*, photos and discussion of postholes at 30–1. See also *eadem*, 'Il Piemonte tra Ostrogoti e Longobardi' in Brogliolo and Chavarria Arnau (eds), *I Longobardi*, 255–65.

68   The figure is cited by C. Giostra, 'Luoghi e segni della morte in età longobarda: tradizione e transizione nelle pratiche dell'aristocrazia', in G. P. Brogliolo and A. Chavarria Arnau (eds), *Archeologia e Società tra Tardo Antico e Alto Medioevo (V–IX secolo)* (Mantua, 2007), 311–44.

69   V. Bierbrauer, 'The cross goes north: from Late Antiquity to Merovingian times south and north of the Alps', in M. O. H. Carver (ed.), *The Cross Goes North. Processes of Conversion in Northern Europe AD 300–1300* (Woodbridge, 2003), 429–42.

70   *HL* V, 34: Foulke, *History of the Lombards*, 238.

71   Pejrani Baricco, *Presenze Longobarde*, 25; G. Roma, *Necropoli e Insediamenti Fortificati nella Calabria Settentrionale: 1 Le Necropoli Altomedievali* (Bari, 2001), 33–49.

72   Bóna, in Bóna and Horváth, *Langobardische Gräberfelder*, 183, notes *perticas* in Pannonian Lombard cemeteries. There may be evidence of one at the head of a grave containing a body at Szentendre-Pannoniatelep, *ibid.*, 101.

73   See A. Zironi, 'Historia Langobardorum V, 34: la "colomba dei morti" fra Bibbia gotica e sepolture franche', in P. Chiesa (ed.), *Paolo Diacono. Uno scrittore fra tradizione longobarda e rinnovamente carolingio* (Udine, 2000), 601–25.

74   C. Mutinelli, 'Scoperta di una necropoli "famigliare" longobarda nel terreno già di Santo Stefano in Pertica a Cividale', *Memorie Storiche Forogiuliesi* XLVI (1960-1), 65–95 and 30 plates; I. Ahumada Silva, P. Lopreato and A. Tagliaferri, *La Necropoli di S. Stefano 'In Pertica'. Campagne di Scavo 1987–8* (Cividale, 1990).

75   Bóna, in Bóna and Horváth, *Langobardische Gräberfelder*, 182, considers depth of burial an indicator of social status: 2–3 m was, according to him, characteristic of interments of free Lombards and exceptional depth (4–5 m), of aristocratic burials, with a 'record' of 7 m, while those of servile status were buried at a depth of only 1 m.

76   For discussions of such reactions to epidemic, see P. Barber, *Vampires, Burial and Death: Folklore and Reality* (New Haven, CT and London), 1988 and Dunn, *Christianization of the Anglo-Saxons,* Chapters 2 and 7.

77   Ahumada Silva, Lopreato and Tagliaferri, *La Necropoli d S. Stefano*, 43–8.

78   See L. K. Little (ed.), *Plague and the End of Antiquity – The Pandemic of 541–750* (Cambridge, 2007).

79   Gregory of Tours *DLH* IV, 31 (Clermont-Ferrand); IX, 22 (Marseilles, 580s); X, 1 (Rome, 590) at Thorpe, *History of the Franks*, 226, 510, 543–7; Paul the Deacon, II, 4 (Liguria, 566) III, 24 (Rome); VI, 5 (Pavia, 680) at Foulke, *History of the Lombards*, 56–8, 127–8, 254–5.

80   See Dunn, *Christianization of the Anglo-Saxons*, Chapters 2 and 7.

81   M. Kulikowski, 'Plague in Spanish Late Antiquity', in Little (ed.), *Plague and the End of Antiquity*, 150–70, at 158–9.

82   See C. Billard, F. Carré, M. Guillon, C. Treffort, D. Jagu and G. Verron, 'L' occupation funéraire des monuments mégalithiques pendant le haut Moyen-Age. Modalités et essai d' interprétation', *Bulletin de la Société Préhistorique Française* 93 (1996), 279–286, especially the discussion at 285.

83   C. Giostra, 'Luoghi e segni della morte in età longobarda: tradizione e transizione nelle pratiche dell' aristocrazia', in Brogiolo and Chavarria Arnau (eds), *Archeologia e Società tra Tardo Antico e Alto Medioevo*, 311–44.

84   Bede *Historia Ecclesiastica* III, 19: see B. Colgrave and R. A. B. Mynors (eds and trans.), *Bede's Ecclesiastical History of the English People* (Oxford, 1969), 268–77; M. Dunn, *The Vision of Fursey and the Development of Purgatory* (Norwich, 2007). I. Moreira, *Heaven's Purge. Purgatory in Late Antiquity* (Oxford, 2010), 113–45, attempts to minimalize the importance of Fursey and argues against suppositions of Irish influence. Dunn traces Fursey's possibly controversial preaching of his vision in Ireland, his stay in England and its setting down in writing in Francia after his death, as well as mentioning the alternative version of the afterlife offered in the seventh-century *Visio Baronti*. See also Dunn, *Christianization of the Anglo-Saxons*, Chapters 2 and 7.

85   E. Emerton, *The Letters of Saint Boniface* (New York, 1940), 23–5.

86   C. H. Talbot, *The Anglo-Saxon Missionaries in Germany* (London, 1954), 110.

87   See B. Colgrave (ed. and trans.), *The Earliest Life of Gregory the Great* (Cambridge, 1985), especially 127–9; Dunn, *Christianization of the Anglo-Saxons*, 172–3.

88   *HL* V, 34: Foulke, *History of the Lombards*, 238; D. A. Bullough, 'Urban change in early medieval Italy: the example of Pavia', *Papers of the British School at Rome* 34 (1966), 82–130.

89   *HL* VI, 55: Foulke, *History of the Lombards*, 300; S. Gasparri, 'Kingship rituals and ideology in Lombard Italy', in F. Theuws and J. Nelson (eds), *Rituals of Power From Late Antiquity to the Middle Ages* (Leiden, Boston and Köln, 2000), 95–114.

90   See F. de Rubeis, 'La scrittura esposta e la società altomedievale: verifica di una possible relazione', in Brogiolo and Chavarria Arnau (eds), *I Longobardi*, 211–25.

91   B. K. Young, 'Exemple aristocratique et mode funéraire dans la Gaule mérovingienne', *Annales ESC* 41 (2) (1986), 379–407.

92   B. Privati, 'La nécropole de Sézegnin', *Société d' Histoire et d' Archéologie de Genève* Série In-4 Tome Dixième (Geneva and Paris, 1983), 3–71.

93   C. Treffort, 'Vertues prophylactiques et sens eschatologique d' un dépôt funéraire du haut Moyen Âge: les plaques boucles rectangulaires burgondes à l' inscription', *Archéologie Médievale* 32 (2002), 31–53; H. Gaillard de Sémainville, 'Nouvel examen de la plaque-boucle mérovingienne de Landelinus découverte à. Ladoix-Serrigny (Côte-d' Or)', *Revue Archéologique de l' Est* 52 (2003), 297–327; B. K. Young, 'The imagery of personal objects: hints of "do-it-yourself" Christian culture in Merovingian Gaul?', in Cain and. Lenski (eds), *Power of Religion*, 229–54.

94   For discussions of buckles in context in Frankish burials see G. Halsall, *Settlement and Social Organization The Merovingian Region of Metz* (Cambridge, 1992), 86, 90, 96, 98,100, 106, 121, 122, 152, 153, 156 162, 186, 266, 268. Also now H. Gaillard de Sémainville, 'À propos de plaques-boucles mérovingiennes à motif chrétien', *Bulletin du centre d' études médiévales Auxerre*, available online: http://cem.revues.org/6752 [accessed 14 July 2013]; DOI: 10.4000/cem.6752.

95   Sørensen, *Cognitive Theory of Magic*, 88–90.

96   Treffort, 'Vertues prophylactiques'.

97   Dan. 14 30–8; Bel. 30–9.

98   Young, 'Imagery of personal objects', 348.

99   Treffort, 'Vertus prophylactiques', 39–40, identifies clerics and deacons among proprietors and wearers of the buckles. This argues against the suggestion, Young, 'Imagery', 342, that these buckles would have been regarded by clerics as 'pagan' or the idea that this is 'do-it-yourself' Christianity.

100 LANDELINUS FICIT NUMEN QVI ILLA PASSE DIRAVIT VIVA[T] VS QVI ANNVS MILI IN D[omin]O – or it could be read as 'Landelinus ficit [fecit] numen, qui illa possedit havit [habet] vita usque annus mille in D[e] o/D[omin]o'.

101   The names of the recipients of the buckles include those of a woman – Iustina
       – and perhaps a Nasvaldus and an Uffila; see Treffort, 'Vertus prophylactiques'.
102   J. Deshusses, 'Le sacramentaire de Gellone dans son contexte historique',
       Ephemerides Liturgicae 75 (1961), 193–210.
103   Paxton, *Christianizing Death*, 117.
104   *Ibid.*, 117–8.
105   *Ibid.*, 119–21.

Bibliography

Primary Sources

Adomnnán, *Vita Sancti Columbae*, trans. R. Sharpe, *Adomnán of Iona. Life of St Columba* (Harmondsworth, 1995).

Agnellus, *Liber Pontificalis sive vitae Pontificum Ravennatum*, trans. D. M. Deliyannis, *Agnellus of Ravenna. The Book of Pontiffs of the Church of Ravenna* (Washington, DC, 2004).

Anonymous, *Life of St Gregory*, ed. and trans. B. Colgrave, *The Earliest Life of Pope Gregory the Great* (Cambridge, 1985).

Anonymus Valesianus, trans. J. C. Rolfe, *Ammianus Marcellinus* vol. 3 (Cambridge, MA, 1939), 508–69.

Augustine, *Confessiones*, trans. P. Schaff, *Confessions Nicene and Post-Nicene Fathers*, 1st series vol. 1 (1886, reprinted Peabody, MA, 1999), 33–207.

—*Collatio cum Maximino*, trans. R. J. Teske *Debate with Maximinus, The Works of St Augustine. A Translation for the 21st Century, I/18: Arianism and Other Heresies* (New York, 1995), 175–336.

—*Sermones* Dolbeau, ed. F. Dolbeau, *Vingt-six Sermons au Peuple d' Afrique* (Paris, 1996).

Avitus of Vienne, *Opera*, selection and translation, D. Shanzer and I. Wood, *Avitus of Vienne: Letters and Selected Prose* (Liverpool, 2002).

Basil of Cæsarea, *Epistolai*, trans. P. Schaff and H. Wace, *Basil: Letters and Select Works, Nicene and Post-Nicene Fathers,* 2nd series vol. 8 (1895, reprinted Peabody, MA, 1999), 109–327.

Bede, *Historia Ecclesiastica Gentis Anglorum*, ed. and. trans. B. Colgrave and R. A. B. Mynors, *Bede's Ecclesiastical History of the English People* (Oxford, 1969).

—*De Temporum Ratione*, trans. F. Wallis, *Bede: The Reckoning of Time* (Liverpool, 1999).

Boethius A. M. S., *Trinitas Unus Deus, Utrum Pater et Filius, Quomodo Substantiae: The Trinity is One God not Three Gods; Whether Father, Son, and Holy Spirit are Substantially Predicated of the Divinity; How Substances are Good in Virtue of their Existence Without Being Substantial Goods*, trans. H. F. Stewart, E. K. Rand and S. J. Tester, *Boethius. The Theological Tractates. The Consolation of Philosophy* (Cambridge, MA, 1997).

Boniface, *Epistolae*, trans. E. Emerton, *The Letters of Saint Boniface* (New York, 1940).

Caesar, *De Bello Gallico*, trans. H. J. Edwards, *The Gallic War, Julius Caesar* (Cambridge, MA, 1917).

Cæsarius of Arles, *Sermones*, trans. M. M. Mueller, *Cæsarius of Arles: Sermons*, 3 vols. (New York and Washington, DC, 1956, 1963, 1973).

Canons of the First and Second Council of Braga, Canons of St Martin (*Canones ex Orientalium Patrum Synodis*), ed. C. W. Barlow, *Martini Episcopi Bracarensis Opera Omnia*, Papers and Monographs of the American Academy in Rome, XII (New Haven, CT, 1950), 80–144.

Carmen de synodo Ticinense, eds L. Bethmann and G. Waitz, *MGH Scriptores Rerum Langobardorum* (Hannover, 1978), 189–91.

Cassian, *Conlationes*, trans. B. Ramsey, *John Cassian. The Conferences* (New York and Mahwah, NJ, 1997).

Cassiodorus, *Variorum Libri xii*, ed. T. Mommsen, *MGH Auctores Antiquissimi* 12 (Berlin, 1894).

Codice Diplomatico del Monastero di San Colombano di Bobbio fino all' anno 1208, ed. C. Cipolla, Fonti per la storia d'Italia 52 (Rome, 1918).

Columbanus, *Letters, Sermons* and *Penitential*, trans. and ed. G. S. M. Walker, *Sancti Columbani Opera* (Dublin, 1970) 1–59, 60–121, 168–81.

Concilia Galliae a. 314–a. 506, ed. C. Munier, *Corpus Christianorum Series Latina* 148 (Turnhout, 1963).

Concilia Galliae a. 511–a. 695, ed. C. de Clercq, *Corpus Christianorum Series Latina* 148a (Turnhout, 1963).

Cyprian, *De Mortalitate*, trans. A. Robertson and J. Donaldson, *On the Mortality, Ante-Nicene Fathers* vol. 5 (1885, reprinted Peabody, MA, 1999), 469–75.

Epiphanius of Salamis, *Panarion*, trans. F. Williams, *The Panarion of Epiphanius of Salamis* (Leiden, New York and Köln, 1994).

Eunapius, trans. R. C. Blockley, *The Fragmentary Classicising Historians of the Later Roman Empire* II (Liverpool, 1983).

Finnian, *Paenitentialis Vinniani*, 'Penitential of Finnian', ed. and trans. L. Bieler, *The Irish Penitentials* (Dublin, 1963), 74–95.

Gildas, *Praefatio Gildae de Poenitentia*, 'Preface of Gildas on Penance', ed. and trans. L. Bieler *The Irish Penitentials* (Dublin, 1963), 60–5.

Gregory I (attributed), *Dialogues*, trans. O. J. Zimmerman, *Saint Gregory the Great Dialogues* (Washington DC, 1959).

Gregory I, *Epistulae*, ed. D. Norberg, *S. Gregorii Magni Registrum Epistularum* vols. I and II, *Corpus Christianorum Series Latina* 140 and 140a (Turnhout, 1982).

Gregory of Tours, *Decem Libri Historiarum*, trans. L. Thorpe, *History of the Franks* (Harmondsworth, 1974).

—*Liber Vitae Patrum*, trans E. James, *Life of the Fathers* (Liverpool, 1985).

—*Liber in Gloria Confessorum*, trans. R. Van Dam, *Glory of the Confessors*, (Liverpool, 1988).

—*Liber in Gloria Martyrum*, trans. R. Van Dam, *Glory of the Martyrs* (Liverpool, 1988).

Hilary of Poitiers, *Adversus Valentem et Ursacium* and *Ad Constantium*, trans. L. Wickham, *Hilary of Poitiers: Conflicts of Conscience and Law in the Fourth-Century Church* (Liverpool, 1997).

Hydatius, *Continuatio chronicon Hieronymianorum*, trans. and ed. R. W. Burgess, *The Chronicle of Hydatius and the Consularia Constantinopolitana* (Oxford, 1993).

Isidore of Seville, 'History of the Kings of the Goths', trans. K. B. Wolf, *Conquerors and Chroniclers of Early Medieval Spain* (2nd edn, Liverpool, 1999), 67–90.

Jerome, *Sancti Hieronymi Epistulae XCVI-CIX*, trans. and ed. J. Labourt, *Saint Jérôme, Lettres* vol. 6 (Paris, 1955).

John of Biclaro, 'Chronicle', trans. K. B. Wolf, *Conquerors and Chroniclers of Early Medieval Spain* (2nd edn, Liverpool, 1999), 51–66.

Jonas of Bobbio, *Vita Columbani II*, selections, trans. I. N. Wood, 'The Abbots of Bobbio from the *Life of Columbanus*', in T. Head (ed.), *Medieval Hagiography* (New York, 2001), 117–35.

Jordanes, *Getica*, trans. C. Mierow, *The Origins and Deeds of the Goths* (Princeton, 1908)

Kottje, R., Körntgen, L. and Spengler-Reffgen, U. (eds), *Pænitentialia Minora Franciae et Italiae Saeculi VIII-IX*, *Corpus Christianorum Series Latina* 156 (Turnhout, 1994).

Leges Langobardorum, trans. K. Fischer Drew, *The Lombard Laws* (Philadelphia, 1996).

Liber Pontificalis, trans. R. Davis, *The Book of Pontiffs (Liber Pontficalis)* (Liverpool, 2000).

Martin of Braga, *De Correctione Rusticorum*, ed. C. W. Barlow, *Martini Episcopi Bracarensis Opera Omnia*, Papers and Monographs of the American Academy in Rome, XII (New Haven, CT, 1950), 159–203.

—*De Pascha*, ed. C. W. Barlow, *Martini Episcopi Bracarensis Opera Omnia*, 259–75.

Miracula sancti Vulfranni, *AASS*, March III, 149–60.

McNeill, J. T. and Gamer, H., *Medieval Handbooks of Penance* (New York, 1938).

Origo Gentis Langobardorum, trans. and ed. A. Bracciotti, *Origo Gentis Langobardorum. Introduzione, testo critico, commento*, Biblioteca di Culture Romanobarbarica 2 (Rome, 1998).

Orosius, *Adversos Paganos*, trans. and ed. A. T. Fear, *Orosius, Seven Books of History Against the Pagans* (Liverpool, 2010).

Paul the Deacon, *Historia Langobardorum*, trans. W. Dudley Foulke, ed. E. Peters, *History of the Lombards* (Philadelphia, PN, 1974).

—*Vitae Sanctorum Patrum Emeretensium*, trans. A. T. Fear, *Lives of the Fathers of Merida, Lives of the Visigothic Fathers* (Liverpool, 1997) 45–106.

Procopius, *De Bello Gothico*, trans. H. B. Dewing, *Procopius, History of the Wars* (New York, 1924).

Salvian, *De Gubernatione Dei*, trans. E. M. Sanford, *Salvian, On the Government of God* (New York, 1930).

Scripta Arriana Latina, ed. R. Gryson, *Corpus Christianorum Series Latina* 87 (Turnhout, 1982).

Sisebut, *Epistola ad Adualualdum*, *MGH Epistolae* vol. III (Berlin, 1892) *Epistolae Wisigoticae*, 671–5.

Socrates Scholasticus, *Historia Ecclesiastica*, trans. P. Schaff and H. Wace, *Ecclesiastical History*, in *Socrates, Sozomenus: Church Histories, Nicene and Post-Nicene Fathers,* 2nd series, vol. 2 (1890, reprinted Peabody, MA, 1999), 1–178.

Sozomen, *Historia Ecclesiastica*, trans P. Schaff and H. Wace, *Ecclesiastical History*, in *Socrates, Sozomenus: Church Histories, Nicene and Post-Nicene Fathers*, 2nd series, vol. 2 (1890, reprinted Peabody, MA, 1999), 179–427.

Stevenson, J. (ed.), *Creeds, Councils and Controversies: Documents Illustrating the History of the Church AD 337–461* (London, 1983).

Sulpicius Severus, *Vita Martini, Historia Sacra*, trans. P. Schaff and H. Wace, *Life of St Martin, Sacred History, Nicene and Post-Nicene Fathers*, 2nd series, vol. 11 (1894, reprinted Peabody, MA, 1999), 1–17, 55–122.

Synodus I. S. Patricii, 'First Synod of St Patrick', ed and trans. L. Bieler, *The Irish Penitentials* (Dublin, 1963), 54–9.

Tacitus, *Annales*, trans. M. Grant, *Tacitus. The Annals of Imperial Rome* (London, 1996).

—*Germania*, trans. A. R. Birley, *Tacitus: Agricola and Germany* (Oxford, 1999).

Talbot, C. H. (trans.), *The Anglo-Saxon Missionaries in Germany Being the Lives of SS Willibrord, Boniface, Sturm, Leoba and Lebuin, together with the Hodoeporicon of St Willibald and a Selection from the Correspondence of St Boniface* (London and New York, 1954).

Tertullian, *De Anima*, trans. A. Robertson and J. Donaldson, *Treatise on the Soul, Ante-Nicene Fathers,* vol. 3 (1885, reprinted Peabody, MA, 1999), 181–235.

Theodoret, *Historia Ecclesiastica*, trans P. Schaff and H. Wace, *Ecclesiastical History, Theodoret, Jerome, Gennadius, Rufinus, Nicene and Post-Nicene Fathers*, 2nd series, vol. 3 (1892, reprinted Peabody, MA, 1994), 33–159.

Tjäder, J-O., *Die nichtliterarischen lateinischen Papyri Italiens aus der Zeit 445-700*, vol. II Papyri 29–59 (Stockholm, 1982).

Vives, J. (ed.), *Concilios Visigóticos e Hispano-Romanos* (Barcelona-Madrid, 1963).

Vita Barbati De S. Barbato Episcopo Beneventano In Italia, AASS Feb. III, 139–42.

Secondary Works

Ahrens, C., 'Ein neues spätsächsisches Gräberfeld mit Dreifach-Pferdebestattung bei Wulfsen, Kreis Harburg', *Hammaburg* NF 2 (1978), 119–24.

Ahumada Silva I., Lopreato, P. and Tagliaferri, A. (eds), *La Necropoli di di S. Stefano 'In Pertica'. Campagne di Scavo 1987-1988* (Cividale, 1990).

Aimone, M., 'Romani e Ostrogoti fra integrazione e separazione. Il contributo dell' archeologia a un dibattito storiografico', *Reti Medievali Rivista* 13 (2012), 31–96.

Almagro Gorbea, M., 'Hallazgos de época visigoda en Almodóvar del Pinar (Cuenca)', *Trabajos de prehistoria* 27 (1970), 311–26.

Antonopoulos, P., 'King Cunincpert and the Archangel Michael', in Pohl, W. and Erhart, P. (eds), *Die Langobarden*, 383–6.

Arbesmann, R., 'The "cervuli" and "anniculae" in Cæsarius of Arles', *Traditio* 35 (1979), 89–119.

Armstrong, G. and Wood, I. N. (eds), *Christianizing Peoples and Converting Individuals* (Turnhout, 2000).

Arnold, M. *Thor. Myth to Marvel* (London, 2011).

Aspöck, E., 'Past "disturbances" of graves as a source: taphonomy and interpretation of reopened early medieval inhumation graves at Brunn am Gebirge (Austria) and Winnall II (England)', *Oxford Journal of Archaeology* 30 (2011), 299–324.

Atran, S., *In Gods We Trust: the Evolutionary Landscape of Religion* (Oxford and New York, 2002).

Augenti, A., Cirelli, E., Mancassola, N., and Manzelli, V., 'Archeologia medievale a Ravenna: un progetto per la città et il territorio', in Fiorillo, R. and Peduto, P., (eds), *Atti del III Congresso Nazionale di Archeologia Medievale (Salerno, 2-5 October 2003)* (Florence, 2003), 271–6.

Ausenda, G., Delogu, P. and Wickham, C. (eds), *The Langobards Before the Frankish Conquest: An Ethnographic Perspective* (Woodbridge, 2009).

Ayres, L., *Nicaea and Its Legacy. An Approach to Fourth-Century Trinitarian Theology* (Oxford, 2004).

Baggieri, G., 'Approccio antropologico sul cavaliere guerriero longobardo della necropoli di San Mauro a Cividale', in Arslan, E. A. and Buora, M. (eds), *L' Oro degli Avari. Popolo delle Steppe in Europa* (Milan, 2000), 206–9.

Barber, P., *Vampires, Burial and Death: Folklore and Reality* (New Haven, CT and London, 1988).

Barbiera, I., *Changing Lands in Changing Memories. Migration and Identity During the Lombard Invasions* (Florence, 2005).

—'Sixth-century cemeteries in Hungary and Italy: a comparative approach', in Pohl, W. and Erhart, P. (eds), *Die Langobarden*, 301–20.

—'Memory of a better death. Conventional and exceptional burial rites in central European cemeteries of the AD 6th and 7th centuries', in Barbiera, I., Choyke, A. M. and Rasson, J. A. (eds), *Materializing Memory* BAR International Series 1977 (Oxford, 2009), 65–75.

Barnes, M. R. and Williams, D. H. (eds), *Arianism after Arius: Essays on the Development of the Fourth Century Trinitarian Controversy* (Edinburgh, 1993).

Barnes, T. D., *Athanasius and Constantius. Theology and Politics in the Constantinian Empire* (Cambridge, MA., and London, 1993).

Barnish, S. J. B., 'The "Anonymus Valesianus II" as a source for the last years of Theoderic', *Latomus* 42 (1983), 572–96.

Barnish, S. J. B. and Marazzi, F. (eds), *The Ostrogoths From the Migration Period to the Sixth Century* (Woodbridge, 2007).

Barrett, J. L., *Why Would Anyone Believe in God?* (Lanham, MD, Boulder, New York, Toronto and Plymouth, 2004).

—*Cognitive Science, Religion and Theology* (West Conshohocken, PA, 2011).

Beck, H. G. J., *The Pastoral Care of Souls in the South-East of France During the Sixth Century* (Rome, 1950).

Bennett, W. H., *The Gothic Commentary on the Gospel of John* (New York, 1960).

Bierbrauer, V., 'Krueuzfibeln in der Mittelalpinen Romanischen Frauentracht des 5–7 Jahrhunderts: Trentino und Südtirol', *Rivista di Studi Alpini* 86 (1992), 1–26.

—'The cross goes north: from Late Antiquity to Merovingian times south and north of the Alps', in Carver, M. O. H. (ed.), *The Cross Goes North. Processes of Conversion in Northern Europe AD 300–1300* (Woodbridge, 2003).

—'Archäologie der Langobarden in Italien: ethnische Interpretation und Stand der Forschung', in Pohl, W. and Erhart, P. (eds), *Die Langobarden*, 21–66.

Billard, C., Carré, F., Guillon, M., Treffort, C., Jagu, D. and Verron, G., 'L' occupation funéraire des monuments mégalithiques pendant le haut Moyen-Age. Modalités et essai d' interprétation', *Bulletin de la Société Préhistorique Française* 93 (1996), 279–86.

Böhner, K., 'Rheinische Grabmäler der Merowingerzeit als Zeugnisse frühen Fränkischen Christentums', in Elbern V. H. (ed.), *Das Erste Jahrtausend – Kultur und Kunst im werdenden Abendland an Rhein und Ruhr* Textband II (Düsseldorf, 1964), 653–78.

Bóna, I., 'Die Langobarden in Ungarn – die Gräberfelder von Várpalota Bezenye', *Acta Archaeologica Hungarica* 7 (1956), 183–244.

—*The Dawn of the Dark Ages* (Budapest, 1976).

Bóna, I. and Horváth, J. B, *Langobardische Gräberfelder in West-Ungarn* (Budapest, 2009).

Boudriot, W., *Die Altgermanische Religion* (Bonn, 1928).

Boyer, P., *The Naturalness of Religious Ideas* (Berkeley, Los Angeles and London, 1994).

—*Religion Explained. The Human Instincts That Fashion Gods, Spirits and Ancestors* (London, 2002).

Bragança, J. O., 'A Carta do Papa Vigílio ao Arcebispo Profuturo de Braga', *Bracara Augusta* 21 (1967), 65–91.

Branston, B., *The Lost Gods of England* (2nd edn, London, 1974).

Brather, S. (ed.), *Zwischen Spätantike und Frühmittelalter: Archäologie des 4. bis 7. Jahrhunderts im Westen* (Berlin, 2008)

Bremmer, J. N., *The Early Greek Concept of the Soul* (Princeton, 1983).

Brennecke, H. C., *Studien zur Geschichte der Homöer* (Tübingen, 1988).

Brogiolo, G. P. (ed.), *Le Chiese Rurali tra VII e VIII Secolo in Italia Settentrionale,* (Mantua, 2001).

Brogiolo, G. P. (ed.), *Gli Scavi al Battistero di Mantova (1984–1987)* (Mantua, 2004).

Brogiolo, G. P. and Possenti, E., 'L' età gota in Italia settentrionale nella transizione tra tarda antichità e alto medioevo', in Delogu, P. (ed.), *Le Invasioni Barbariche nel Meridione dell' Impero: Visigoti, Vandali, Ostrogoti* (Catanzaro, 2001), 257–95.

Brogiolo, G. P. and Chavarria Arnau, A. (eds), *Archeologia e Società tra Tardo Antico e Alto Medioevo (V-IX secolo)* (Mantova, 2007).

Brown, P. R. L., *The Rise of Western Christendom Triumph and Diversity 200–100* AD (Oxford, 1996 and 2003).

Brown, T. S., 'Everyday life in Ravenna under Theoderic: an example of his "tolerance" and "prosperity"?', in *Teoderico Il Grande e i Goti D' Italia* (Spoleto, 1993), 77–99.

—'Lombard religious policy in the late sixth and seventh centuries: the Roman dimension' in Ausenda, G., Delogu, P. and Wickham, C. (eds), *The Langobards*, 289–308.

Brozzi, M., 'Das Langobardische Gräberfeld von S. Salvatore bei Maiano', *Jahrbuch des Römisch-Germanisches Zentralmuzeums* 8 (1961), 157–63.

Bullough, D. A., 'Urban change in Early Medieval Italy: the example of Pavia', *Papers of the British School at Rome* 34 (n.s. 21) (1966), 82–129.

Cain, A. and Lenski, N. (eds), *The Power of Religion in Late Antiquity* (Farnham and Burlington, VT, 2009).

Carey, J., 'From David to Labraid: sacral kingship and the emergence of monotheism in Israel and Ireland', in Ritari, K. and Bergholm, A. (eds), *Approaches to Religion and Mythology in Celtic Studies* (Cambridge, 2008), 2–27.

Carletti, C. and Otranto, G. (eds), *Culto e Insediamenti Micaelici nell' Italia Meridionale fra Tarda Antichità e Medioevo* (Bari, 1994).

Cartocci, M. C., 'Alcune precisazioni sulla intitolazione a S. Agata della "Ecclesia Gothorum" alla Suburra', in *Teoderico Il Grande e i Goti D' Italia* (Spoleto, 1993), 611–20.

Castellanos, S. and Martín Viso, I., 'The local articulation of central power in the north of the Iberian Peninsula (500–1000)', *Early Medieval Europe* 13 (2005), 1–42.

Cecchelli, M., '"Spazio Cristiano" e monumenti eretici in Roma', in *Atti del VI Congresso Nazionale di Archeologia Cristiana* (Florence, 1985), 287–96.

Cecchelli, M. and Bertelli, G., 'Edifici di culto Ariano in Italia', *Actes du XIe Congrès Internationale d' Archéologie Chrétienne* vol. I, Collection de l'École française de Rome 123 (Rome, 1986), 233–47.

Chapman, J., *Notes on the Early History of the Vulgate Gospels* (Oxford, 1908).

Charles-Edwards, T. M., 'The Penitential of Columbanus', in Lapidge, M. (ed.), *Columbanus: Studies on the Latin Writings* (Woodbridge, 1997), 217–39.

—*Early Christian Ireland* (Cambridge, 2000).

Christie, N., *The Lombards. The Ancient Longobards* (Oxford, 1995).

Ciglenečki, S., 'Langobardische Präsenz in Südostalpenraum im Lichte neuer Forschungen', in Pohl, W. and Erhart, P. (eds), *Die Langobarden*, 265–80.

Cirelli, E., *Ravenna: Archeologia di una Città* (Borgo S. Lorenzo, 2008).

Cohen, E., Lanman, J. A., Whitehouse, H. and McCauley, R. N., 'Common criticisms of the Cognitive Science of Religion – answered', *Council of Societies for the Study of Religion Bulletin* 37 (4) (2008), 112–15.

Collins, R., 'King Leovigild and the conversion of the Visigoths', in *idem*, *Law, Culture and Regionalism in Early Medieval Spain* (Aldershot, 1992), II, 1–12.

—*Early Medieval Spain* (2nd edn, New York, 1995).

—*Visigothic Spain* (Oxford, 2004).

—*Early Medieval Europe 300–1000* (3rd edn, Basingstoke, 2010).

Conti, M., *The Life and Works of Potamius of Lisbon* (Steenbrugge, 1998).

Conway, M., 'St. Radegund's reliquary at Poitiers', *Antiquaries' Journal* 3 (1923), 1–12.

Crawford, S, 'Children, death and the afterlife in Anglo-Saxon England', *Anglo-Saxon Studies in Archaeology and History* 6 (Oxford, 1993), 83–9.

Cusack, C. M., *The Rise of Christianity in Northern Europe 300–1000* (London, 1998).

—*The Sacred Tree: Ancient and Medieval Manifestations* (Newcastle upon Tyne, 2011).

Daim, F., Mehofer, M., and Tobias, B., 'Die Langobardischen Schmiedegräber aus Poysdorf und Brno. Fragen, Methoden, erste Ergebnisse', in Pohl, W. and Erhart, P. (eds), *Die Langobarden*, 201–24.

Danforth, L. M., *The Death Rituals of Rural Greece* (Princeton, 1982).

David, P., *Études Historiques sur la Galice et le Portugal du VIe au XII Siècle* (Lisbon and Paris, 1947).

Davies, W., Graham-Campbell, J., Handley, M., Kershaw, P., Koch, J. T., Le Duc, G. and Lockyear, K., *The Inscriptions of Early Medieval Brittany* (Oakville, CT and Aberystwyth, 2000).

De Aguilera, A. B., 'El Priscilianismo: Herejia o Movimento Social?', *Cuadernos de Historia de España*, 37–38 (1963), 5–41.

De Cáceres, E. C. M., 'El mundo funerario y religioso en época visigoda', in *III Congreso Nacional de Arqueología Medieval Española. Ponencias* (Oviedo, 1989), 91–110.

De Las Heras, I. B. and Guerrero, R. D., 'La necrópolis visigoda de Zarza de Granadilla (Cáceres)', *Trabajos de prehistoria* 27 (1) (1970), 327–36.

Deliyannis, D. M., *Ravenna in Late Antiquity* (Cambridge, 2010).

Delogu, P., 'Conclusion: The Lombards – power and identity', in Pohl, W. and Erhart, P. (eds), *Die Langobarden*, 549–54.

Derks, T., 'The perception of the Roman pantheon by a native elite: the example of votive inscriptions from Lower Germany', in Roymans, N. and Theuws, F. (eds), *Images of the Past* (Amsterdam, 1991), 235–65.

—*Gods, Temples and Ritual Practices. The Transformation of Religious Ideas and Values in Roman Gaul* (Amsterdam, 1998)

Deshusses, J., 'Le sacramentaire de Gellone dans son contexte historique', *Ephemerides Liturgicae* 75 (1961), 193–210.

Díaz, P. C., 'El Parrochiale Suevum: organización ecclesiástica, poder político y poblamiento en la Gallaecia Tardoantigua', in Alvar, J. (ed.), *Homenaje a José Maria Blázquez*, vol. VI (Madrid, 1998), 35–47.

Dick, S., "'Langobardi per annos regem non habentes, sub ducibus fuerunt." Formen und Entwicklung der Herrschaftsorganisation bei den Langobarden. Eine Skizze', in Pohl, W., and Erhart, P. (eds), *Die Langobarden*, 335–44.

Dodds, J. D., *Architecture and Ideology in Early Medieval Spain* (Philadelphia, PN, 1993).

Dowden, K., *European Paganism: The Realities of Cult from Antiquity to the Middle Ages* (London, 2000).

Dumézil, B., *Les Racines Chrétiennes de l' Europe. Conversion et Liberté dans les Royaumes Barbares, Ve-VIIIe siècle* (Paris, 2005).

Dunn, M., *The Emergence of Monasticism* (Oxford, 2003).

—*The Vision of Fursey and the Development of Purgatory* (Norwich, 2007).

—*The Christianization of the Anglo-Saxons c.597–c.700* (London, 2009).

—'Intuiting gods: creed and cognition in the fourth century', *Historical Reflections/ Reflexions Historiques* 38 (2012), 1–23.

—'Paradigms of penance', *Journal of Medieval Monastic Studies* 1 (2012), 17–39.

—'Lombard religiosities reconsidered: "Arianism", syncretism and the transition to Catholic Christianity', in Roach, A. P. and Simpson, J. R. (eds), *Heresy and the Making of European Culture. Medieval and Modern Perspectives* (Farnham, 2013), 85–105.

Effros, B. *Merovingian Mortuary Archaeology and the Making of the Middle Ages* (Berkeley, Los Angeles and London, 2003).

Ellis Davidson, H. R., *The Road to Hel: A Study of the Conception of the Dead in Old Norse Literature* (Cambridge, 1943).

—*Gods and Myths of Northern Europe* (Harmondsworth, 1964).

—*Myths and Symbols in Pagan Europe: Early Scandinavian and Celtic Religions* (Manchester, 1988).

—*The Lost Beliefs of Northern Europe* (London and New York, 1993).

Escher, K., *Genèse et Évolution du Deuxième Royaume Burgonde: les Témoins Archéologiques*, BAR International Series 1402 (I–II) (Oxford, 2005).

—*Les Burgondes, Ie-VIe Siècle apr. J.-C.* (Paris, 2006).

Everett, N., 'How territorial was Lombard law?', in Pohl, W. and Erhart, P. (eds), *Die Langobarden - Herrschaft und Identität* (Vienna, 2005), 345–60.

Fanning, S., 'Lombard Arianism reconsidered', *Speculum* 56 (1981), 241–58.

Fehr, H., 'Germanische Einwanderung oder kulturelle Neuorientierung? Zu den Anfängen Reihengräberhorizontes', in *Zwischen Spätantike und Frühmittelalter: Archäologie des 4. bis 7. Jahrhunderts im Westen* (Berlin, 2008), 67–102.

Fernández Galiano Ruiz, D., 'Excavaciones en la necrópolis hispano-visigoda del Camino de los Afligidos (Alcalá de Henares)', *Noticiaro Arqueológia Hispánico* 4 (1976), 5–90.

Ferreira, C. J. A., 'A necrópole tardo-romana e visigótica da Pedreira. Rio de Moinhos-Abrantes', *Arqueologia Medieval* (1992), 91–110.

Ferreiro, A., 'The missionary labor of St Martin of Braga in 6th century Galicia', *Studia Monastica* 23 (1981), 11–26.

Ferreiro, A., 'St Martin of Braga's policy towards heretics and pagan practices', *American Benedictine Review* 34 (1983), 372–95.

—'Braga and Tours: some observations on Gregory's *De virtutibus Sancti Martini*', *Journal of Early Christian Studies* 3 (2) (1995), 195–210.

—(ed.), *The Visigoths, Studies in Culture and Society* (Leiden, 1999).

Filotas, B., *Pagan Survivals, Superstitions and Popular Cultures in Early Medieval Pastoral Literature* (Toronto, 2005).

Fletcher, R., *The Conversion of Europe From Paganism to Christianity 371–1386* AD (London, 1997).

Flint, V. I. J., *The Rise of Magic in Early Medieval Europe* (Oxford, 1991).

Fomin, M., Mac Mathúna, S. and Vertogradova, V. (eds), *Sacred Topology of Early Ireland and Ancient India* (Washington, DC, 2010).

Fontes, L. F. de O., 'O Norte de Portugal no período suevo-visigótico. Elementos para seu estudo', in *XXXIX Corso di Cultura sull' arte Ravennate e Bizantina* (Bologna, 1992), 217–48.

Freeman, C., *Holy Bones, Holy Dust. How Relics Shaped the History of Medieval Europe* (New Haven, CT, and London, 2011).

Friedrichsen, G. W. S., *The Gothic Version of the Gospels* (London, 1926).

Füzes, M. F., 'Die Pflanzenfunde des Langobardischen Gräberfeldes von Vörs', *Acta Archaelogica Hungarica* 16 (1964), 409–42.

Gaillard de Sémainville, H., 'Nouvel examen de la plaque-boucle mérovingienne de Landelinus découverte à Ladoix-Serrigny (Côte-d' Or)', *Revue Archéologique de l' Est* 52 (2003), 297–327.

—'À propos de l'implantation des Burgondes: réflexions, hypothèses et perspectives', in Passard, F., Gizard, S., Urlacher, J-P. and Richard, A. (eds) *Burgondes Alamans Francs Romains* (Besancon, 2003), 17–39.

—'À propos de plaques-boucles mérovingiennes à motif chrétien', *Bulletin du centre d' études médiévales Auxerre*; available online: http://cem.revues.org/6752; DOI: 10.4000/cem.6752 [accessed 14 July 2013].

García Moreno, L. A., 'La arqueología y la historia militar visigoda en la península ibérica', *Arqueología Medieval Española* II Congreso (Madrid, 1987), 331–6.

—*Historia de España Visigoda* (Madrid, 1989).

—'La Iglesia y el Cristianismo en la Galecia de época sueva', in *Espacio y tiempo en la percepción de la Antigüedad Tardía, Antigüedad Cristiana* XXIII (Murcia, 2006), 39–55.

—'Prosopography and onomastic: the case of the Goths', in Keats-Rohan, K. S. B. (ed.), *Prosopography Approaches and Applications A Handbook* (Oxford, 2007), 338–50.

Gasparri, S., *I Duchi Longobardi* (Rome, 1978).

—'Le tradizioni germaniche nell' Italia dei Goti', in *Teoderico Il Grande e i Goti D' Italia* (Spoleto, 1993), 201–26.

Geary, P., 'Humiliation of saints', in Wilson, S. (ed.), *Saints and Their Cults* (Cambridge, 1983), 123–40.

Gennep, A. van, *The Rites of Passage*, trans. Vizedom, M. B., and Caffee, G. L. (London, 1960).

George, J. W., *Venantius Fortunatus, A Latin Poet in Merovingian Gaul* (Oxford, 1992).

Ginzburg, C., *Ecstasies* (London and Sydney, 1990).

Giostra, C., 'Aspetti del ritual funerario', in Micheletto, E. (ed.), *Longobardi in Monferrato. Archeologia della 'Iudiciaria Torrensis'* (Casale Monferrato, 2007), 99–112.

Giostra, C., 'Luoghi e segni della morte in età longobarda: tradizione e transizione nelle pratiche dell' aristocrazia', in Brogiolo, G. P., and Chavarria Arnau, A. (eds), *Archeologia e società tra tardo antico e altomedievale (V-IX secolo)* (Mantua, 2007), 311–43.

—'Goths and Lombards in Italy: the potential of archaeology with respect to ethnocultural identification', *Postclassical Archaeologies* 1 (2011), 7–36.

Godoy, C. and Vilella, J., 'De la Fides Ghotica a la orthodoxia Nicena: inicio de la teologia politica visigotica', *Antigüedad y Cristianismo* 3 (1986), 117–44.

Grange, A., Parriat, H. and Perraud, R., 'La nécropole Gallo-Romaine et barbare de Briord (Ain) - découverte d'une basilique paléochrétienne', *La Physiophile* 58 (1963), 3–92 and 12 plates.

Gray, P. T. R., and Herren, M. W., 'Columbanus and the Three Chapters controversy - a new approach', *Journal of Theological Studies* 45 (1994), 160–71.

Green, D. H., 'The influence of the Merovingian Franks on the Christian vocabulary of Germany', in Wood, I. (ed.), *Franks and Alamanni in the Merovingian Period - an Ethnographic Perspective* (Woodbridge, 1998), 343–60.

Gregg, R. C. and Groh, D. E., *Early Arianism: A View of Salvation* (London, 1981).

Gurevich, A. I., *Medieval Popular Culture. Problems of Belief and Perception* (Cambridge, 1988).

Gwynn, D. M., 'Archaeology and the "Arian Controversy"', in Gwynn, D. M. and Bangert, S. (eds), *Religious Diversity in Late Antiquity* (Leiden, 2010), 229–63.

Hakenbeck, S., '"Hunnic" modified skulls: physical appearance, identity and the transformative nature of migrations', in Sayer, D. and Williams, H. (eds),

Mortuary Practices and Social Identities in the Middle Ages (Exeter, 2009), 64–80.

Halfond, G. I., *The Archaeology of Frankish Church Councils AD 511–768* (Leiden, 2010).

—'Vouillé, Orléans (511) and the origins of the Frankish conciliar tradition', in Mathisen, R. W. and Shanzer, D. (eds), *Battle of Vouillé*, 151–65

Hall, A., *Elves in Anglo-Saxon England. Matters of Belief, Health, Gender and Identity* (Woodbridge, 2007).

Halsall, G., *Settlement and Social Organization. The Merovingian Region of Metz*, (Cambridge, 1992).

—'The origins of the Reihengräberzivilisation: forty years on', in Drinkwater, J. and Elton H. (eds), *Fifth Century Gaul. A Crisis of Identity* (Cambridge, 1992), 196–333.

—'Social change around AD 600: an Austrasian perspective', in Carver, M. O. H. (ed.) *The Age of Sutton Hoo* (Woodbridge, 1992), 265–78.

—*Early Medieval Cemeteries: An Introduction to Burial Archaeology in the Post-Roman West* (Skelmorlie, 1995).

—'Social identities and social relationships in Early Merovingian Gaul', in Wood, I. (ed.), *Franks and Alamanni in the Merovingian Period – an Ethnographic Perspective* (Woodbridge 1998), 141–64.

—'Archaeology and the late Roman frontier in northern Gaul: the so-called Föderatengräber reconsidered', in Pohl. W. and Reimitz, H. (eds), *Grenze und Differenz in Frühenmittelalter* (Vienna, 2000), 167–80.

—*Barbarian Migrations and the Roman West 376–568* (Cambridge, 2007).

—*Cemeteries and Society in Merovingian Gaul. Selected Studies in Archaeology and History 1992–2009* (Leiden, 2010).

—'Ethnicity and early medieval cemeteries', *Arqueología y Territorio Medieval* 18 (2011), 15–27.

Handley, M. A., *Death, Society and Culture: Inscriptions and Epitaphs in Gaul and Spain*, BAR International Series 1135 (Oxford, 2003).

Hanson, R. P. C., The *Search for the Christian Doctrine of God* (Edinburgh, 1988).

Haperen, M. C. van, 'Rest in pieces: an interpretive model of early medieval "grave robbery"', *Medieval and Modern Matters* 1 (2010), 1–36.

Harmening, D., *Superstitio: Überlieferungs- und theoriegeschichtliche Untersuchungen zur kirchlich-theologischen Aberglaubensliteratur des Mittelalters* (Berlin, 1979).

Haubrichs, W., 'Amalgamierung und Identität – Langobardische Personennamen in Mythos und Herrschaft', in Pohl, W. and Erhart, P. (eds), *Die Langobarden*, 67–102.

Heather, P., 'The crossing of the Danube and the Gothic conversion', *Greek, Roman and Byzantine Studies* 27 (1986), 289–318.

—'The historical culture of Ostrogothic Italy', in *Teoderico Il Grande e i Goti D' Italia* (Spoleto, 1993), 317–51.

—*The Goths* (Oxford, 1996).

—(ed.), *The Visigoths - From the Migration Period to the Seventh Century. An Ethnographic Perspective* (Woodbridge, 1999).

—'Roman diplomacy and the Gothic problem', in Bersani, S. G. (ed.), *Romani e Barbari - Incontro e scontro di culture* (Atti del Convegno - Bra, 2003), 141–55.

—'Merely an ideology? Gothic identity in Ostrogothic Italy', in Barnish, S. J. and Marazzi, F. (eds), *The Ostrogoths From the Migration Period to the Sixth Century* (Woodbridge, 2007), 31–60.

—'Goths in the Roman Balkans c. 350–500', in Poulter, A. (ed.), *The Transition to Late Antiquity, on the Danube and Beyond* (Oxford, 2007).

Heather, P. and Matthews, J., *The Goths in the Fourth Century* (Liverpool, 1991).

Heil, U., *Avitus von Vienne und die homöische Kirche der Burgunder* (Berlin and Boston, 2011).

Heinrich-Tamaska, O., 'Deutung und Bedeutung von Salins Tierstil II zwischen Langobardia und Avaria', in Pohl, W., and Erhart, P. (eds), *Die Langobarden*, 281–300.

Hen, Y., 'Clovis, Gregory of Tours and pro-Merovingian propaganda', *Revue Belge de Philologie et d' Histoire* 71 (2) (1993), 271–6.

—*Culture and Religion in Merovingian Gaul A.D. 481–751* (Leiden, New York and Köln, 1995).

—'Paganism and superstitions in the time of Gregory of Tours: *une question mal posée!*' in Mitchell, K. and Wood, I. (eds), *The World of Gregory of Tours* (Leiden, Boston and Köln, 2002), 229–40.

—*Roman Barbarians* (Basingstoke and New York, 2007).

Hen, Y. and Meens, R. (eds), *The Bobbio Missal - Liturgy and Religious Culture in Merovingian Gaul* (Cambridge, 2009).

Hertz, R., trans. Needham R., and C., *Death and the Right Hand* (London, 1960).

Hillgarth, J. N. 'Popular religion in Visigothic Spain', in James, E. (ed.), *Visigothic Spain: New Approaches* (Oxford, 1980), 3–60.

Hillgarth, J. N., *The Conversion of Western Europe, 350–750* (Englewood Cliffs, NJ, 1969).

Horton, R., 'African conversion', *Africa* 41 (1971), 85–108.

—'On the rationality of conversion', *Africa* 45 (1975), 219–35; 373–99.

Hummer, H. J., 'Franks and Alamanni, a historical sketch', in Wood, I. (ed.), *Franks and Alamanni in the Merovingian Period - an Ethnographic Perspective* (Woodbridge, 1998), 9–21.

Hunt, E. D., 'Did Constantius II have "court bishops"?', *Studia Patristica* 19 (1989), 86–90.

Hunter, M. J., 'The Gothic Bible' in Lampe, G.W. H. (ed.), *The Cambridge History of the Bible* vol. 2, *The West From the Fathers to the Reformation* (Cambridge, 1969), 338–62.

Isaacs, B., *The Invention of Racism in Classical Antiquity* (Princeton, NJ and Oxford, 2004).

James, E. (ed.), *Visigothic Spain: New Approaches* (Oxford, 1980).

—*The Franks* (Oxford, 1991).

—*Europe's Barbarians AD 200-600* (London, 2009).

Jensen, R. M., *Face to Face. Portraits of the Divine in Early Christianity* (Minneapolis, 2010).

—*Understanding Early Christian Art* (Abingdon, 2010).

Jepure, A., 'Interpretationsprobleme der Westgothenarchäologie', in Brather, S. (ed.), *Zwischen Spätantike und Frühmittelalter: Archäologie des 4. bis 7. Jahrhunderts im Westen. Ergänzungsbände zum Reallexikon der germanischen Altertumskunde 57* (Berlin and New York, 2008), 193–209.

Johnson, M. J. 'Pagan-Christian burial practices of the fourth century: shared tombs?', *Journal of Early Christian Studies* 5 (1997), 37–59.

Jolly, K. L., *Popular Religion in Late Anglo-Saxon England* (Chapel Hill, NC, 1996).

Kazanski, M., and Périn, P., 'Identité ethnique en Gaule à l' époque des grandes migrations et des royaumes barbares: étude de cas archéologiques', *Antiquités Nationales* 39 (2008), 181–216.

—' "Foreign" objects in the Merovingian cemeteries of northern Gaul', in D. Quast (ed.), *Foreigners in Early Medieval Europe* (Mainz, 2009), 149–67.

Keely, A., 'Arians and Jews in the "Histories" of Gregory of Tours', *Journal of Medieval History* 23 (1997), 103–15.

Keys, D., *Catastrophe - An Investigation into the Origins of the Modern World* (London, 1999).

Kieckhefer, R., 'The specific rationality of medieval magic', *AHR* 99 (1994), 813–34.

Kingsley, M., *Travels in West Africa. Congo Français, Corisco and Cameroons* (London, 1897).

—*West African Studies* (3rd edn, London, 1964).

Klingshirn, W., *Caesarius of Arles: The Making of a Christian Community in Late Antique Gaul* (Cambridge, 1994).

Kopecek, T. A., *A History of Neo-Arianism* (Cambridge, MA, 1979).

Künzel, R., 'Paganisme, syncrétisme, et culture religieuse au haut moyen âge. Réflexions de méthode', *Annales ESC* 4–5 (1992), 1055–69.

Kulikowski, M., 'Plague in Spanish Late Antiquity', in Little, L. K. (ed.), *Plague and the End of Antiquity*, 150–70.

—'Wie Spanien gotisch wurde: der Historiker und der archäologische Befund', in Brather, S. (ed.), *Zwischen Spätantike und Frühmittelalter*, 27–43.

Kümmel, C., *Ur- und frühgeschichtlicher Grabraub. Archäologische Interpretation und kulturanthropologische Erklärung* (Münster, New York, Munich and Berlin, 2009).

La Baume, P., 'Das fränkische Gräberfeld Junkersdorf bei Köln', in Elbern, V. H. (ed.), *Das Erste Jahrtausend – Kultur und Kunst im werdenden Abendland an Rhein und Ruhr, Textband II* (Düsseldorf, 1964), 679–86.

La Rocca, C., 'Una prudente maschera "Antiqua". La politica edilizia di Teoderico', in *Teoderico Il Grande e i Goti D' Italia* (Spoleto, 1993), 451–516.

Lansival, R., 'La nécropole mérovingienne de Metzervisse (Moselle)', *Revue Archéologique de l' Est* 56 (2007), 231–310.

Laumon, A., 'La nécropole mérovingienne de Bettborn', *Annuaire de la Société d' Histoire et d' Archéologie de Lorraine* 77 (1977), 51–71.

Laux, F., 'Der Reihengräberfriedhof in Oldendorf, Samtgemeinde Amelinghausen Kr. Lüneburg/Niedersachsen – Ein Beitrag zu den frühgeschichtlichen Gräberfeldern im Bardengau', *Hammaburg* NF 5 (1983), 91–147.

Lawson, E. T., 'The wedding of psychology, ethnography, and history: methodological bigamy or tripartite free love?', in Whitehouse, H. and Martin, L. H. (eds), *Theorizing Religions Past: Archaeology, History and Cognition* (Walnut Creek, CA, Lanham, New York, Toronto and Oxford, 2004), 1–6.

Leyser, C., '"Divine power flowed from this book": ascetic language and episcopal authority in Gregory of Tours' *Life of the Fathers*', in Mitchell, K. and Wood, I. (eds), *World of Gregory of Tours*, 291–4.

Liebeschuetz, J. H. W. G., *Barbarians and Bishops. Army, Church and State in the Age of Arcadius and Chrysostom* (Oxford, 1990).

Lifshitz, F., *The Norman Conquest of Pious Neustria. Historiographic Discourse and Saintly Relics 684–1090* (Toronto, 1995).

Little, L. K. (ed.), *Plague and the End of Antiquity – The Pandemic of 541–750* (Cambridge, 2007).

Lixfeld, H., 'Die Guntramsage (AT 1645 A)', *Fabula* 13 (1972), 62–107.

Löhr, W. A., *Die Entstehung der homöischen und homöousianischen Kirchenparteien – Studien zur Synodalgeschichte des 4 Jahrhunderts* (Bonn, 1986).

—'A sense of tradition: the Homoiousian church party', in Barnes, M. R. and Williams, D. H. (eds), *Arianism After Arius: Essays on the Development of Fourth Century Trinitarian Conflicts* (Edinburgh, 1993), 81–100.

—'Western Christianities', in Casiday, A. and Norris F. W. (eds) *The Cambridge History of Christianity* vol. 2, *Constantine to c. 600* (Cambridge, 2007), 9–51.

Lüdemann, H., *Mehrfachbelegte Gräber im Frühen Mittelalter* (Würzburg, 1990).

Lyman, R., 'A topography of heresy: mapping the rhetorical creation of Arianism', in Barnes, M. R. and Williams, D. (eds), *Arianism After Arius*, 45–62.

Manzelli, V., *Ravenna* (Rome, 2000).

Marenbon, J., *Boethius* (Oxford, 2003).

Markus, R. A., *Gregory the Great and His World* (Cambridge, 1997).

Marti, R., 'La région de Bâle entre Burgondes, Francs et Alamans (V^e – VIIe siècle)', in Passard, F., Gizard, S., Urlacher, J.-P. and Richard, A. (eds), *Burgondes Alamans Francs Romains*, 205–11.

Martin, J-M., 'À propos de la vita de Barbatus, évêque de Bénévent', *Mélanges de l'École française de Rome, Moyen Âge, Temps Modernes* 86 (1) (1974) 137–64.

—'La Longobardia meridionale', in Gasparri, S. (ed.), *Il Regno dei Longobardi in Italia* (Spoleto, 2004), 327–65.

Martinez Diez, G., 'La coleccion canonica de la iglesia sueva: los Capitula Martini', *Bracara Augusta* 21 (1967), 224–43.

Martinez Santa Ollala, J., *Excavaciones en la necropólis visigoda de Herrera de Pisuerga* (Madrid, 1933).

Mastrelli, C. A., 'Prestiti lessicali gotici: un aggiornamento', in *Teoderico Il Grande e i Goti D' Italia* (Spoleto, 1993), 183–99.

Mathisen, R., 'Ricimer's church in Rome: how an Arian barbarian prospered in a Nicene world', in Cain, A. and Lenski, N. (eds), *Power of Religion*, 307–26.

Mathisen, R. W., 'Barbarian bishops and the churches "in barbaricis gentibus" during Late Antiquity', *Speculum* 72 (1997), 664–97.

Mathisen, R. W. and Shanzer, D. (eds), *The Battle of Vouillé, 507 CE. Where France Began* (Boston and Berlin, 2012).

McCulloh, J. M., 'The cult of relics in the letters and "Dialogues" of Pope Gregory the Great', *Traditio* 32 (1976), 145–84.

McKenna, S., *Paganism and Pagan Survivals in Spain up to the Fall of the Visigothic Kingdom* (Washington, DC, 1938).

McLynn, N. B., *Ambrose of Milan. Church and Court in a Christian Capital* (Berkeley, Los Angeles and London, 1994).

—'From Palladius to Maximinus: passing the Arian torch', *Journal of Early Christian Studies* 4 (4) (1996), 477–93.

McNeill, J. T. and Gamer, H., *Medieval Handbooks of Penance* (New York, 1938).

Meens, R., 'Reforming the clergy: a context for the use of the Bobbio penitential', in Hen, Y. and Meens, R. (eds), *The Bobbio Missal*, 154–67.

—'Remedies for sins', in Noble, T. F. X. and Smith, J. M. H. (eds), *Cambridge History of Christianity. Early Medieval Christianities c. 600–c. 1100* (Cambridge, 2008), 399–415 and 736–47.

Menghin, W., *Die Langobarden – Archäologie und Geschichte* (Stuttgart, 1985).

Menis, G. C. (ed.), *I Longobardi* (Milan, 1992).

Mercier, C. and Mercier-Rolland, M., *Le Cimetière Burgonde de Monnet-la-Ville* (Paris, 1974).

Merrills, A. H., *History and Geography in Late Antiquity* (Cambridge, 2005).

Meslin, M., *Les Ariens d' Occident 335–430* (Paris, 1967).

—'Persistences paiennes en galice, vers la fin du VIᵉ siècle', in Bibauw, J. (ed.), *Hommages à Marcel Renard* vol. II (Brussels, 1969), 512–24.

—*La Fête des Kalendes de Janvier dans l' Empire Romain* (Brussels, 1970).

Metcalf, P. and Huntington, R., *Celebrations of Death. The Anthropology of Mortuary Ritual* (rev. edn, Cambridge, 1991).

Micheletto, E., 'Materiali di età gota in Piemonte: un aggiornamento', in Fiorillo, R. and Peduto, P. (eds) *Atti del III Congresso Nazionale di Archeologia Medievale*, Società degli Archeologi Medievisti Italiani (Florence, 2003), 697–704 .

—'Lo scavo di Mombello e l' archeologia della "Iudiciaria Torrensis"', in Micheletto, E. (ed.), *Longobardi in Monferrato. Archeologia della 'Iudiciaria Torrensis'* (Casale Monferrato, 2007), 43–61.

Micheletto, E. and Pejrani Baricco L., 'Archeologia funeraria e insediativa in Piemonte tra V e VII secolo', in Paroli, L. (ed.), *L' Italia centro-settentrionale in età longobarda* (Firenze, 1997), 295–344.

Molinero Perez, A., 'La necropolis visigoda de Duraton (Segovia)', *Acta Arqueologica Hispanica* IV (Madrid, 1948).

Montes Moreira, A., 'Le retour de Potamius de Lisbonne à l' orthodoxie nicéenne', *Didaskalia* 5 (1975), 330–54.

Moorhead, J., *Theoderic in Italy* (Oxford, 1992).

Moreira, I., *Heaven's Purge. Purgatory in Late Antiquity* (Oxford, 2010).

Motschi, A., 'La nécropole de Oberbuchsiten (canton de Soleure, Suisse): L' évolution des pratiques et la question du peuplement (fin IVᵉ – VIIᵉ siècle)', in Passard, F., Gizard, S., Urlacher, J-P. and Richard, A. (eds), *Burgondes Alamans Francs Romains* (Besancon, 2003), 191–2.

Moyano, I. T. and Lizana, M. R., 'Las necrópolis de las Delicias y El Almendral. Dos necrópolis visigodas en el llano de Zafarraya (Granada)', in *Arqueología Medieval Española II Congreso* (Madrid, 1987), 385–94.

Murray, A., 'Missionaries and magic in dark-age Europe', *Past and Present* 136 (1992), 186–205.

Mutinelli, C., 'Scoperta di una necropoli "famigliare" longobarda nel terreno già di Santo Stefano in Pertica a Cividale', *Memorie Storiche Forogiuliesi* XLVI (1960–1961), 65–95 and 30 plates.

—'Das Langobardische Gräberfeld von S. Stefano in Pertica in Cividale', *Jahrbuch des Römisch-Germanischen Zentralmuseums* 8 (1961), 139–56.

Nedoma, R., 'Der altisländische Odindname Langbarðr: "Langbart" und die Langobarden', in Pohl, W. and Erhart, P. (eds), *Die Langobarden*, 439–44.

Neugebauer, J-W., 'Langobarden im 6. Jahrhundert im unteren Traisental. Die Gräberfelder von Pottenbrunn (Landeshauptstadt St. Pölten) und Oberndorf in der Ebene (Stadtgemeinde Herzogenburg)', in Pohl, W. and Erhart, P. (eds), *Die Langobarden*, 321–34.

Nie, G. de, 'Cæsarius of Arles and Gregory of Tours: two sixth-century Gallic bishops and 'Christian magic', in Edel, D. (ed.), *Cultural Identity and Cultural Integration. Ireland and Europe in the Early Middle Ages* (Dublin, 1995), 170–96.

Noble, T. F. X., 'Theodoric and the Papacy', in *Teoderico Il Grande e i Goti D' Italia* (Spoleto, 1993), 395–423.

North, R., *Heathen Gods in Old English Literature* (Cambridge, 1997).

O' Loughlin, T., *Celtic Theology* (London, 2000).

Okely, J., *The Traveller-Gypsies* (Cambridge, 1983).

Old, H. O., *The Reading and Preaching of the Scriptures in the Worship of the Christian Church* vol. 3, *The Medieval Church* (Grand Rapids, MI and Cambridge, 1999).

Orlandis, J., 'El Arrianismo visigodo tardio', *Cuadernos de Historia de España* 65 (1981), 5–20.

Palmieri, S., 'Duchi, principi e vescovi nella Longobardia meridionale', in *2. Convegno Internazionale di Studi Promosso dal Centro di Cultura dell' Università Cattolica del Sacro Cuore* (Benevento, 1992), 43–99.

Pantò, G. and Pejrani Baricco, L., 'Chiese nelle campagne del Piemonte in età tardolongobarda', in Brogiolo, G. P. (ed.), *Le Chiese Rurali tra VII e VIII Secolo in Italia Settentrionale* (Mantua, 2001), 17–52.

Parriat, H. and Perraud, R., 'Les inscriptions paléochrétiennes de Briord (Ain)', *La Physiophile* 79 (1973), 14–37.

Parriat, H., Laugrand, R., and Perraud, R., 'La necropole gallo-romane et mérovingienne des Plantées a Briord (Ain). Les Plantées-Sud. Synthèse et rèsultats des fouilles de 1958 a 1973', *La Physiophile* 92 (1980), 15–52.

Parvis, S., *Marcellus of Ancyra and the Lost Years of the Arian Controversy 325–345* (Oxford, 2005).

Passard, F. and Urlacher, J-P., 'Architectures funéraires de la nécropole de Saint-Vit (Doubs): des significations sociales et culturelles?', in Passard, F., Gizard, S., Urlacher, J.-P. and Richard, A. (eds), *Burgondes Alamans Francs Romains*, 143–53.

Passard, F., Gizard, S., Urlacher, J-P. and Richard, A. (eds), *Burgondes Alamans Francs Romains dans l' est de la France, le sud-ouest de l' Allemagne et la Suisse* (Besançon, 2003).

Paxton, F. S., *Christianizing Death. The Creation of a Ritual Process in Medieval Europe* (Ithaca and London, 1990).

Peduto, P., 'Insediamenti longobardi del ducato di Benevento (sec. VI–VIII)', in Gasparri, S. (ed.), *Il Regno dei Longobardi in Italia* (Spoleto, 2004), 367–442.

Pejrani Baricco L. (ed.), *Presenze Longobarde – Collegno nell' Alto Medioevo* (Torino, 2004).

—'Il Piemonte tra Ostrogoti e Longobardi', in Brogliolo, G. P. and Chavarria Arnau, A. (eds), *I Longobardi. Dalla caduta dell' Impero all' alba dell' Italia* (Milan, 2007), 255–65.

Pérez, F., Agüero, M. S., de Silva, C. P. and de Robles, F. C. S. (eds), *Historia de España – Los Visigodos* (Madrid, 1978).

Petrucci, A., *Writing the Dead. Death and Writing Strategies in the Western Tradition* (Stanford, 1998).

Pieper, P., 'Autopsie und Experimenta zur Runeninschrift auf dem Goldreif von Pietroasa', in Heizmann, W. and Nahl, A. van (eds), *Runica-Germanica-Mediaevalia, Ergänzungsbände zum Reallexikon der Germanischen Altertumskunde* (Berlin and New York, 2003), 595–646.

Pina, A. A. de, 'S. Martinho de Dume e la sobrevivencia de la mitologia suevica', *Bracara Augusta* 9–10 (1958), 58–66.

Pohl, W., 'I Goti d' Italia e le tradizioni delle steppe', in *Teoderico Il Grande e i Goti D' Italia* (Spoleto, 1993), 227–51.

—'Deliberate ambiguity: the Lombards and Christianity', in Armstrong, G. and Wood, I. (eds), *Converting Peoples and Christianizing Individuals*, 47–58.

—'Geschichte und Identität im Langobardenreich', in Pohl, W. and Erhart, P. (eds), *Die Langobarden*, 555–66.

—'Heresy in Secundus and Paul the Deacon', in Chazelle, C. and Cubitt, C. (eds), *The Crisis of the Oikoumene. The Three Chapters and the Failed Quest for Unity in the Sixth-Century Mediterranean* (Turnhout, 2007), 243–64.

Pohl, W. and Erhart, P. (eds), *Die Langobarden – Herrschaft und Identität* (Vienna, 2005).

Polomé, E.,'L' étymologie du terme germanique *ansuz*, "Dieu souverain"', *Études Germaniques* 8 (1953), 36–44.

Poulain, R., 'Les plaques-boucles à motifs chrétiens en Burgondie mérovingienne: approche méthodologique', in Passard, F., Gizard, S., Urlacher, J-P. and Richard, A. (eds), *Burgondes Alamans Francs Romains*, 59–66.

Privati, B., 'La nécropole de Sézegnin', in *Société d' Histoire et d' Archéologie de Genève*, Série In-4 Tome Dixième (Geneva and Paris, 1983), 3–71.

Richert, H-G., 'Ni Ibon Ak Galeika Sweriþa – Überlegungen zum dogmatischen Standpunkt des Skeireinisten', in Burger, H. O. and Von See, K. (eds), *Festschrift Gottfried Weber* (Bad Homburg, 1967), 11–45.

Rigaud de Sousa, J. J., 'Novas considerações sobre a necropole do Beiral (Ponte de Lima)', *Gallaecia* 5 (1979), 293–303.

Rock, S., *Popular Religion in Russia. Double Belief and the Making of an Academic Myth* (Abingdon, 2007).

Rodriguez, C. G., *El Culto de Los Santos en La España Romana y Visigoda* (Madrid, 1966).

Roma, G., *Necropoli e Insediamenti Fortificati nella Calabria Settentrionale: 1 Le Necropoli Altomedievali* (Bari, 2001).

Róna-Tás, A., *Hungarians and Europe in the Early Middle Ages* (Budapest and New York, 1999).

Roselló, N., 'Necrópolis de Vistalegre (Aspe, Alicante)', *Arqueología Medieval Española* 11 (1987), 374–8.

Rosenwein, B. H., 'Perennial prayer at Agaune', in Farmer, S. and Rosenwein, B. H. (eds), *Monks and Nuns, Saints and Outcasts. Religion in Medieval Society* (Ithaca, NY, 2000), 37–56.

Rouche, M., *L' Aquitaine Des Wisigoths Aux Arabes* (Paris, 1979).

Rousselle, A., *Croire et Guérir. La Foi en Gaule dans l' Antiquité Tardive* (Paris, 1990).

Rowell, G., *The Liturgy of Christian Burial* (London, 1977).

Rubeis, F. de, 'Scritture epigrafiche e scritture librarie in Italia meridionale', in Pohl, W. and Erhart, P. (eds), *Die Langobarden*, 525–32.

—'La scrittura esposta e la società altomedievale: verifica di una possible relazione', in Brogiolo, G. P. and Chavarria Arnau, A. (eds), *I Longobardi*, 211–25.

Rummel, P. von, 'Ambrosius, Julianus Valens und die "gotische Kleidung" – eine Schlüsselstelle historisch-archäologischer Interpretation', in Brather, S. (ed.), *Zwischen Spätantike und Frühmittelalter: Archäologie des 4. bis 7. Jahrhunderts im Westen* (Berlin, 2008), 45–63.

Russell, J. C., *The Germanization of Early Medieval Christianity: A Sociohistorical Approach to Religious Transformation* (Oxford, 1994).

Sadowski, S., 'The youngest phase of Wielbark Culture cemetery in Swaryczów, site 1', in Niezabitowska-Wiśniewska, B., Juściński, M., Łuczkiewicz, P., and Sadowski, S. (eds), *The Turbulent Epoch* (Lublin, 2008), 303–14.

Salin, E., *La Civilisation Mérovingienne – d' après les Sépultures, les Textes et le Laboratoire* (Paris, 1959).

Schäferdiek, K., 'Die Anfänge des Christentums bei den Goten und der sogenannte Gotische Arianismus', *ZKG* 112 (2001), 295–310.

—'Germanic and Celtic Christianities', in Casiday, A. and Norris, F. W. (eds), *The Cambridge History of Christianity*, vol. 2, *Constantine to c. 600* (Cambridge, 2007), 52–69.

Schmitt, J- C., 'Les superstitions', in Goff, J. Le (ed.), *Histoire de la France Religieuse*, vol. 1 (Paris, 1988), 425–53.

Schwarcz, A., 'Cult and religion among the Tervingi and Visigoths and their conversion to Christianity', in Heather, P. (ed.), *The Visigoths*, 447–59.

See, K. von, 'Der Spottvers des Hjalti Skeggjason', *Zeitschrift für Deutsches Altertum* 97 (1968), 155–8.

Shanzer, D., 'So many saints – so little time: the *Libri Miraculorum* of Gregory of Tours', *Journal of Medieval Latin* 13 (2003), 19–60.

Shaw, P. A., *Pagan Goddesses in the Early Germanic World. Eostre, Hreda and the Cult of Matrons* (London, 2011).

Shepard, J., 'Manners maketh Romans? Young barbarians at the emperor's court', in Jeffreys, E. (ed.), *Byzantine Style, Religion and Civilization In Honour of Sir Steven Runciman* (Cambridge, 2001), 135–58.

Simek, R., *Götter und Kulte der Germanen* (Munich, 2004).

Simmer, A.,'Le nord du Département de la Moselle à l' époque mérovingienne', *Revue Archéologique de l' Est et du Centre-Est* 38 (1987), 333–96.

—*Le Cimitière Mérovingien d' Audun-le-Tiche* (Paris, 1988).

Simonetti, M., 'Osservazioni sull' "Altercatio Heracliani cum Germinio"', *Vigiliae Christianae* 21 (1967), 39–58.

—*La Crisi Ariana nel IV Secolo* (Rome, 1975).

Snee, R., 'Gregory Nazianzen's Anastasia Church: Arianism, the Goths, and hagiography', *Dumbarton Oaks Papers* 52 (1998), 157–86.

Sørensen, J., *A Cognitive Theory of Magic* (Lanham, MD, New York, Toronto and Plymouth, 2007).

Stead, C., *Divine Substance* (Oxford, 1977).

Stein, F., 'Verhaltensweisen der Bestattungsgemeinschaft von Rency/Renzig bei Audun-le-Tiche in Lothringen', in Hägermann, D., Haubrichs, W., Jarnut, J., and Giefern, C. (eds), *Akkulturation: Probleme einer germanisch-romanischen Kultursynthese in Spätantike und frühem Mittelalter* (Berlin and New York, 2004), 274–310.

—'Der Helm von Steinbrunn – ein ostgotisches Ehrengeschenk?', in Pohl, W. and Erhart, P. (eds), *Die Langobarden*, 225–46.

Tejral, J., 'Zur Unterscheidung des vorlangobardischen und elbgermanisch-langobardischen Nachlasses', in Pohl, W. and Erhart, P. (eds), *Die Langobarden*, 103–200.

Thacker, A. and Sharpe, R. (eds), *Local Saints and Local Churches in the Early Medieval West* (Oxford, 2002).

Thompson, E. A., *The Historical Work of Ammianus Marcellinus* (Cambridge, 1947).

—'Constantine, Constantius and the Lower Danube Frontier', *Hermes* 84 (1956), 372–81.

—*The Visigoths in the Time of Ulfila* (Oxford, 1966).

—'The conversion of the Spanish Suevi to Catholicism', in James, E. (ed.), *Visigothic Spain: New Approaches* (Oxford, 1980), 77–92.

—*The Huns* (Oxford, 1996).

—*The Goths in Spain* (Oxford, 1969 and 2000).

Tjäder, J.-O., 'Der Codex Argenteus in Uppsala und der Buchmeister Viliaric in Ravenna', in Hagberg, U. E. (ed.), *Studia Gotica* (Stockholm, 1972), 144–64.

—*Die nichtliterarischen lateinischen Papyri Italiens aus der Zeit 445-700*, vol. II, Papyri 29–59 (Stockholm, 1982).

Todd, M., *The Early Germans* (Oxford, 1992).

Tomka, P., 'Langobardenforschung in nordwestungarn', in Pohl, W. and Erhart, P. (eds), *Die Langobarden*, 247–64.

Treffort, C., 'Vertues prophylactiques et sens eschatologique d' un dépôt funéraire du haut Moyen Âge: les plaques boucles rectangulaires burgondes à l' inscription', *Archéologie Médievale* 32 (2002), 31–53.

Urbano, A., 'Donation, dedication, and Damnatio Memoriae: the Catholic reconciliation of Ravenna and the church of Sant' Apollinare Nuovo', *Journal of Early Christian Studies* 13 (2005), 71–110.

Vaggione, R. P., 'Of monks and lounge lizards: "Arians", polemics and asceticism in the Roman East', in Barnes, M. R. and Williams, D. H. (eds), *Arianism After Arius*, 181–214

Valentini, R. and Zuchetti, G. (eds), *Codice Topografico della Città di Roma*, vol. II (Rome, 1942).

Van Dam, R., *Leadership and Community in Late Antique Gaul* (Berkeley, Los Angeles and London, 1985).

—*Saints and Their Cults in Late Antique Gaul* (Princeton, 1993).

Veas Ruiz, N. and Sanchez, J. C., 'El elemento acuático en las iglesia visigoda', *Cristianismo y Acculturación en Tiempios del Imperio Romano. Antigüedad Cristiana* (Murcia) VII (1990), 487–93.

Verhoeven, M., *The Early Christian Monuments of Ravenna : Transformations and Memory* (Turnhout, 2011).

Viana, A., 'Necrópole Romano-Suevica (?) de Beiral', *Arquivo do Alto Minho* 10 (1961), 115–23.

Vieillard-Troiekouroff, M., *Les Monuments Religieux de la Gaule d' Après les Oeuvres de Grégoire de Tours* (Paris, 1976).

Villa, C. and Lo Monaco, F., 'Cultura e scrittura nell' Italia longobarda', in Pohl, W. and Erhart, P. (eds) *Die Langobarden*, 503–24.

Vingo, P. de, 'Il fenomeno della sovrapposizione della popolazione nel Piemonte centro-meridionale: le trasformazioni di una società mista tra Tardoantico e Altomedioevo', *Archeologia Medievale* XXXIV (2007), 303–27.

—*From Tribe to Province to State*, BAR International Series 2117 (Oxford, 2010).

Violante Branco, M. J., 'St Martin of Braga, the Sueves and Gallaecia', in Ferreiro, A. (ed.), *The Visigoths, Studies in Culture and Society* (Leiden, 1999) 63–97.

Voinot, J., *Les Fouilles de Chaouilley, Cimitière Mérovingien* (Nancy, 1904).

Volp, U., *Tod und Ritual in den christlichen Gemeinden der Antike* (Leiden-Boston, 2002).

Wallace-Hadrill, J. M., *The Frankish Church* (Oxford, 1983).

Ward-Perkins, B., 'Where is the archaeology and the iconography of Germanic Arianism?', in Gwynn, D. M. and Bangert, S. (eds), *Religious Diversity in Late Antiquity* (Leiden, 2010) 265–89.

Watkins, O. D., *A History of Penance*, vol. 2 (London, 1920).

Webster, J., ' "Interpretatio": Roman word power and the Celtic gods', *Britannia* 26 (1995), 153–61.

—'Necessary comparisons: a post-colonial approach to religious syncretism in the Roman Empire', *World Archaeology* 28 (1997), 324–38.

—'Creolizing the Roman provinces', *American Journal of Archaeology* 105 (2001), 209–25.

Whitehouse, H., 'Rites of terror: emotion, metaphor and memory in Melanesian initiation cults', *Journal of the Royal Anthropological Institute* 2 (4) (1996), 703–15.

—*Arguments and Icons: Divergent Modes of Religiosity* (Oxford, 2000).

—'Theorizing religions past', in Whitehouse, H. and Martin, L. H. (eds), *Theorizing Religions Past*, 215–32.

Whitehouse, H. and Martin, L. H. (eds), *Theorizing Religions Past: Archaeology, History and Cognition* (Walnut Creek, CA, Lanham, New York, Toronto and Oxford, 2004).

Wickham, C., *Early Medieval Italy. Central Power and Local Society 400–1000* (London, 1981).

Wiles, M., *Archetypal Heresy. Arianism Through the Centuries* (Oxford, 1996).

—'Attitudes to Arius in the Arian Controversy', in Barnes, M. R. and Williams, D. H. (eds), *Arianism After Arius*, 31–43.

Williams, D. H., 'Another exception to later fourth-century "Arian" typologies: the case of Germinius of Sirmium', *Journal of Early Christian Studies* 4 (1996), 335–57.

—*Ambrose of Milan and the End of the Nicene-Arian Conflicts* (Oxford, 1995).

Williams, H, 'Monuments and the past in early Anglo-Saxon England', *World Archaeology* 31 (1998), 90–109.

Williams, R., *Arius* (2nd edn, London, 2001).

Wilson, D., *Anglo-Saxon Paganism* (London and New York, 1992).

Wolfram, H., *History of the Goths*, trans. Dunlap, T. (Berkeley, 1987).

—*The Roman Empire and Its Germanic Peoples*, trans. Dunlap, T. (Berkeley, Los Angeles and London, 1990).

Wood, I. N., 'Gregory of Tours and Clovis', *Revue Belge de Philologie et d' Histoire* 63 (2) (1985), 249–72.

—*The Merovingian Kingdoms, 450–751* (London and New York, 1994).

—(ed.), *Franks and Alamanni in the Merovingian Period. An Ethnographic Perspective* (Woodbridge, 1998).

—'Constructing cults in early medieval France: local saints and churches in Burgundy and the Auvergne 400–1000', in Thacker, A. and Sharpe, R. (eds), *Local Saints and Local Churches*, 155–87.

Woodruff, H., 'The iconography and decoration of the mosaics of La Daurade', *The Art Bulletin* 13 (1931), 80–104.

Young, B. K., 'Exemple aristocratique et mode funéraire dans la Gaule mérovingienne', *Annales ESC* 41 (2) (1986), 379–407.

—'The imagery of personal objects: hints of "do-it-yourself" Christian culture in Merovingian Gaul?', in Cain, A. and Lenski, N. (eds), *Power of Religion*, 229–54.

—'Has anyone seen the barbarians? Remarks on the missing archaeology of the Visigoths in Gaul', in Mathisen, R. W. and Shanzer, D. (eds), *Battle of Vouillé*, 183–201.

Zeiller, J., *Les Origines Chrétiennes Dans Les Provinces Danubiennes de l' Empire Romain* (Paris, 1918).

Zielinski, H., 'Elemente der Stabilität im Dukat Benevent in vorfränkischer Zeit', in Pohl, W. and Erhart, P. (eds), *Die Langobarden*, 409–28.

Zironi, A., 'Historia Langobardorum V, 34: la "colomba dei morti" fra Bibbia gotica e sepolture franche', in Chiesa, P., (ed.), *Paolo Diacono. Uno scrittore fra tradizione longobarda e rinnovamente carolingio* (Udine, 2000), 601–25.

Websites

Excavations at Lagny-sur-Marne, France:
http://www.inrap.fr/archeologie-preventive/Ressources-multimedias/Audiovisuels/Reportages-videos/Reportages-2011/p-13082–lg0–Les-tombes-merovingiennes-de-Lagny-sur-Marne.htm [Accessed 14 July 2013].

Excavations at Romans d' Isonzo, Italy:
www.archeologia.beniculturali.it/index.php?it/142/scavi/scaviarcheologici_4e048966cfa3a/5 [Accessed 14 July 2013].

Index

Lightning Source UK Ltd.
Milton Keynes UK
UKOW06f0432030915

257939UK00006B/128/P